1980

D1112807

COOP

COOP

The Life
and Legend
of Gary Cooper

STUART M. KAMINSKY

——————— ST. MARTIN'S PRESS ———————
——————— New York ———————

Library of Congress Cataloging in Publication Data

Kaminsky, Stuart M
    Coop.

    1. Cooper, gary, 1901–1961. 2. Moving-picture actors and actresses
—United States—Biography.
I. Title.
PN2287.C59K3   791.43′028′0924 [B]   79–22534
ISBN 0–312–16955–8

To the memory of Sandra Lieb Cimaglia.
And for those who loved her.

CONTENTS

ACKNOWLEDGMENTS

My initial thanks go to the following people who knew and worked with Gary Cooper and who were kind enough to be interviewed for this book—Ingrid Bergman, Julian Blaustein, Frank Capra, Carl Foreman, Colleen Moore Hargrave, Charlton Heston, Patricia Neal, Deborah Kerr, Karl Malden, Charles "Buddy" Rogers, Walter Seltzer, Don Siegel, Richard Widmark, Cornel Wilde, Fay Wray, King Vidor and Fred Zinnemann.

My thanks also go to Dorothy Adams of Dunstable, England, who knew Cooper as a child in England and who was very helpful in providing information about his life as a child.

B. J. Gainsley, Registrar, Dunstable College, Kingsway, Dunstable, England, went far beyond my initial request of him and provided a great deal of valuable material. Others who were extremely helpful in providing information about Cooper's life include Dan L. Rieder, Executive Secretary, Alumni Association, Montana State University, and Janet W. German, Director of Alumni Programs of Grinnell College.

Great assistance in providing information about Gary Cooper's career and helping to arrange interviews was given by Anthony Slide, Coordinator of the National Film Information Service of the American Academy of Motion Picture Arts and Sciences. David Bradley should also be singled out for his assistance and valuable suggestions.

Research for this book was done principally by Linda Obalil, Steve Seidman and Carol Slingo. The often difficult task of typing the manuscript was done by Carol Slingo, Amy Levy and Jean Lindburg.

Finally, invaluable editing at all stages was done by my wife, Merle Gordon Kaminsky.

COOP

ONE

INTRODUCTION: IMAGE AND ACTING

One night in London, in 1958, during the filming of The Wreck of the Mary Deare, Charlton Heston and Gary Cooper went out to dinner at a steakhouse in the Mayfair district.

"We went in," recalled Heston, "had dinner in this very small, very crowded restaurant, with the tables close together, and then tried to make our way out, threading carefully through the crowded aisles. We passed a table with a few young couples, kids really, around twenty or twenty-two, swaggering types. As Coop was just passing their table, one of the kids said sarcastically, 'There goes the big cowboy star.' Coop stopped, turned, looked down at the kid, and said quite distinctly, 'When you wanna call me that, smile.' The kid didn't know it was a line from *The Virginian,* and Coop said it perfectly straight.

"Everybody at the table sat still, nobody moved, nobody said anything. The kid looked up at Coop kind of wide-eyed, and suddenly it wasn't a crowded restaurant in London. It was the middle of a street in Dodge City, with the sun beating down, and somebody standing fifty feet away from him.

"Nobody said anything for about thirty seconds. Then Coop gave a little nod and walked out. I was still behind him. The kids didn't say anything or break up. They were looking down. I walked out and caught up with Coop, who was settling into the back of his Rolls-Royce, and I said, 'You read that line well, Coop.' 'Well,' said Coop, 'I've had a lot of practice.' "

Gary Cooper had more than thirty-five years of practice in American films. Of the eighty-four feature-length films in which he starred—not counting guest shots in such films as

1

Hollywood Boulevard, Alice in Wonderland and *Alias Jesse James*—Cooper played a Westerner twenty-five times, fewer than one-third of his roles. He played a soldier, military pilot, or sailor twenty-three times, and the rest of his roles were a wide variety ranging from artists, architects, department store clerks, explorers and baseball players to gangsters, dentists, hoboes, professors and soldiers in the Foreign Legion.

Throughout his career, whether he had been doing a melodrama, a Western, or a comedy, Cooper was often criticized for playing the same role over and over. Furthermore, critics and the public were convinced that he was always playing himself. What he was doing, they said, was not acting. They weren't sure what it was, but in spite of four Academy Award nominations and two Oscars, in spite of public admiration for his work from people as diverse as John Barrymore, Ernst Lubitsch, and Graham Greene, the critics were sure it wasn't acting.

Strangely enough, Gary Cooper was usually the first to agree. Throughout his life, Cooper maintained a remarkable humility about his work. He never thought of himself as an accomplished actor. In fact, the one time he tried out for a play in college, he failed to make the cast. He always had a fear of appearing in public and did his best to avoid it, except during World War II, when he toured military bases.

Once, quite late in his career, after the Oscars, Cooper asked to sit in on acting classes conducted by veteran character actor Jeff Corey. Although invited to participate, Cooper sat silently and respectfully, trying to learn what he could of the craft he had devoted his life to.

That Cooper's lanky body and sorrowful, often naive-looking face became the touchstone for determined, goodwilled Americanism for three decades is seldom questioned. His popularity is proven by the years he was a top box-office draw in the United States. Cooper and the public, however, often failed to appreciate the contributions he made to the art of film-acting.

For example, though many actors have claimed that they recognized early in their careers the camera's ability to pick up slight gestures and facial movements, Cooper was a master almost from the beginning. Certainly his gestures came from his own character, his own shyness before the camera, but he soon cultivated them, made the slight gulp, the pointing of a finger, the twitch of a facial muscle, the almost undetectable slouch of the shoulder part of what he called his "bag of tricks." But Cooper didn't only practice tricks; he developed a broad range of reactions he could call upon and mold to a wide range of characters. There was, as the critics noted, a continuity to his roles, but within that he could become many people. In fact, according to Lee Strasberg, Cooper was one of the first Method actors. Cooper either didn't, or chose not to, understand this, but it was quite clear what Strasberg meant. Cooper studied the characters he would play and then "became" the roles. He didn't just enact them; the actor and performance became inseparable. Certainly there are notable exceptions, exceptions usually the result of Cooper's own physical problems, his overburdened acting schedule, or directors who did not understand what he was doing and forced him to obliterate or mask his talent. Still, the number of times, in eighty-four starring roles, that Cooper's art is evident is remarkable.

Novelist Graham Greene was an early admirer of Cooper's who recognized the actor's ability to "become" the character. In a review of *The Real Glory*, written for *The Spectator* in 1940, Greene said: "Sometimes his lean photogenic face seems to leave everything to the lens, but there is no question here of his not acting. Watch him inoculate the girl against cholera— the casual jab of the needle and the dressing slapped on while he talks, as though a thousand arms had taught him where to stab and he doesn't have to think anymore."

Cooper wasn't born an actor. He learned to be one, and, as he said, he had "a lot of practice." Cooper's cultivated image on film was that of the man of few words, but when the role called for it, he could be just as convincingly talkative as a sideshow barker. In fact, most of his major roles required him to give at least one major speech, a speech that determined to what degree the audience would put their faith in this man of supposedly few words. From *A Farewell to Arms* to *Meet John Doe* to *The Court-Martial of Billy Mitchell,* Coop's character would rise to defend himself and what he believed in.

Cooper's mastery of underplaying made that final speech a point of public outcry for the underplayers of the world, the individuals who don't get a chance to say what they mean and want, and in fact probably couldn't articulate it if they got the chance. But Cooper's character always had the words, and the commanding presence to make them listened to and believed —even when his speeches were contradictory or filled with simple catch phrases.

Early in his career, Cooper realized his power to underplay, to call attention to his presence by refusing the flamboyant gesture, the loud laugh, the shout. He learned to welcome scenes with actors other people shunned for fear of being overwhelmed. Cooper enjoyed playing opposite such scene-chewers and -stealers as Akim Tamiroff in *The General Died at Dawn* and *For Whom the Bell Tolls.* He relished playing opposite his friend Walter Brennan in many movies, including *Meet John Doe, Sergeant York* and *The Westerner.* He welcomed playing opposite Lee J. Cobb, Thomas Mitchell, Burt Lancaster and Charles Laughton, for no matter how flagrantly they acted, viewer attention invariably went to Cooper, who would underplay and use his knowledge of small movements on the large screen to draw attention.

During the course of my research for this book, several actors and directors recalled the story of Akim Tamiroff's perplexity at Cooper's ability to steal scenes and shots. The more Tamiroff overacted, the better Cooper looked in the rushes (the daily screenings) for *The General Died at Dawn.* Frantically, Tamiroff, who had been sure he would steal the picture, began "to play Cooper's game." But now he found himself outclassed by the master of underplaying. The more Tamiroff underplayed, the better Cooper looked. Tamiroff couldn't win.

It has often been assumed that Gary Cooper was a naive man

of little depth, and in many ways he surely was. He clung to his mother well into adulthood. He had great difficulty with women early in his life, particularly Clara Bow, Lupe Velez and the Countess Dorothy DiFrasso. He surely had problems with his political ideas, which occasionally caused him trouble. However, he molded his own career, getting the roles he wanted and rising to become the highest-salaried individual in the United States. In spite of the publicity surrounding his early romances, he married only once and, with the exception of a major romantic involvement with Patricia Neal rather late in his life, managed to keep his private life separate from his public image. Although he was an outspoken Republican of a very conservative nature who cooperated quite fully with the House Un-American Activities Committee in the 1940s, he never gave that committee a single name it could follow up on, nor did he cite a single script he had ever seen that could get anyone into difficulty with the committee. In fact, his testimony before that committee is so amazingly true to his screen persona that it is difficult to tell if Cooper was acting or really unable to remember scripts and names.

In spite of rare insults flung at him publicly, normal human provocations and irritations throughout a public lifetime, and the pains of illness, Cooper rarely said a public word against any man or woman. Considering his influence and stature, it is notable how few enemies the man had.

It would be false to imply by all this that Cooper was some kind of flawless individual. Surely, he was no intellectual. Surely, too, he was a highly ambitious man who could strike a hard bargain and was not averse to feigning an illness or withholding his services if it could get him what he wished, and that usually meant a choice role or money.

In addition, Cooper employed a rather fanciful imagination in interviews dealing with his life and professional career. He was not above letting a publicity man come up with a tale of poverty or heroism. Cooper's various interviews about his life are filled with contradictions and clear errors. Sometimes the errors can be attributed to poor or selective memory. Often the errors are clearly the result of some creative autobiography on Cooper's part.

Toward the end of his life—he was only sixty when he died of cancer of the lung—a long string of illnesses and injuries dating back to childhood and a lifetime of smoking began to take a heavy toll on his acting. He was slow, in pain and often tired, but he never complained.

Shortly before he died, Cooper, like his friends Ernest Hemingway and John Wayne, converted to Catholicism and claimed that he was calmly awaiting his fate.

The road to that hospital bed from the hills of Montana was a long and eventful ride on horses and in fast sports cars, through Europe, the United States and the South Pacific, with companions who were, to a great degree, makers of the history of American film.

In Japan, where he was a great favorite, Cooper was known as "the dry actor," and to a great extent he was. From the smooth boyish look of the 1920s and early 1930s, he became the tall, dry stick of a man whose face looked like the map of America and whose body was brittle but unafraid. It is the image of a dry Gary Cooper walking out alone to face a mad trio of villains or a hostile crowd that will almost certainly be remembered, not the picture of a sick man in a hospital.

Appropriately enough, the road through Gary Cooper's life begins in the American West a century ago.

TWO

BABY PICTURES, SPILLS, AND GROWING UP IN MONTANA

If General George Armstrong Custer and his more than 200 men had not been killed by Sitting Bull and his Sioux warriors on June 25, 1876, in Montana, there might have been no movie star named Gary Cooper.

Cooper's paternal family dates far back into history in Houghton Regis, a corner of Bedfordshire, in England. A reporter for England's *Film Pictorial* went to the area's local churchyard in the summer of 1936 and found some of the Cooper gravestones of past centuries so worn by time that they were almost unreadable. As far back as anyone could remember, the Coopers had been farmers, but by the 1800s, a few of them had moved slightly higher in status and were considered agriculturalists and landowners. Descendants of the clan still reside in the area. Farms near the villages of Tingrith and Houghton Regis are still owned by Coopers.

In the late 1800s, children of the Cooper clan, like most children in the United States and England, were avid consumers of legends of the American West through pulp novels and distorted newspaper accounts. One such English boy was Walter Cooper. When the news of Custer's death reached Bedfordshire, Walter was in his late teens. He immediately began to save money for passage to America with the goal of becoming an Indian fighter and avenging the death of Custer and his men. It took Walter a few years to save his money, book passage, and make his way across the United States to Montana —just in time to find that the Indian wars were over. With no desire to turn back, Walter Cooper settled in the mining town of Last Chance Gulch. The town's name had recently been changed to Helena when it was designated the territorial capital, but many of the old-timers had never accepted the dandified new name.

Walter's disappointment at the lack of hostile Indians was apparently short-lived. He got a job working for the Northern Pacific Railroad and in a few years worked himself up to the job of locomotive engineer. In letters home to England to his younger brother Charles, Walter painted a glowing picture of his own responsibilities and opportunities on the dwindling western frontier.

Although he was a skinny, quiet boy of seventeen, Charles had every bit of his brother's determination. With only two shillings and sixpence in his pocket, Charles packed a small bag and set out in 1883 to join his brother by working his way across the ocean. Charles made it as far as Wisconsin, where he got trapped by the winter snow and managed to land a job as a shoe salesman. He made enough to get to Helena when the weather broke in the spring. By the time he entered Montana, he was nineteen years old. His journey had taken two years. Walter welcomed his younger brother and got him a job with the Northern Pacific as an engine cleaner working twelve hours a day, from six in the morning till six at night.

The ambitious Charlie considered that to be a lot of free time, so he got another job from four till six in the morning making deliveries for a bakery. In addition, he went to a small business school in the evenings, learning shorthand and studying to be a lawyer. On Sunday, his day off, he picked up commission money searching out new customers for the bakery. Whatever free time he had beyond this was devoted to reading Shakespeare aloud to his brother, to learn eloquence for his future law career.

Charlie was such a good bakery salesman that he soon was making enough to quit Northern Pacific and devote most of his day to studying law. He picked up a few extra dollars as a court reporter and by doing clerical work for local lawyers and an occasional task for the Montana Supreme Court. Even before he was officially declared a lawyer, Charles Cooper was also practicing a bit of law.

When Walter Cooper had heard the cry of Indians in 1876, he was not the sole English boy to respond. A young engineering trainee named Alfred Brazier from Gillingham in Kent had also been moved by the tales of Custer's defeat and had vowed to make his way to Montana. The Braziers had been shipbuilders in the port town of Gillingham for generations, but Alfred broke the pattern. He headed West, landing in Helena about the same time as Walter Cooper. Ironically, Alfred Brazier the engineer, on discovering that there were no Indians for him to fight, decided to become a farmer. His farm became a ranch, and soon he had enough money to marry and have children. He wrote to England, suggesting that his younger sister Alice come to Montana to help with the family and start a new life.

Alice, a cautious girl known as "Cousin Dolly," made her way to Montana, retaining her return fare to England just in case. When she hit Helena, she deposited her money in a local bank, where it was promptly lost when all the banks in Montana failed in a silver market panic in 1893.

In 1894 Charles Cooper, the up-and-coming lawyer, and Alice Brazier met, fell in love and were married. In 1895 their first child, Arthur, was born. And six years later, on May 7, 1901, Frank James Cooper, who would become Gary Cooper, was born.

Shortly after the death of her husband in 1946, Alice Louise Brazier Cooper wrote a biographical sketch of him that is on file with the Montana State Historical Society. Her sketch of Gary Cooper's father is brief and loving:

> Charles Henry Cooper was born at Houghton Regis, Bedfordshire, England in 1865. He went to Private School where the Coopers had all attended for over one hundred years.
> His father owned several farms, raised stock, and had a Dairy Business in London. One of nine living children,

he decided he would like to come to America, arriving in Helena in 1885. He worked with his brother on the Northern Pacific Railroad for a short time. He went to Business College and studied Law and Stenography. Charles worked with John S. Shelton, attorney, for his law office experience. Later passing his bar exam, he was office lawyer to Colonel Sanders for some time, while Col. Sanders prosecuted the Chinese cases in Butte. He was also secretary to Governor Leslie for a short time. Charles also had stenographic offices for Court Reporting and law offices with J. U. Sanders.

Later, Charles was elected to the Supreme Court (in 1918). He resigned in 1924 to come to California in order to take executorship of his cousin's estates. Poor health and a bad accident forbade his return to Montana.

He took up writing and made it his hobby. An earnest Shakespearean scholar, he could recite pages of plays. . . . We would take him to visit the boys in hospitals. He would recite to them (from a wheelchair) and treat them to Ice Cream, and had a wonderful time. At a baseball game, he took cold, and turning to pneumonia, he passed away on September 17, 1946; two days after his 81st birthday.

He was buried in Forest-Lawn Memorial Park.

Charles was married to Alice Louise Brazier Gillingham, Kent, England in 1894. Arthur L. Roy born 1895. Frank James Gary born 1901. He was 32nd Mason Algeria Lodge in good standing, Helena, Montana.

One hobby was his ranch on the Missouri River, spending summer and vacations there. He raised cattle and alfalfa. He received an Honorary Degree of Law at Missoula University.

The Colonel Sanders referred to by Mrs. Cooper was Wilbur Sanders, territorial governor of Montana. "I know in my own hometown, Helena," Gary Cooper told *McCall's* magazine in a 1961 interview, "there was a man named Colonel Sanders with whom my father studied law. Colonel Sanders had been educated in Europe and was a student of Greek. He was a quiet, scholarly man, and yet when road agents began holding up gold shipments in Montana Territory, often killing the guards, Colonel Sanders saw his duty and became one of the leaders of a vigilante organization." J. U. Sanders was the colonel's son, with whom Charles went into the law business. But business was so bad Charles had to give up the practice and become legal secretary for the next territorial governor, Preston H. Leslie.

Arthur and Frank spent their first years in a two-story brick house on Eleventh Avenue in Helena. Running behind the house was the original Last Chance Gulch that had been the cause of the town's rise when gold was discovered there in 1864. When they were old enough, the Cooper brothers sought gold in the gulch that had been probed and reprobed thousands of times.

In an autobiographical piece in *The Saturday Evening Post,* in 1956, Cooper wrote: "Even the cracks in the bedrock had been probed with knitting needles to bring up the last flakes of gold. Yet after every spring flood we kids could still find enough gold to keep us in licorice and all-day sucker money for a week."

In the same article, Cooper admitted that in previous interviews he had exaggerated and colored his life story a bit for publicity purposes. Since even the *Post* article has some tales that are more than a bit exaggerated, it sometimes becomes a bit difficult to rely on Cooper's own tales about his life. Two of these unverified tales of childhood were told by Cooper to *St. Nicholas, The Magazine of Youth,* in November of 1935.

> Got my first lesson riding a horse when I was four years old. Roy Smith, a typical plainsman, was my teacher. He was a tall, angular, silent man who wore his hair long after the fashion of Buffalo Bill. No one knew where he came from—and when he disappeared one day, no one knew where he went and no one ever found out.
>
> We were great friends. We rode the range together and it was in his company that I had the first of these two unforgettable experiences. It was my first visit to the outside world. He and I took a carload of cattle to St. Paul. Bunking in the cattle car and awaking in the morning to the excitement of a large city—this was adventure. I came home feeling that at last I had become a man.

Since Frank Cooper first left for England when he was eight years old, the preceding adventure would have to have taken place when he was seven or less. Cooper also told the magazine:

> Even more vivid is the memory of the time the Hauser Dam burst. I was little more than a baby, and I remember that my father and mother and I were almost drowned in the flood that followed.
> We were sleeping in a tent when it happened. I do not know what would have happened if the dogs hadn't begun to bark. They made an awful racket and we woke up. The water had overflowed the banks of the Missouri River and was washing up on the tent flaps. My mother leaped up, lifted me to a horse—and the three of us galloped away to safety.
> Had we delayed another twenty minutes, none of us would have survived.

In 1929, Cooper had told of another old-timer he admired, a "taciturn old ranger" named Ashburton Carter, who had been snowbound for six months in Colorado. Carter, according to Cooper, had "held long conversations with his horse."

Another old-timer turns up in the *Saturday Evening Post* article. The old-timer is a stagecoach driver who was robbed by the Plummer brothers (who emerge, among other places, as the villains in John Ford's 1939 film *Stagecoach*) and enjoyed telling the Cooper boys about his adventure. In later years Gary Cooper's image of the Westerner would be built greatly on Colonel Sanders, Carter and real and imagined characters from his youth.

During those first eight years of his life, Frank and his brother were fairly free to do what they liked outside of school. They roamed the hills, strode through the mud and went downtown to watch for drunks being thrown out of the saloons.

Charles Cooper was hard at work in his law practice during these early years and would appear only briefly at meals and then retire to his study to work. Alice Cooper became interested in chemistry and photography and was one of the first women in the country who not only took pictures but processed and printed them herself. Later Gary Cooper was to claim that his mother's interest in photography had taught him how to pose for pictures and how to hold still for the long exposures necessary with the still rather primitive film available.

With the family income improving and Charles fast becoming a respected trial lawyer, Alice began thinking of her sons' education. When Frank came in one afternoon and casually used a western swearword, Alice insisted that the boys be taken to England for some Old World refinement. Charles agreed, and, leaving her husband to his work, she spent the summer of 1909 in Bedfordshire with her boys.

Throughout his life Cooper told interviewers that he had an awful time in England as he longed for the open territory of Montana. While attending Dunstable School, the Cooper boys lived in the home of Mr. and Mrs. Walter Barton. The Bartons' young daughter Dorothy played with Frank. In a letter to this author, Dorothy Barton Adams, who still lives on Houghton Road in Dunstable, recalled that Frank was good in sports at school and did not seem at all unhappy.

"They say he was miserable here," she reported, "that he yearned for his father's ranch in Montana. That's not true. Gary was a happy-go-lucky kid, and I'm sure he thoroughly enjoyed himself at our house in the High Street. They say he was sickly. He was not terribly robust, but he had only the usual childish ailments, and his main trouble was biliousness. Still, that didn't rob him of his appetite.

"He was always a little bundle of mischief and not a great lover of school books. He was a real boy, in fact."

Biographical sketches written about Cooper through the years have occasionally mentioned an English fiancée acquired and abandoned when he was at school in England. Since his English education ended when he was eleven, the most likely candidate was Alice Adams. "Yes," is Mrs. Barton's reply, she was the fiancée. "Only Gary was eleven and I was six."

In school, Frank was enrolled in the third grade, where he was taught and promptly forgot Latin and French. His only real interest was art, an interest that had started just before he and his brother were taken to England. His father had taken the eight-year-old to the state capitol building, where the boy saw a massive mural of explorers, Indians, and horses. It was Charles Russell's painting of Lewis and Clark at Ross Hole. The painting so moved the young Cooper that he began to think about becoming a painter.

After three years in England, in which the elder brother excelled at athletics, the Cooper boys returned to Helena, where their English education did not impress the local school board. Frank found himself behind everyone else and hampered by a temporary British accent overlaying his Montana drawl, which made him a figure of ridicule in class. Things got worse when he began to grow and soon towered over his classmates.

While Mrs. Cooper and the boys had been in England, Charles Cooper had taken a serious interest in the Seven Bar Ranch in Sunnyside, fifty miles outside of Helena along the Missouri River. He had purchased it a few years earlier as a hobby, and while they were away, he began to invest in the ranch, hire help and build his cattle herd.

Ranch responsibilities increased in 1917 when Arthur, along with all the ranch's Indian workers, joined the U.S. Army to fight in World War I. Charles was busy at the capitol, and the main responsibility for the 500 head of cattle and the ranch fell on Frank and his mother.

Frank, sixteen, dropped out of school to work the ranch. His memories of that period included his mother's swinging an axe to break frozen hay bales in minus-twenty-degree weather and six-foot snowdrifts that had to be overcome to feed hungry cattle. When he finally went back to school after Arthur returned, the contrast between him and his schoolmates at Helena High School was embarrassing. He had grown thirteen inches and stood almost six-foot-three, the height he would usually be given in studio releases, though occasionally the publicity would list him as six-foot-four. Cooper later said that a teacher, knowing his interest in art, pointed out to the seventeen-year-old that Montana had a special law for farm boys allowing them to bypass much of their education.

In fact, Frank Cooper was dismissed from Helena for disciplinary reasons and was sent to Gallatin County High School in Bozeman so that he could graduate, according to a Montana State University source.

After finishing high school, Cooper enrolled in a few courses at Wesleyan College in Helena. There he became friends with another student, Harvey Markham, who had been stricken with polio as a child and was unable to move his legs. Markham's father had altered a Model T Ford for his son to drive, and Harvey would pick up his friend Frank and drive to school over the hills. On one of these trips, Harvey's hand brake failed at the top of a hill.

"I remember, as yesterday," Cooper recalled in a 1929 article for *Photoplay,* "the automobile accident that knocked me out of active life for many months and sent me to Sunnyside. I can recall the big touring car I was driving as it whizzed along. The sudden impact. How it rolled over. How I got up and walked to the curb, not dizzy, nor weak, my senses sharpened to a superhuman degree. And then how my left side failed me. It hung like a heavy dead thing. And everything went blue. I guess that is the way you feel when you faint. I awakened in a hospital. They said I had a broken leg and complications too numerous to mention."

While the Model T has changed to a touring car and Harvey is no longer the driver, the incident itself did take place. Doctors told Cooper to stay off his feet.

The recovery at Sunnyside took two years, during which Frank did a lot of drawing and horseback riding. He found it less painful to ride than to walk. Years later, he would find that his two years of riding were the worst thing he could have done. X-rays showed that he had a pelvic separation. The riding increased the separation and caused him pain and problems for the rest of his life.

In 1942 Cooper's mother remembered those two years in an interview with *Photoplay*. "Frank," she said, "would go off into the hills, walking or shooting, with the Indian boys. Those Indians never talked much—and Frank would spend hours with them without speaking a word."

The family fortune and prestige had improved. Charles had been appointed to the state supreme court, and the ranch was prospering.

In 1922, sufficiently recovered, Frank Cooper enrolled at Grinnell College in Grinnell, Iowa, to pursue his art career. Although biographical sketches of Cooper had indicated that he was a cartoonist for the school newspaper, the alumni association of Grinnell College states that "there is no evidence that he was on the newspaper staff. One *Scarlet and Black* [school newspaper] article mentions Cooper's being Art Editor of the Yearbook." However, the *Cyclone,* Grinnell's yearbook, for 1922, 1923 and 1924, does not have a picture of Cooper; he is not mentioned as a staff member nor are there credits to him on any of the drawings.

While at Grinnell, Cooper lived in Room 226 in Langan Hall. He showed some interest in theater, trying out for the Grinnell College Dramatic Club, which refused to vote him into membership. An article in the *Scarlet and Black* on January 4, 1933, quotes Homer N. Abegglen, who was then a faculty member at Miami of Ohio. Abegglen had been the president of the Grinnell dramatic club in 1923, and according to him, "Gary was only a freshman, tall and lanky, and we seniors naturally thought he'd have another chance to make our club."

In fact, Cooper was in his second year at Grinnell when he tried for the dramatic club. Years later he was given honorary membership in the club, and he accepted. His public recollections of Grinnell appeared in the May, 1930, issue of the college humor magazine. He said:

> I spent two years at Grinnell. . . . It has never been clear in my mind whether or not one can claim to be a college

man if he hasn't received a degree. But one thing is clear to me. I wouldn't trade that two years I spent in Langan Hall at my alma mater—well, for a good many things that the world seems to set a high price upon.

My only regret is that the exigencies of life forced me to leave college two years too soon. It isn't the loss of the degree that I regret so much . . . but the loss of two years of association with men whom I had come to know as brothers.

A 1933 article from the Grinnell College Library and supplied by the college indicates that at one time during his career at Grinnell, Cooper "decked himself in a ten-gallon Stetson and led the torchlight parade on horseback, his plainsman yells giving new flavor to the affair." On another occasion, according to the article, "he blacked up as a Numidian guard and stood outside of the Egyptian temple background erected for the senior banquet, but all the appearances he made under protest. He preferred to remain in his room to fret over Spanish and Greek, a combination that confounded him mightily."

The article goes on to say that he was known on campus as "Cowboy Cooper," and, in addition to failing to get into the drama club in his sophomore year, he also tried and failed to make the cast of Eugene O'Neill's *Beyond the Horizon.*

He was also reported to have "led a student raid on a five-gallon can of apple cider he had himself as Saturday handyman pressed out for Professor H. W. Tatlock's Halloween party." Rather tame stuff, it is true, but a bit out of keeping with the image of Cooper as the shy boy from a Montana ranch.

While at Grinnell, Cooper apparently fell in love for the first time, a love he referred to at various times in his life, indicating that he had come near marriage. According to the Grinnell newspaper, the girl was a "campus vocalist," for whose company there was much competition, and from which the taciturn sophomore was completely eliminated. When he proposed marriage, she sent him west to find a job.

The rejection may well have been the "exigencies" of life Cooper said were the cause of his leaving college two years early. In 1929 Cooper would return as a distinguished alumnus for Grinnell's Diamond Jubilee and Homecoming.

During his two summers at Grinnell, Frank Cooper worked in Yellowstone Park as a bus driver for tourists. Boots Dunlap, later a Warner Brothers special police officer, worked with Cooper there. He recalled his days at Yellowstone for *Photoplay:*

> Frank Cooper and I were gear-jammers together in the park. We drove busses and spieled for the tourists. Frank worked there during the summer while he was at Grinnell and we called him "The Sheik."
>
> Frank was a fine driver, but not much of a spieler. One fellow claimed that his Yellowstone experience was his first real acting for pay. To get tips out of the tourists, he would make the treacherous drive through the park seem even more treacherous by grimaces and exaggerated pulls at the wheel.

In addition to working at Yellowstone, Frank did some cartooning for the campaign his father was working on to get Joseph Dixon elected governor of Montana. Dixon was a Republican, and Frank's father was a staunch Republican, a tradition his son would take up in later years.

Leaving Grinnell, Frank Cooper was convinced that his future lay in advertising. His parents had moved to Los Angeles, and his brother had entered the banking business. Before heading east to the Mecca of his chosen field, Frank decided to see his parents for a brief visit. He arrived on Thanksgiving Day in 1923. Then, instead of going east, Frank tried to get a job as an artist for one of the local newspapers, but failed. He couldn't land an advertising job either and finally took a job soliciting family photographs door to door. He failed miserably. Then he tried to sell real estate, but that was even worse.

According to Cooper, in 1929, "It wasn't much fun living in a dinky, smelly room and eating sinkers and coffee. But I wouldn't write home for money."

On March 3, 1935, a *New York Times* reporter asked him if

it was true that he had spent his last dime for a loaf of bread just before he got his first movie job. "That story's garbled considerably," he remarked. "I already had my first movie job. Time I spent my last dime it was for a bed."

Twenty years later, Cooper popped the myth of his poverty days in Los Angeles. He had lived, in fact, with his parents, and, far from going hungry, he was probably overfed by his doting mother. "I think," he said, "my starvation diet at the time ran to no less than a dozen eggs a day, a couple of loaves of bread, a platter of bacon, and just enough pork chops between meals to keep me going until I got home for supper."

Eventually, Cooper did land a job as an artist. In 1942, Cooper described the job to Frank S. Nugent of the *New York Times Magazine:* "This guy made the curtains for small movie and vaudeville houses. You know: the kind with the posters painted on, advertising so-and-so's hardware shop or meat market. I'd chase over to the theatre manager and sell him the idea. Then I had to line up the local merchants, get them to buy space on the curtain. Then we'd make up the curtain. I worked on commission."

But vaudeville was on the way out in 1924, and with it went Cooper's curtain job. He had saved about $400 and was determined to head for Chicago and enroll in a professional art course, but he took his time deciding, and the $400 disappeared.

Wondering what to do next, Frank Cooper was walking near Vine Street in December, 1924, when he was stopped by two beat-up cowboys who recognized him. They were boyhood friends from Montana, Jimmy Galen and Jimmy Calloway. Both, like Cooper, were the sons of Montana lawyers. Both were working in movies as extras, jobs they had obtained through another Montana friend, Slim Talbot, a championship rodeo rider who had made a small name for himself as a stunt rider in Western movies.

The two Jimmys announced that they were making an easy ten dollars a day falling off horses. Of course if Frank Cooper wanted to get in on it, he'd probably make only five a day beginner's salary, but that was five dollars more than Frank Cooper was making. Five dollars a day for riding a horse— Cooper decided he had nothing to lose. So he joined his friends to try out for extras on a new picture called *The Vanishing American* with Richard Dix.

THREE

STUNT MAN TO "IT" BOY: TIED IN KNOTS BY CLARA BOW

Frank Cooper got a job as an extra that day in December, 1925.
Cooper's getting the job was indeed remarkable since he was,
according to his memory of the event, the only one of 200
would-be extras not in cowboy gear. Years later he would credit
Slim Talbot with gallantly stepping back and giving him the
job though the more experienced stunt rider could easily have
had it.

Whether Talbot did actually stand aside to give his Montana
friend his first job or not is not known. What is known is that,
when Cooper became a star, Talbot began a more than thirty-
year career doubling for him.

The name of that first picture Cooper appeared in is a matter
of conjecture. Five years after the event, he told *Photoplay* that
the first film was not *The Vanishing American* but "a Tom Mix
picture. He was using 200 extras in some sort of legendary
flashback taking place in Sherwood Forest in Robin Hood's
heyday."

Ten years from the event, he still remembered the film as a
vehicle starring Tom Mix, and he recalled being fitted into his
first movie costume, a pair of green tights and a leather cap and
jerkin.

He told *The New York Times:* "They gave me a bow and an
arrow. I got into the costume and wandered down to the set.
There were a lot of other archers walking around, and pretty
soon Billie Dove was brought in on one of those chariot things
that they carry around. Four big blacks were carrying it. And
Tom Mix came riding in, all laces and wearing one of those
cavalier hats with a plume."

The movie was probably *Dick Turpin,* a 1925 costume film for Mix set in eighteenth-century England, and not a flashback sequence for a Mix Western.

As time passed, Cooper's memory of the film grew more hazy. In 1942 he told the *New York Times* that he went to work as an extra on his first movie after a makeup man had fixed him up with a square beard and a black hat pulled low over his eyes.

"Never saw a cowhand dressed like this," Cooper said he protested.

"You're not supposed to be a cowhand, chump," was the reply. "We're shooting the Boer War."

Another fourteen years removed from the event, and Cooper told the *Saturday Evening Post* that his first film as an extra was a cavalry picture: "The twenty of us represented the United States Cavalry. I think there were nineteen officers and Private Cooper. As a detachment, we would ride through an oak grove. As another, we would sweep across a prairie."

There is no doubt that Frank Cooper worked on a lot of movies in his first eleven months, but which one was first and in what order the others followed is difficult to determine. He can, however, be seen in prints and publicity stills of *The Thundering Herd, Wild Horse Mesa, The Vanishing American, The Enchanted Hill* and *Watch Your Wife,* all made in 1925 and 1926.

What is known is that his parents were mildly skeptical about his working in movies, though his father simply assumed he would grow out of it. Early in the morning, Frank would get up and put on his makeup—hoping that no one, especially his family, would see him in unmanly powder—and make his way to the cattle call at Gower Gulch in Burbank where the Westerns were being made. Directors wanted to shoot only one take, and extras were an expendable commodity. Cooper remembered frequent accidental falls from horses with the director of the silent epic calling for the cameras to keep rolling to catch real blood.

The skinny young extra—he weighed about 160 pounds and

seldom in his life went over 170 pounds—made extra money by taking falls off his horse for the camera. Once he took a tumble on his head. Another time a fall left him numb on his left side for days. The damage to the horses was even more severe in those pre-anticruelty days, and it wasn't unusual for a purposely tripped horse to break its legs. Cooper was soon making ten dollars a day instead of five and working regularly, but the tumbles and contusions coupled with the permanently injured hip were to take a heavy toll later in his life and greatly affect some of his most memorable portrayals.

Ambition hit Frank in 1926, when he learned Tom Mix was earning $1,700 a week. Cooper began to have dreams of being something besides a nameless villain who takes fearful tumbles from a crippled horse. He paid a makeup man ten dollars to teach him how to cupid's-bow his lips and apply the eyepencil and shadow necessary for photography in those days of high-intensity light and insensitive film. Cooper then went to his old boss at the photographic studio and had a batch of stills made. In addition to poses with a Western hat, he had pictures made in a Valentino manner. He then invested sixty-five dollars in a few seconds of audition film he could show to producers or anyone who would look at it.

"I galloped up on a horse," he recalled, "pulled him back on his haunches and made a running dismount. Long shot. Then I walked up, took off my hat, rubbed the sweat off my forehead. Medium shot. Then I yelled 'Hello,' and grinned."

While he tried to move upward in the movie business, Cooper continued to work in whatever films he could get. He recalled one of his big early moments involved catching Tom Mix as he fell off a horse and another big moment when he got to lean over in a scene and pet Rin-Tin-Tin.

His first break came not through an unknown producer but through his father. In 1925, Marilyn Mills was one of the queens of two-reel Westerns. She had her own production company and was turning out a weekly film starring her, her horse and an actor named J. Frank Glendon. Marilyn Mills's father, manager of the largest bakery in Los Angeles, sought some legal advice from Charles Cooper. The two men started to talk about their children in the film business and agreed that Frank would show up the next day for a talk with Marilyn Mills.

"I was only doing my dad a favor when I said I'd see the boy, and the next day, up popped this Frank Cooper," Marilyn Mills Davis told the *New York Herald Tribune* years later.

> I never saw so much humanity before in one piece. He said the closest he'd ever been to a studio was waiting outside a casting director's office. He had never been interviewed. He had some photographs of himself and showed them to me. They were very sophisticated and George Raftish—hair sleeked down and most of them had cigarette smoke curling up. Or else a pipe in his hand.
>
> I was sorry for the kid because even though he was as old as I was, he seemed bewildered by the whole business. I told him I'd try to give him a break in my next picture, a little opus called *Tricks*. When Cooper arrived on location, Bruce Mitchell, the director, said he looked like a human string bean and refused to put him in the picture.
>
> I finally insisted the kid get a break, but we never put him in a scene with our leading man, the late J. Frank Glendon, unless one of them was on a horse because he made Glendon look like a shrimp.

Cooper played a Western villain in *Tricks* and a pencil-moustached Eastern villain in his second Marilyn Mills film, *Three Pals*. "They made him wear five extra shirts so he wouldn't look too skinny," she recalled.

One of Marilyn Mills's suggestions to Frank Cooper was that he get himself an agent. She suggested a woman named Nan Collins. One of the first things Collins insisted on was that Cooper change his name. There was nothing wrong with Frank Cooper, but there were too many Frank Coopers around, including one in the news at the time who was accused of murdering his wife. She suggested the name Gary because she had been born in Gary, Indiana. He accepted the name without too much thought but was never totally comfortable with it even though, in the mid-1930s, he had his name legally changed to

Gary. He encouraged his friends and acquaintances to call him "Coop," and they took to it easily. Nan Collins did not remain Gary Cooper's agent for long. In fact, through much of his career, Coop served as his own agent and did exceedingly well in that capacity.

Although, in 1925, Cooper was earning fifty dollars a week as a villain in Marilyn Mills's two-reelers, his lanky frame was beginning to mark him, and Mills began using him less and less. So Cooper gathered his publicity stills and his one-reel self-directed screen test and began making the studio rounds. He did occasional extra work, appearing, for example, as a bearded Cossack behind Rudolph Valentino in *The Eagle* and with Lightnin' the Super Dog in *Lightnin' Wins*. With time on his hands, he went to the movies to study the leading men of his time.

He took his screen test and list of credits to John Waters, who was directing a series of Zane Grey Westerns for Paramount. Waters liked what he saw but said he had nothing at the moment though he would call Cooper back when he did.

Cooper was no longer sure he had a future, but he took his film and stills to Samuel Goldwyn's office and patiently sat waiting till the producer would have a moment or two to look at him and his material. Goldwyn claimed to have discovered Cooper, and this claim has been repeated frequently. For example, Richard Griffith, in his book *Samuel Goldwyn: The Producer and His Films,* referred to "Cooper, discovered waiting in Mr. Goldwyn's outer office by the producer himself . . ."

For years, the director Henry King also claimed that he spotted the lean young man in that office and began talking to him. Henry King, who had acted on the stage in his teens, had begun directing movies in 1916. At the time he met Cooper, he had already been acclaimed for such movies as *Tol'able David, The White Sister* and *Stella Dallas.* He would go on to a long career in sound-film, directing such films as *Seventh Heaven, Jesse James, Stanley and Livingstone, The Song of Bernadette, Twelve O'Clock High* and *The Gunfighter.*

Cooper had no idea who King was and was a bit reluctant at first to let this stranger look at his precious few seconds of film. When King came back from the projection room, he returned Cooper's small reel and offered him $65 a week. He needed someone who could ride a horse and look natural. Cooper gulped, and King told him if he could keep that gulp it would get him some extra footage in the film he was doing, *The Winning of Barbara Worth.* Cooper kept the gulp for more than thirty-five years and called upon it frequently.

Yet another version of Cooper's "discovery" comes from Frances Marion, who wrote the screenplay for *The Winning of Barbara Worth.* Marion would go on to write dozens of screenplays and win Academy Awards for two of them, *The Big House* in 1930 and *The Champ* in 1932. In her autobiography, *Off With Their Heads,* Marion reported that Cooper had been dating Samuel Goldwyn's secretary. The secretary asked Marion one day to take a look at her boyfriend outside the window.

Marion immediately said, "That's our man," seeing him in the role of Abe Lee. But, according to her, "Neither Sam nor Henry King . . . thought much of the test made of Cooper." Marion reports that she then suggested that the studio secretaries be brought in to view all the screen tests. They sat through the tests without comment until Cooper appeared. Then they let out a chorus of "ahhs."

The Winning of Barbara Worth starred Ronald Colman and Vilma Banky. Colman played an Eastern engineer building dams in the West. Cooper was to have the small role of his dispatch rider. The rival for Miss Banky in the film was a simple Western character, Abe Lee, scheduled to be played by an actor named Harold Goodwin. Goodwin was working on another film when King began shooting *Barbara Worth.* Because Cooper looked somewhat like Goodwin, King began to use the young actor in Goodwin's costume for over-the-shoulder shots and various angles where Cooper's face wouldn't show. When King had exhausted all the shooting he could do in a Los Angeles studio and it was time to move on to location work in

Nevada, there was still no Goodwin. King decided to cast Cooper in Goodwin's role as Abe Lee, a name certainly suggestive of the Abraham Lincoln–type figure Cooper was to become so often in movies.

Goldwyn was apparently worried about using a relatively untried young actor in a major role in his film, but King assured Goldwyn that Cooper would do fine in the dramatic scenes. The big test would be the scene in which Abe Lee, after a twenty-four-hour desert ride, drags himself up a flight of hotel stairs, knocks on the door, and collapses in exhaustion in front of Ronald Colman.

According to one of Cooper's later accounts, King had him run for ten miles, threw dust in his face and sent him through the door, at which point Cooper fell flat on his face, with Colman moving forward just in time to catch his head before it hit the floor.

More than forty years later, King changed his story and told Kevin Brownlow in *The Parade's Gone By* that he had noticed Cooper sitting outside not Goldwyn's office but that of casting director Bob McIntyre. Cooper reportedly said he wanted to play the role of Abe Lee, and King told him the part was taken. However, King did look at Cooper's test film and recalled that it ended with Cooper's getting off his horse and going into a saloon. King said he then hired Cooper for fifty dollars a week for a small role, but when his Abe Lee actor didn't show up, he decided to try Cooper.

He told Cooper all he had to do was keep his eyes on Vilma Banky. "Do you know," said King, "that man stood there from eight in the morning till twelve? No matter where Vilma Banky went, his eyes followed her—whether we were shooting or not."

For the big scene in which Cooper collapses after coming through the door, King said he walked him all morning and worked with him for an hour before asking him to come on the set. Then he told Cooper to go through the door when the camera started and fall flat on his face, "even if it smashes you to pieces." Cooper agreed. Cooper did as he was told, and King assured him that the part of Abe Lee was his with no strings.

Goldwyn had been watching the shooting through a hole in a curtain and wanted to sign Cooper for a contract while he was still weak. He gave the job of signing Cooper to Abe Lehr. King suggested they offer Cooper $100 a week. Lehr offered $75. Meanwhile, Nan Collins had been in touch with Paramount and John Waters, who had promised Cooper work, and Paramount offered the suddenly hot young actor $125 a week.

According to Alva Johnston in *The Great Goldwyn* published in 1937, Goldwyn "generously released Cooper when the young actor got an offer of $200 a week." Ten years later Goldwyn would hire Cooper for $3,000 a week and consider his letting Cooper go in 1925 one of the major blunders of his career as a producer.

According to Cooper in an interview just before he died, he did get a $65-a-week offer from Goldwyn, but members of the *Barbara Worth* cast advised him to turn it down and hold out until the picture was released and hopefully got good reviews, which would force Goldwyn to increase his offer. However, the Paramount offer was too good to turn down.

Although Cooper later remembered his first Paramount film as *Wings,* he actually appeared in four other films first. His initial effort at Paramount was in *Arizona Bound,* which was directed by John Waters and shot in two weeks on location, but not in Arizona. The cast and crew moved to Bryce Canyon, Utah. The female lead in the film was Thelma Todd, a blond former schoolteacher who would later become a well-known comedienne in her own films, in addition to playing semi-straight roles in several Laurel and Hardy films and Marx Brothers' efforts, including *Monkey Business.*

As happened to Cooper frequently in his early career, a moment came while the film was being shot when he froze, unable to act. In this case, he went blank in the love scenes with Thelma Todd, scenes that did not even call for a kiss. Simple shyness might have been part of the reason, but Cooper was not unaware of women. He did, however, suffer from embarrassment throughout most of his film career. The reasons are not totally clear, but they stemmed initially from a lack of confidence in himself as an actor, a lack of confidence that never left him. Cooper simply never thought he was an actor. Considering his success and his willingness to appear in films with some of the biggest scene-stealers in history, his humility, which never wavered, was quite rare in Hollywood.

Since the film was silent, director Waters set up the camera over Thelma Todd's shoulder and talked Cooper through the scene as they shot. Cooper's massive appetite and ability to consume large quantities of food were already well known, and Waters simply told Cooper that he was a man who hadn't eaten in days, that he was looking at not Thelma Todd but a table loaded with chicken and ham. According to Cooper, this brought a look of love to his eyes. In the film, Cooper even licks his lips as he looks at Todd as if she were a plate of mashed potatoes.

In another scene of *Arizona Bound,* Cooper has a barroom brawl with the villain, played by Jack Dougherty. Cooper claimed that though the fight started out staged, it soon developed into a real free-for-all when Dougherty belted him in the mouth. If this is so, it is difficult to tell from the film. What can be determined from the film is that Cooper has few long-take scenes, scenes in which the camera records his acting for more than a few seconds. Much of Cooper's performance was constructed in the editing room with pieces of several takes and angles for a scene. The edited Cooper looked good to Paramount, and Waters immediately began to direct the blue-eyed actor's second starring film, *Nevada.*

While shooting was going on for *Nevada,* with Evelyn Brent as Cooper's co-star and William Powell as a villain with a sense of humor, reviews were coming in on *Barbara Worth* with high praise for Cooper. *Motion Picture* said Cooper "played the most consistent and convincing characterization of the picture." *Va-*

riety Weekly wrote, "An outstanding performance was given by Gary Cooper as Abe Lee, played in a most sympathetic manner, who came near taking the stuff away from Colman." A few previews had also been held for *Arizona Bound,* and the word was that Cooper looked terrific. When it was released, *Variety* said of the young man who did his own stunts, "Cooper is a tall youth, with a boyish smile and enough swagger to give him character." To Cooper, it seemed as if the scissors-and-paste actor in the film was not him at all.

At night after shooting on *Nevada,* Paramount began giving Cooper fencing lessons. The idea was to keep him busy and moving from one film to another. The long hours of shooting on *Nevada* and fencing at night took their toll on the already lean Cooper, who lost 15 pounds he could ill afford to lose. At 150 pounds, he made a rather dehydrated desert star. Filming on the desert, with mirrored reflectors to direct the hot sun on him for eight hours a day, he found it almost impossible to keep up his strength.

In the film Cooper plays Jim Lacy, who helps a friend break out of jail and then seeks a new life only to run into a band of rustlers. He deals with the rustlers and makes his peace with the law in a land, as a title in the film tells us, where "the quickest man on the draw was always right." When the film was released, *Photoplay* praised Cooper as "a hero with a sense of humor." *Variety Weekly* wrote: "Cooper is improving in his work and serving his masters well in everything but his love-making."

The chronology of Cooper films is a bit jumbled at this point. All three of his next movies—*It, Children of Divorce* and *Wings* —starred Clara Bow, and this was not a coincidence. In fact, Cooper's relationship with Clara Bow is about all that can account for the up-and-coming young actor's walk-on role in *It,* his near disastrous role in *Children of Divorce* and his less-than-a-minute appearance in *Wings.* As it turned out, the brief appearance in *Wings* was an important point in his career, but he didn't know or expect it at the time.

In most of his recollections about Clara Bow, Cooper maintained that their love relationship was concocted for publicity, though he did say in one interview at the time that "Clara was helpful. She is that kind of a girl, generous with her friendship and praise. I had never before known an actress. She was a new type of girl, glamorous, full of fun, devoid of jealousy. I was grateful to her and admired her. We went around together."

Clara Bow, already a star, had met Cooper at a Hollywood party. She introduced herself, according to her biographers Joe Morella and Edward Z. Epstein, and invited him to her house that night. At the time, Clara Bow was apparently juggling several men friends, including director Victor Fleming, who would later direct both *Gone With The Wind* and *The Wizard of Oz.* Clara Bow insisted that Cooper have a role in *It,* and the studio was happy to let him do a walk-on as a reporter with one brief scene.

The film made Clara Bow one of the top stars in Hollywood, and had columnists referring to Cooper as the "It" boy, which he detested, but he couldn't resist Bow's offer to co-star with him in her next picture, *Children of Divorce.* In *Children of Divorce,* he had a major role as a contemporary young man of the urban East. According to Hedda Hopper, the columnist, who was an actress in the film, "Gary was miscast as any guy could be. Fresh off a Montana ranch, he was given the part of a New York smoothie. Camille in her death scene couldn't have topped his misery."

Adela Rogers St. John, who also worked on the picture, recalled that Cooper and Clara Bow "had the same sense of humor. There was a lot of giggling and laughing during the production." In addition to giggling and laughter, there were also battles between the two lovers. Director Frank Lloyd recalled one morning when Cooper came to work with distinct scratches on his face. In fact Lloyd wanted to get rid of Cooper, and Cooper, uncomfortable in his fancy suit and unfamiliar role, might not have had great objections, but Clara Bow did.

Finally, a shot in the film turned out to be the most traumatic episode in Cooper's long career. In a party scene with many extras, Cooper was supposed to walk into a room, talk to several people and make his way through the crowd to someone at the far end of the room. The idea was to shoot in a single take. It seemed a relatively easy shot, but the first take developed minor problems and then the second and then Cooper spilled some champagne. By the fourth take, Cooper was in panic, seeing the distance across the room as an enormous gulf.

According to Hedda Hopper, "Frank Lloyd, our director, tried the scene twenty-two times before finally giving up on Coop." Cooper turned from the disgruntled director and walked off the set and out of the studio. The next morning Lloyd told Cooper that, in spite of Clara Bow, he was through on the picture.

"I jumped into my car," Cooper recalled two years after the event, "and beat it for the Mojave, driving like the devil. I stayed all night on the desert in a ramshackle hotel. . . . The next day I came back down the coast road, through Malibu, with the mountains rising on one side, the ocean beating on the other."

At about noon, the ever-hungry Cooper headed for a favorite restaurant, where director Lloyd was waiting for him. Lloyd had called the police out to look for Cooper, afraid he had become suicidal. "You're back on the picture," Lloyd told Cooper. The rushes on the third day's work had shown improvement, and he was back in the cast.

What had happened was that Lloyd and the studio executives had discovered what dozens of others in the film industry were to learn. There was something about Cooper that photographed well almost in spite of what he seemed to be doing on the set. His shyness led him to underplay, and his underplaying, coupled with his intense look of sincerity, made him stand out in the screening room even if he appeared lost on the set.

The reviews for Clara Bow for *Children of Divorce* were outstanding. Her death scene was singled out as particularly moving. Cooper did not fare so well. *Variety* wrote that "Cooper will likely find himself more at home in Westerns," and *Film Daily* stated that Cooper didn't do "anything to distinguish himself." Paramount had just decided to sink three million dollars into an airplane epic directed by twenty-nine-year-old newcomer William Wellman. To insure the box-office draw of the film, they expanded a part in the film for Clara Bow. Since location shooting was done in San Antonio, Texas, Clara Bow asked Wellman to give Cooper a small role so he would have an excuse for accompanying her. Wellman agreed.

When they got to San Antonio, Clara Bow was the center of attraction, and Cooper grew jealous. According to Wellman, "She kept Cooper, [Buddy] Rogers, [Richard] Arlen . . . and a few whose names I don't remember plus a couple of pursuit pilots from Selfridge all in line. They were handled like chessmen, never running into one another."

According to Morella and Epstein, Bow dropped Cooper, saying he was too jealous of her, though the two saw each other on and off for several years after. The Bow biographers, who are not at all sympathetic to Cooper, picture him at this point in his life as an opportunist who was not above "accepting the attentions of a wealthy young tobacco heiress who had influence with certain members of Hollywood's hierarchy."

Richard Arlen later recalled Cooper's day of work on *Wings*. Arlen had, like Cooper, started his career as an extra. A pilot in World War I, he was particularly suited for his role in *Wings,* a role that led to friendship with Cooper and a fifty-year movie career. Cooper, said Arlen, "had been told to come to our hotel in the morning ready to go out to the location with us. We were expected on the set about ten. Gary didn't show up until ten-thirty. The driver tried to hurry him into the car. But Cooper couldn't be stampeded and wanted to know, 'Where do we have breakfast?' And then, with everybody hopping around trying to get him started, he had a nice quiet breakfast of pretzels and near beer.

"It was twelve when we arrived at the field, and Gary was

through with the picture by three and on the train for Hollywood at seven."

In an interview with Richard Schickel more than forty-five years after the shooting, director Bill Wellman had a different impression of Cooper's role in *Wings*. Wellman remembered looking at at least thirty-five actors for the small role that "had to be something that an audience would remember."

Wellman said he waited to shoot Cooper's scene till the rest of the shooting in San Antonio was finished. They rehearsed the scene in Wellman's hotel room one night and did it in one take the next day.

Wellman then went up to his room and took a shower. When he got out, he heard a knock at the door. It was Cooper asking that the scene be shot again. Wellman responded, "It was great or I wouldn't have printed it. . . . Tell me why you didn't like it."

Cooper reportedly responded that he had inadvertently picked his nose in the middle of the scene. According to Wellman, he then advised Cooper not to worry about it, and added, "Never be the aggressor. Always back away from everything until you can't back any farther." The director then comments, "And he did. And he became one of the greatest stars we've ever had."

Aside from the fact that Cooper most certainly does not pick his nose in the footage used in *Wings*, Wellman's recollection smacks of a high degree of retrospective self-appreciation.

When *Wings* was released, Cooper got seventh billing and an enormous amount of fan mail for his brief part. In describing the film, reviewer after reviewer mistakenly recalled Cooper's role as that of a training officer. In fact, he plays a cadet several weeks ahead of new recruits Charles "Buddy" Rogers and Arlen. In the film, Cooper is shown walking up, rubbing his nose and shaking hands with Arlen and Rogers. He smiles slightly, flicks his right hand to his cap and, according to the title card, goes out to do some figure eights. And that is Cooper's performance. After he is gone, Arlen and

Rogers discover he has forgotten his lucky piece. We see the shadow of a plane, and then a soldier comes in to tell Arlen and Rogers to gather the cadet's things, that he has died in a crash. The two men find a picture of Cooper's old aunt and a partly eaten Hershey's chocolate bar. Cooper always admitted that much of the reaction to him in the film was based not on his acting but on how Rogers and Arlen handled the scene after he departed. And he was quite right.

Rogers was twenty-four years old when he made *Wings.* An accomplished pilot, he had made only one major film, *Fascinating Youth,* prior to this. Following his success in *Wings,* Rogers, who later married Mary Pickford, starred in a long string of silent and sound films including *Abie's Irish Rose* and *This Reckless Age.*

"I met Gary Cooper when we were filming *Wings,"* Rogers told this author. "My first impression was that he was super quiet. We didn't consider him a great actor, but his strong personality made him a star." Rogers also recalled that Cooper's small role was altered slightly by Wellman to suit the lanky actor.

Following the making of *Wings,* Rogers, Arlen, Cooper and Jack Oakie became close friends. In fact, Rogers said, the four of them made a pact the next year that "if one wouldn't have his contract renewed the others would share their money and food with him. It was in the days when talkies were first coming, and voices cost many stars their careers."

Away from Clara Bow, Cooper went to what he knew best, action films. Cooper made *Doomsday* and *The Last Outlaw* and moved on to *Beau Sabreur.* There had been some difficulty concocting this sequel to *Beau Geste,* which had been a huge success. The problem was that at the film's end, everyone was killed, leaving no star for a possible sequel. *Beau Sabreur* simply picked up the tale with the hero as a member of the relief party to recapture Fort Zinderhoff from the Arabs. A decade later Cooper would star in a remake of the original tale, thus becoming the only actor to star in a sequel before he made the original.

During *Beau Sabreur* Cooper began a relationship with co-star Evelyn Brent. "In Evelyn Brent," he said a few years later, "I found the companionship of a woman who was wise and brilliant. I was first attracted to her as a woman who had her feet on the ground and was not riding the clouds"—a rather clear reference to the stormy relationship with Clara Bow.

Cooper's next film was *Legion of the Condemned,* in which he co-starred with Fay Wray, with whom he would appear in four films. Cooper was still trying to live down the "It"-boy tag and the public comments by Clara Bow about his childish jealousy.

Cooper later recalled one scene in the picture in which he had to run into a field as planes dive-bombed, pick up Fay Wray and run across the rest of the field while fake rocks blew up all around them. Although he thought he knew the path through the exploding rocks, he made a wrong turn and found the blasts coming dangerously close to him and his leading lady. With eyes smarting from the dust of exploded cork rocks, Cooper staggered out of range and collapsed.

Fay Wray, who had a long and distinguished career in films, is best known as *King Kong*'s love interest in the first version of that film. In an interview for this book, she recalled that Cooper "had a nice, easy quality. A little shy, but I was too at that time. He never seemed very articulate, but he was famous for that. He had a great, slender face and smoky gray eyes and long eyelashes, a very captivating appearing person."

Wray and Cooper remained friends for years after, but there was never a romantic connection. "We saw each other in social situations constantly," she said. "I always thought of Gary as being my big brother. After we did *Legion,* the studio wanted to team us on a continuing basis. They called us 'Paramount's Glorious Young Lovers.'" In fact, the studio did apparently plant romantic stories about the two to build publicity for a second film, *The First Kiss,* in 1928.

"That particular picture," she said, recalling *The First Kiss,* "was not a good one for him or for me. He would have done better with a more—aggressive is not the word—someone who did not have the same temperament and style. He did better with more vigorous and aggressive ladies." Wray also recalled what many who worked with Cooper marveled at. "He always had the capacity to relax to such a degree that he could fall asleep between scenes."

Cooper's next film was *Lilac Time* opposite Colleen Moore. Colleen Moore was twenty-eight years old when she made *Lilac Time.* She had been in movies more than a dozen years, including featured roles in *Intolerance, Little Orphan Annie* and *So Big.* Colleen Moore Hargrave reports that she had chosen Cooper to be her co-star in *Lilac Time.* "The first time I saw Gary Cooper was in a Western picture, a B-type film. I was at Catalina making exteriors for my picture, *Oh Kay.* Every night our whole company would go to the movies, and when I saw Gary in this picture I thought he would be perfect for the part of the English aviator in *Lilac Time.* I telephoned the studio, and they called me back later to tell me that he was under contract to Paramount Pictures and that they had negotiated with the company to loan him to us for the picture."

Mrs. Hargrave recalled that Cooper "was very easy to work with. He was not temperamental and was popular with everyone in my crew." In answer to a question about Cooper's difficulties with acting at this point in his career, she responded, "I would say his main problem was that he found it very difficult to be an actor and was self-conscious doing some scenes. However, when we would look at the rushes next day he came across on the screen with such charisma that he didn't have to act."

She also recalled that Cooper "was very tired most of the time and used to fall asleep in his chair on the set. Of course, that may have been due to his girl friend, Lupe Velez, keeping him up all night.

"I did know he was going to be a big star in spite of the fact that his acting ability was, shall we say, limited at this time. Every day, at some time during the day, my set would be visited by every girl who worked at the studio. They never came before to my set, and it was interesting to see the girls stare at Cooper, giggle, and go back to their desks in the front office.

"What Cooper had was a wonderful, boyish, clean-cut quality that appealed to both men and women. There was no pretense about him; he was completely natural all the time and this showed through on the screen. He had a romantic quality but the kind that one would find in a Western outdoor man."

Although she wanted to do another picture with Cooper following the success of *Lilac Time,* Cooper's salary was suddenly too high for her budgets at First National. "There was," she said, "no room in either of our financial budgets for the two of us to be in the same picture."

Marquis Busby in the *Los Angeles Times* wrote that Cooper gave a "fine performance" and was "a sincere and manly lover." *Motion Picture Classic,* however, found him "too restrained." The song that had been written to be played with the silent film became a national favorite. With his roles in *Wings* and *Lilac Time,* Cooper was indeed a big star.

In *Lilac Time* Cooper, who was now being cast in more flying pictures than Westerns, was an English pilot in France. The twenty-seven-year-old star falls in love with a little French girl played by Moore, and in his key scene, he puts on a false front of bravery before going up to fight the infamous Von Richtoffen. Despite the comments on Cooper's early troubles as an actor, this scene is an even more outstanding piece of acting than the brief appearance in *Wings.* Instead of putting on a broad false grin, Cooper manages to choke off his concern with a pained smile. Later, after he is injured and presumed dead, Cooper, wrapped in bandages like a mummy, strains to rise so he can go to the window of his room. Again underplaying serves him well, and the stoic tensing of the lips implies much more pain than the frenzied gestures that might mark the work of another actor. Cooper was learning.

His next film was *Half a Bride,* in which he played a sea captain marooned on a desert island with a rich married woman played by Esther Ralston. Then Cooper made *The Shop-worn Angel* with Nancy Carroll. *Shopworn Angel* is note-worthy for at least one thing. It was begun just as the studios were frantically converting to sound, and it was decided to add a scene at the end with dialogue, so the film could be released as a talkie.

In the wedding scene at the end of the film, Nancy Carroll says her "I do," and Cooper responds with his first spoken words in film, "I do." In the film Cooper plays a naive soldier charmed by wealthy Nancy Carroll. Cooper's reviews in this non-Western were his best yet. The *New York Daily Mirror* wrote that he "gives a great performance," and Mordaunt Hall in the *New York Times* referred to Cooper's "wonderfully sensi-tive performance as the love-smitten doughboy."

FOUR

SOUND, FURY, AND MEXICAN SPITFIRE: ENCOUNTERS WITH LUPE VELEZ

Lupe Velez, née Guadelupe Velez de Villalobos, was twenty-one when she met Gary Cooper. The Mexican actress had been in movies for almost two years and was already known for her acts of mayhem against the English language, a wild temper and her quick emotions. The pair had met when *Wolf Song* was in the talking stage, and both immediately decided to go beyond the talking. Cooper was still getting some residue of publicity for his "It"-boy image, and the Cooper/Velez romance became big news. Not only the fan magazines but daily papers, including the relatively staid *New York Times,* were covering the couple.

"In Lupe Velez," Cooper said in 1929, "I find a girl who takes the same joy out of primitive, elemental things that I do." *Wolf Song* was not a loser in the publicity; the part-talkie picture turned out to be a success for Paramount, certainly in part because of the notoriety surrounding the two stars. The crooner Russ Columbo appeared in the film and sang the theme song, which became a national hit. The talking part of the film was a brief dialogue scene between Velez and Cooper and two songs sung by Velez.

Although he recalled Lupe Velez as a creature as elusive as quicksilver, Cooper admitted that he was in love with her. He had difficulty understanding the public interest in his personal life, but he was always willing to take advantage of publicity that might help to promote his career. Cooper attributed the massive publicity caused by his relationship with Velez to the fact that the Depression had just hit and the public was happy to lose itself in the far-removed love life of movie stars.

During one interview at the time, Cooper casually remarked that falconry interested him as a possible future hobby. A Montana fan sent him a "pair of love birds," a male and female eagle. Cooper, who was twenty-eight years old, was still living with his parents, who had no room in their home at 1919 Argyle in Los Angeles for a pair of eagles. Lupe Velez had a huge yard and was happy to let Coop house his eagles in a cage there. An enterprising reporter came up with the story that Cooper had given the birds to Velez as a bizarre love gift. Reports of gifts escalated, and twenty-five years later magazines were still referring to the eagles and wildcats the couple had given each other. To get away, the couple went to Catalina to hunt mountain goats, but reporters found them; they spent a month or more in Velez's yard, painting her swimming pool, but photographers, ever enterprising, found ways to get their picture.

Cooper recalled later that Velez never really minded the publicity. Her father had been a Mexican general who had the unfortunate inability to choose the right side in revolutions. The family had fled to San Antonio, where Lupe decided to become an actress. When the family went back to Mexico, Lupe, then sixteen and with no musical or dance training and certainly no experience in acting, talked her way into the leading Mexican theaters—and, by audacity, became a star. When she came to Hollywood at eighteen, she brought her reputation with her and was known to throw props about when she got angry and launch into Spanish tirades against helpless directors, and if someone called her "wild," it would indeed drive her wild.

Cooper got up enough nerve one day to bring Lupe Velez home to his parents. His mother remained forever baffled by her, but his father was completely taken in, even to the point of laughing when she had fits of emotion in the living room. According to Coop, she would then sit on his father's lap and reduce the judge to jelly.

Apparently, the couple were close to marriage several times.

On February 21, 1929, the *New York Times* solemnly reported the denial of Velez that she and Cooper were engaged. One magazine actually prepared a story announcing the marriage but pulled it just before press time.

Around the same time, Cooper told a reporter, "I am going to marry. I want, like almost every man, a home and a family. I want a permanent union, not one of these weekend impermanences." Since he mentioned Lupe Velez in the interview as one of the leading ladies about whom "the most casual linking of our names caused dynamite," it was assumed that the marriage partner in the future was not likely to be Lupe Velez.

However, under Velez's influence, Cooper may have loosened up a bit. On April 22, 1929, he was ticketed for driving forty-five miles an hour in a fifteen-mile-an-hour zone on Wilshire Boulevard. The minor event made the New York newspapers.

To capitalize on their public heat, Paramount rushed Cooper into *Betrayal* with Esther Ralston and Velez into *Lady of the Pavements*. A re-pairing of Velez and Cooper would have seemed more likely.

Betrayal actually starred the German actor Emil Jannings, winner of the first Academy Award for acting. In the film, his last silent picture, Cooper played a young Viennese artist.

Director Lewis Milestone, who would work with Cooper later on *The General Died at Dawn,* had no trouble with Cooper, but Jannings was apparently a problem. "Jannings was very difficult to work with," Milestone recalled later. "You had to know how to handle him. Like most Germans, he could understand a shout, bark or command, but if you tried to be a gentleman with him he would mistake it for weakness.

"He [Jannings] always referred to himself in the third person. If he was asked to lunch, and they served soup, he would taste the soup and say: 'That's wonderful soup—the best thing for Emil.'"

Cooper decided in 1929 that it was time to get back to what

he felt most comfortable in, a Western. When shooting began on his first all-talking picture, *The Virginian,* publicity was in full swing.

"It's like a vacation," he told reporters, "playing in a Western picture. I get the exercise that I don't have time for otherwise. I ride horseback and wear comfortable clothes. There's a great future for Westerns, I think. Good Westerns. I was crazy about them when I was a kid." (In fact, Cooper frequently reported later, he had seen almost no movies as a child and had only really begun going to them after he decided to become an actor in 1924.) "The talkies," Cooper went on, "will give the Westerns new life; that is, if they're good and there aren't too many of them."

The publicity also reported that Cooper had turned Sunnyside into a dude ranch. Paramount began a campaign to compare Cooper to William S. Hart, whose career as the premier cowboy of the silent film had just come to an end. Actually, the comparison was quite reasonable. They both had images as strong, silent heroes. Both had long, serious faces and both, the publicists were quick to point out, had come from a Western background, Hart from Dakota, Coop from Montana. Hart—who actually had moved to Westerns from a stage career in Shakespeare—had even written a book about his supposed adventures in the wild West. Cooper never went quite that far, but he did begin to talk about his adventures with friendly Indians on the ranch. The family even dug out a picture of Coop at sixteen with an Indian headdress.

The *Saturday Evening Post* wanted Coop for a future cover and commissioned Norman Rockwell to do the painting. In his book *A Rockwell Portrait,* the artist described the meeting: "We had a wonderful time. He was as nice a guy as ever you'd meet. I didn't know what to expect from a famous movie star; maybe that he'd be sort of stuck-up, you know. But not Gary Cooper. He had fun, too. He horsed around so much . . . that I had a hard time painting him."

The Cooper painting ran on the *Post*'s cover of May 24, 1930, and clearly visible in it is a slate with the title of Cooper's film *The Texan* written on it.

The director of *The Virginian* was Victor Fleming, who had been Cooper's principal rival for Clara Bow's affection. The film was based on Owen Wister's turn-of-the-century novel, already filmed twice and destined to be the most popular Western novel of all time. *The Virginian* was one of the first major talking pictures to be shot outdoors. The other major outdoor talkie in 1929 was *In Old Arizona*, the film for which Warner Baxter would win his Academy Award as the Cisco Kid.

Exterior filming was done in Sonora in the Sierras, and the problems were great. The sound equipment required elaborate rigging and trucks, and the equipment and microphone had to be right next to the actors but just out of sight of the camera. A young actor from Virginia named Randolph Scott was hired as dialogue coach to work on Cooper's accent. Fleming was irritated by the tyranny of the sound crew, and Cooper was completely flustered. He recalled one scene with Richard Arlen, who played his pal Steve. It was a particularly poignant moment; the Virginian (Cooper) has caught his old friend rustling. Both know that the posse will have to hang Steve. The two friends sit on the ground and have a pained conversation. As soon as the slapsticks clacked in front of Coop's face to announce the take and give a sound cue for the future editor, the actor went blank. The unfamiliar crack of wood under his nose completely unnerved him. For take after take, Cooper was unable to do the scene. It was a pattern he recognized. After something had broken his concentration, it was difficult for Cooper to perform. Repeated takes only made it worse.

No longer could a John Waters tell Cooper to think of a chicken dinner while he looked at Thelma Todd. The microphones were there, and Cooper was on his own.

It was Arlen who came up with a solution that would be adopted over and over again in films—right up to the present. Since his back was to Cooper during the shot, why couldn't they simply tape Cooper's lines to Arlen's shirt, out of sight of the camera? Cooper could simply read them a foot away from his face. The next morning they tried it and got the shot in one take. In the finished film, the scene is remarkably effective. Cooper's eyes are downcast, and he speaks haltingly. It looks as if emotion over his friend's plight has almost broken him down. The eyes are clearly down to read the dialogue, and the stammer was a result of an awkward reading, but film is a medium of illusion, and Cooper was quickly becoming an inadvertent master of the medium.

In *The Virginian,* Cooper's co-star, with equal billing, was Walter Huston, the first in a long series of character actors who, according to logic, should have made the underplaying Cooper disappear. Remarkably, Cooper always looked best in scenes with such actors. The more they snarled and raged, the more Cooper underplayed.

The Virginian also marks the start of many Cooper characteristics that were to symbolize the actor. In his first appearance, he delivers a rather stock "Well, I'll be gol'darned" line while he absently twirls a piece of braid with his right hand. Cooper's hands were huge and long. They almost looked as if they didn't belong on that lean, lanky body, but Cooper learned to use them constantly, to keep them busy doing little things that would be natural for the character he was playing. Movements of his hands and body were frequently more important to defining his screen characters than his dialogue, and the body movements always remained totally natural and unobtrusive. Cooper was also experimenting with "tricks" he could use effectively if the director controlled them. The timely innocent gulp had stayed with him, and in *The Virginian,* after delivering the line, "Well, Steve, I reckon I gotta learn you all over again," he literally puts his tongue in his cheek. The gulp comes after the rescue of the schoolmarm on a runaway horse.

In the famous scene in the bar in which *The Virginian* is called a supposedly foul name by Trampas, Cooper says, "When you wanna call me that, smile," after calmly rolling a cigarette in his massive and potentially threatening fingers.

In an outdoor dinner scene, Cooper wanders through with his thumbs in his pockets. His elbows are out, and he appears large and awkward in this civilized setting. In a conversation later in the scene, Cooper avoids looking into someone's eyes by rubbing his hands together and looking at his fingernails.

For years it was felt essential that a comedy scene be included in most Cooper films. In *The Virginian,* Cooper and Arlen purposely mix up half a dozen babies at a christening, and, in the midst of their antics, Cooper announces that it's "getting mighty swampy around this bed."

Another Cooper trademark that began with *The Virginian* was his ability to refer to spaces in the film as if they were real, not just sets or nonexistent reference spots just beyond the end of the frame. In *The Virginian,* he announces to the girl, "I aim to stay here," and points down decisively. He would gradually play with this until he could point someplace off the screen without looking at it and give the impression that the farm, office, ship or battle was so clearly there that it needed no reference beyond his character's assertion of its existence.

The extremely thin Cooper also made it a point to lean distinctly to the left, off center, in the saddle when talking to someone. It drew attention to him and underlined his character's comfort in the saddle. In fact, the left-hand list was related to his damaged pelvis, which made such a move more comfortable. It became, however, one of Cooper's tricks.

Cooper had one scene in *The Virginian* that was reminiscent of the silent days. As directors grew further and further away from the belief in the early 1930s that the new sound had to exist constantly, Cooper would frequently go back to individual scenes that required, instead of dialogue, a wide range of small facial and body reactions in a single shot. After Steve is hanged, a forlorn Virginian rides away. A quail whistles. It is the whistle Steve always used. Cooper, riding toward the camera, looks up—not quite hopefully—knowing it can't be Steve—unable to resist the dead hope.

The Virginian blames Trampas for leading his friend Steve

into a life of crime that causes his death. In his final showdown
with Trampas, Cooper shows his anger by talking through
clenched teeth, and his jaws quiver with controlled rage. Early
in the film, Cooper wears his white hat at the back of his head
in an almost childlike way, but as the film moves forward,
Cooper's hat does too, to the point where it is pulled low over
his eyes for the final gunfight.

The film's end is remarkably like that of Cooper's other
major Western, *High Noon.* The Virginian is about to marry
the schoolmarm, played by Mary Brian, but he finds Trampas
in town on their wedding day. She tries to stop him with a quite
reasonable argument, but he gives the classic Cooper argument, an argument that became symbolic of American self-
righteousness: There are some things a man just can't walk
away from. The Virginian triumphs, and, even though she has
threatened to leave, the waiting fiancée gladly takes him back.

In the film, Cooper's accent, in spite of Randolph Scott's
coaching, is crude. Gradually, he would refine his Western accent to give only the suggestion of a mythic West and not its
caricature.

The Virginian also helped to establish the Cooper image as
one of a man of few initial words besides "Yes, ma'am" when
confronting a woman. In fact, his sparseness of conversation
even at this early date is turned into a joke. In answer to a
series of questions from Mary Brian after they meet, Cooper
answers only "No, ma'am" and "Yes, ma'am."

"Is that all you have to say for yourself?" Brian asks in
exasperation. To which Cooper replies, "No, ma'am. Yes
ma'am," and breaks out laughing.

Cooper had mixed feelings about cultivating his image. At
times, especially in interviews, he would nurture it. At other
times, he would complain that he was a normal, in fact, quite
garrulous, individual. In a few of his pictures, as we will see, he
went out of his way to play men who had a great deal to say
and loved to talk.

But this was 1929—*The Virginian* was a smash, and Cooper

was a sensation. The *London Times* said Cooper was "everything he should be as the Virginian; strong, attractive, and serious." Over about a year, Paramount put him in six films—*Seven Days' Leave, Only the Brave, The Texan, Paramount on Parade, The Man from Wyoming,* and *The Spoilers.*

Seven Days' Leave was an adaptation of James Barrie's play, *The Old Lady Shows Her Medals.* The setting was England, and Cooper played an innocent Scottish soldier in kilts befriended by a lonely old woman while he is on leave. *Only the Brave* was a Civil War tale. He had only a cameo appearance in *Paramount on Parade,* which marked his first appearance in color, but *The Texan* and *The Spoilers* (which was based on a silent film) were both action-filled Westerns and wound up with excellent reviews for Cooper. *The Man From Wyoming* was an army film set in France and not a Western as has frequently been assumed. During this time, Cooper was literally confused about which picture he was appearing in, and for much of the year he would work on two films at the same time, with different directors.

During the shooting of one of these films, in the fall of 1930, he was again thrust into the news when reports came out that he and the cast were trapped by a snowstorm in the Sierras. According to one newspaper:

> Two state highway department snowplow tractors nosed their way up the steep automobile road, clearing the snow, which was reported to be eighteen inches deep. The flock of sheep, also marooned at Dardanelle, was first to plod down the mountain road after the tractors had opened the way. This, highway experts said, hardened the remaining snow and made the road smoother for the automobiles and trucks of the motion picture company.
>
> The company was on location at Dardanelle, a tiny summer resort, filming a Western picture.
>
> Several thousand dollars worth of motion picture equipment was reported buried in three feet of snow on the summit of the Sierra Nevada 5700 feet above sea level . . .

Cooper fans waited anxiously for news about their star's safety. Strangely, the story of the snowstorm was carried by papers across the country, but no one seemed to have checked to see if it was true. In fact, it wasn't. The snowstorm was the idea of a publicity man on the picture. Cooper made a slight protest about the fraud but did not think it a major incident.

FIVE

IN HIGH SOCIETY: THE COUNTESS AND A DEB FROM NEW YORK

Cooper's next picture was Morocco, *in which he co-starred* with Marlene Dietrich in her first American movie. The director was Josef von Sternberg. Born Josef Stern in Vienna in 1894, Sternberg came to the United States at the age of seven. He served in the U.S. Army in World War I, making army training films. After some independent film work, he did various jobs patching up films made by other directors, by shooting additional scenes and working on the editing. Two such films had been *It* and *Children of Divorce.* He got his first major break in 1927, when he directed *Underworld,* and solidified his position as a top director with *The Last Command* in 1928. It was in that year that Von Sternberg went to Germany and made his only German film, *The Blue Angel,* in which he "discovered" Marlene Dietrich.

Although he got along well with Dietrich, Cooper later said he instantly disliked Sternberg, who took a great deal of time setting up his lighting and ignored his actors. The only one Sternberg really talked to at length was Dietrich, and he spoke to her only in German. When Cooper complained, Von Sternberg stalked off the set.

Sternberg's attitude began to undermine Cooper's growing confidence, and Cooper complained to his friend Adolphe Menjou, who also appeared in the film, that the director did not see him as a co-star but as a decorative prop.

Menjou, who frequently made the list of America's best-dressed men, told Cooper that he could make his legionnaire's uniform work for him, could tilt the cap at various angles, play with the buttoning and unbuttoning of his tunic. Cooper took the advice willingly and from that point on, tried whenever he could to get hats for the characters he played.

Von Sternberg's version of the shooting of *Morocco* differs greatly from Cooper's. In his autobiography, *Fun in a Chinese Laundry,* Von Sternberg remembers Cooper as "one of the nicest human beings I have ever met." However, says Von Sternberg, in response to Cooper's claims about him, "I spoke German only to an actress [Dietrich] who could not understand English and this should not have bothered him as they rarely played in the same scene."

Von Sternberg also recalled his difficulties with Cooper. To get the proper reaction shots of Cooper, "I was forced to replace her [Dietrich] with some of my assistants, who clowned and made comic grimaces to induce Cooper to overcome his shyness."

Von Sternberg also denied that he had ever walked off the set when confronted by Cooper and added, "I was never displeased with him, and as far as I knew, we were always good friends."

Von Sternberg also recalled working with Cooper when he reshot scenes for *Children of Divorce.* Cooper, he said, was so reluctant to look directly at the director that he turned his eyes constantly toward the lights and developed a rather painful occupational trauma of actors in the late twenties and early thirties, klieg eyes.

Eventually the film was finished, and Cooper was satisfied with his performance as French Foreign Legionnaire Tom Brown, a cad with women. He was not satisfied with the ad campaign, however, believing that Von Sternberg highlighted Marlene Dietrich and virtually ignored Cooper and Menjou.

In any case, he was not ignored by the critics. In the *New York Herald Tribune,* Richard Watts, Jr., wrote: "The understandably popular Gary Cooper, who underacts more completely than any other player within memory, never has been as effective and certainly never as expert an actor as he is in the role of the hero." In the *New York Evening Post,* Thornton

Delehanty said, "Gary Cooper gives one of his best performances in this picture, a restrained and telling piece of work."

Cooper was rushed into shooting *Fighting Caravans* with Lilly Damita. The film, based on a novel by Zane Grey, was quite similar to *The Covered Wagon,* with Cooper playing a guide who leads a wagon train across the country. Paramount saw it as a major project and employed two directors, two cinematographers and nine composers to arrange the musical score. So much footage was eventually shot that there was enough left over to provide the background for another film, *Wagon Wheels,* starring Randolph Scott, which was released two years later.

Some of the film was shot at Sonora, and then the cast and crew moved to the mountains. During the day, Cooper would nearly suffocate. At night, he would jump into his car and drive the hundred miles back to Hollywood to do scenes for *City Streets*. Originally, *City Streets* was to have starred Clara Bow, but the re-pairing was not to be. Bow backed out, and Sylvia Sidney got the role.

In one shot, filmed after midnight, Cooper was driving a prop car. The shot was entirely inside the studio on a set, and the fake car never moved. The script called for Cooper to pretend to swerve to miss an accident. Worn out from his schedule, Cooper said that a moment came when he confused fiction and reality and was convinced that he was in a real car about to have an accident. There may have been memories of his hip-fracturing accident a few years earlier, or maybe Cooper had attained the ultimate in Method acting and become the fictional character for a brief moment, in spite of the props and lights.

Whatever the reason, the next thing he knew, he was in a hospital looking up at a small crack in the white ceiling. The doctors said he was suffering from exhaustion, that he had lost too much weight and was working too hard. He needed a rest. He finished both *Fighting Caravans* and *City Streets* and sailed for Europe before the two films were released.

Ironically, the *Motion Picture Herald* wrote of his performance in *Fighting Caravans* that "No great demands are made upon him, but he gives an interesting performance." His reviews for *City Streets* were excellent.

City Streets was made from a screenplay by Dashiell Hammett, the creator of the Thin Man and Sam Spade. It was his only original screenplay. Hammett had been working at Paramount when he met director Rouben Mamoulian. Mamoulian told Hammett he was looking for ideas, so Hammett did a four-page outline Mamoulian liked. In the course of working on the film, Hammett met Cooper and discussed the possibility of Cooper's starring in a film version of Hammett's novel *The Glass Key.* Cooper, in fact, moved to purchase film rights to the book. Eventually *The Glass Key* would be made with George Raft in the starring role. A later remake starred Alan Ladd.

Rouben Mamoulian, director of *City Streets,* was proud of his treatment of film gangsterism and told the press, "You know, there are ten killings in this film, and you don't actually see one of them." In the film, Cooper plays a Westerner, complete with white cowboy hat, who works in a traveling carnival. When the film opens, the carnival is in a big city. Recognition of Cooper's romantic appeal is underlined by his first appearance. His back is to the camera; we see only his hat; then he turns around, with a match in his mouth, to give a broad smile. His first line further underscores his image. He says only, "Yup." Since he is running a shooting gallery, he then has the opportunity to twirl his guns and fire at some targets.

Walking through the carnival with Sylvia Sidney, Cooper throws a ball behind his back at some milk bottles, scratches his neck with his right hand and munches on a hot dog.

When his girl friend goes to prison, the straight Kid joins the gang and discards his cowboy hat for a cap. His Western gun skills and fighting ability are going to be used by the gang.

In one scene, Cooper, as the Kid, visits his girl in prison. They try to touch through the mesh separating them, and he keeps his huge right hand against the wire as they talk. The scene is handled primarily with a single take and not as an edited scene. The kiss at the end of the take is a further example of the characters' difficulty in getting to each other. The film, as is true of most films, was not shot chronologically, that is, the way we see it is not the way it was shot. Scenes in a single location used throughout the picture were shot at the same time. As we see the film, Cooper gradually loses his Western accent. This quite reasonably indicates the passage of time and his absorption into the urban environment. Cooper had to keep track from shot to shot of where his accent was supposed to be, and he handled this flawlessly.

A new Cooper trick is seen in *City Streets*. When the character is impatient, he bounces on his heels slightly. Considering his build and his immediate recognition by an audience, even if he is not in the center of the frame, it is difficult to ignore the vibrating figure.

There is nothing in Cooper's performance in the film to indicate the exhaustion he claimed. It is improbable that Cooper is masking it, since in many later films his exhaustion and pain are clearly evident in his movements and performance. Though Paramount was convinced that Cooper's exhaustion was in part an excuse to get a vacation and gain greater control of his roles, there was little they could do about it. The departure was blamed by various sources on jaundice, flu, a nervous breakdown and a broken heart.

Newspaper columnists suggested strongly that Cooper really wanted to get away from Lupe Velez, who was apparently putting an end to their relationship. According to Cooper, he and Velez just "drifted apart." Velez, however, blamed Cooper's mother for ending the affair. "He may be an idol to his mother," she said, "but he's less than nothing to me." Velez told reporter Marion Leslie that whenever Cooper didn't do as his mother wanted him to, she became ill. "She is just trying to hold him by sickness," she added.

Although Velez remained a star, she gradually moved to

lower and lower budget films, while Cooper continued to rise. She married and divorced Johnny Weissmuller, and in the 1940s starred in a series of highly popular B-budget "Mexican Spitfire" comedies co-starring comedian Leon Errol. In 1944, despondent over her career, despite the success of her series, she committed suicide in her Beverly Hills home.

On his trip to Europe, Cooper visited relatives in England, stopped briefly in Algiers, where he was recognized by Arab boys who shouted "Boom! Boom!" at him and pointed their fingers, and wound up in Venice. Lounging around on the beach in an attempt at serious rest, he was nagged by depression. "Nobody recognized me there," he said later, "so I began getting depressed again. I was nothing more than a hunk of celluloid pieced together in cutting rooms by the directors."

At this point, Cooper got a telegram from Walter Wanger, the producer. Wanger urged Cooper to look up his old friend, the Countess Dorothy diFrasso, at her Villa Madama in Rome. The Countess, born Dorothy Taylor in a wealthy New York family, "took me in hand like the lost lad I was," Cooper recalled. "Her villa was a meeting place for the international set, and rubbing elbows with assorted noblemen, heiresses and celebrated characters made me forget my fears."

In fact, Cooper and the countess, who was older than he and married to the count, had a rather open affair. She was eventually to number among her conquests the gangster Bugsy Siegel, but in 1931, she concentrated on turning Gary Cooper into a gentleman of high society, as she would later try to do with Siegel. The countess, who had spent a million dollars fixing up her villa, escorted Cooper across Europe and helped him earn high rank in the equivalent of the 1930s jet set. His exploits, including a well-publicized ride over the steeplejack course at an Italian cavalry school, resulted in a telegram from Paramount telling Cooper that he was clearly recovered and should get back quickly.

It was agreed, however, that Cooper would not have to come

all the way back to Hollywood. He could make his next picture in New York, so he could continue to mingle with his new friends and with the countess and the count.

It was August, 1931, when he arrived in New York and plunged right into shooting *His Woman* with Claudette Colbert. Old studios in Astoria were used, and Cooper remembered the unbearable heat in those pre-air-conditioning days. The studio had been built for silent film and was an enormous barnlike place that picked up echoes. Blankets were placed along the walls, resulting in better sound—and more heat. Hot lights made it worse, but Cooper had no relapse of whatever had caused his European flight.

In the film, Cooper played Sam Whalan, captain of a tramp freighter whose crew picks up a baby drifting in a boat. Needing a mother for the baby, Whalen hires Sally Clark (Colbert), who really wants passage home from the tropical port where they find her. Eventually, she learns to love Cooper and the baby, and they live happily ever after. The *New York Times* thought Cooper was "outrageously" miscast. Most of the reviews praised the baby and ignored the stars. Cooper always claimed that his habit of sleeping between takes began with *His Woman,* but others had remarked about it much earlier.

Cooper's next film was *I Take This Woman,* which was originally supposed to star him and Fay Wray. Instead, Carole Lombard, a rising star, was cast in this comedy-romance in which Cooper played a contemporary cowboy in love with a sophisticated heiress who introduces him to society, ridicules him and eventually falls in love with him. There may have been some wish to capitalize on the diFrasso-Cooper romance in making the film, but it was a bust as a financial idea. The diFrasso situation was generally regarded in Hollywood as a joke on Cooper. Tallulah Bankhead said that she was once asked at a Santa Barbara party why she thought Gary Cooper had not yet arrived. "He's probably worn to a frasso," responded Tallulah.

When he finished the two films, Cooper began to complain

that his exhaustion was returning, that he didn't care if he made another picture. He had, in fact, run into two of the countess's friends, Jimmie and Willie Donahue, who were planning an African safari. He also met some European friends who owned a ranch in Tanganyika and invited him to come. "They suggested it would be a fine place to recuperate," Cooper recalled.

From Africa, the countess and Cooper went on to the Riviera in the spring of 1932. Newspapers in the United States covered Cooper's progress through Monte Carlo, Cannes, Nice and Paris. The tour ended when Cooper found that he had gone broke trying to keep up with the millionaires. He was thirty years old and more than a bit scared. This time Paramount had not sent him a telegram urging him to come home to work. In fact, Paramount had begun to groom what the movie magazines termed a new Gary Cooper. The new face belonged to Cary Grant. It was suggested that the similarity of names was not at all coincidental. It was also suggested that the two actors looked remarkably alike, a suggestion, surprisingly, that no one publicly laughed at.

As it turned out, Paramount was happy to have Cooper come back. His European jaunt and the attendant publicity had made him an even hotter property. Back on the payroll, Cooper was cast with Tallulah Bankhead and Charles Laughton in *The Devil and the Deep*. Paramount also cast Cary Grant in a major role in the film, possibly just to remind Cooper of what might happen if he took it into his head to have another breakdown.

Bankhead had met Cooper a year earlier, when Walter Wanger sent him over on a blind date. Wagner knew she had admired Cooper and arranged the meeting. Two days after that single date, a New York gossip columnist announced the engagement of the two stars. "Never," she said, "was an engagement coined on such slight evidence." When Reuter's, the English news bureau, asked Bankhead for confirmation, she sent a telegram saying that she was engaged to eight-year-old Jackie Cooper, not Gary Cooper.

While they were making *The Devil and the Deep,* Bankhead and Cooper made a guest appearance as themselves in *Make Me a Star,* a remake of *Merton of the Movies,* starring Stuart Erwin.

To prepare for *The Devil and the Deep,* Cooper began to read books about submarines. He read technical books, histories and even fictional pieces, including Jules Verne's *20,000 Leagues Under the Sea.* It was a procedure he would use in almost every film he made. When he knew what his role would be, he plunged into research and tried to become that character, to make the character's movements, feelings, and knowledge so much a part of his actions that he felt he wasn't even acting. To prepare for *The Devil and the Deep,* he talked extensively to the naval officer who served as technical advisor for the film and arranged to rehearse not the actual role but the way a submarine officer would act and react. For example, working on a mock-up of a submarine, Cooper practiced learning how to behave in a crash dive and how to handle routine moves.

One afternoon Tallulah Bankhead found Cooper on the submarine set, practicing with the controls and tensing his jaws for imaginary dives.

"What," she asked, "has this to do with acting?"

Cooper explained that he had learned through the technical advisor that submarine crews got tense from their jaws to their toes when they went into a dive, that they held themselves differently underwater. Cooper was trying to get the feel of being underwater.

"The point is," he said, "if I know what I'm doing, I don't have to act."

Years later Bankhead was to work with Cooper again on radio. She was hosting a radio variety show, and Cooper was the guest.

"It was our custom," she said, "to end each performance of 'The Big Show' with each of the notables involved singing one line of Meredith Willson's hymn, 'May the Good Lord Bless and Keep You.' Gary blanched when told he, too, must sing one line of this anthem. He's tone-deaf. He was scared, but steeled himself to the task. The rest of us rehearsed this bit for a bare ten minutes, but Gary rehearsed his one line for a solid week."

Actually, Cooper does sing in a few of his movies, most notably *Good Sam* and *Along Came Jones* and while his voice is far from operatic, he can keep a tune. He also sang regularly and in public while performing for troops during World War II and even recorded a song from *Friendly Persuasion.*

In his next effort, *If I Had A Million,* Cooper appeared in one segment of the multistory film as a tough marine named Gallagher who gets a check for a million dollars, thinks it's a gag, and gives it away to a lunchstand operator. Norman McLeod directed the segment, and Cooper received top billing over George Raft, Charles Laughton and Jack Oakie.

Cooper's European image stayed with him for much of this time. Reporter Muriel Babcock interviewed the star and said that he had a flock of new suits, ties and shoes. She said that Cooper preferred Italian tailors to the British and that he was now smoking a "very aristocratic and mild brand of cigarettes instead of the good old cowboy brand."

She also reported that Cooper now had a pet chimpanzee, a "cute little thing that loves to curl up affectionately in Gary's lap and climbs trees in his backyard."

Cooper's backyard was in a rented home at 1027 Chevy Chase Drive in Beverly Hills. The count and countess moved in a few doors away. Cooper's landlord would later sue him for $1,014 for damage done to the property, particularly to the glassware and a bronze statue. Whether the damage was caused by the chimp or Cooper's now frequent parties was never made clear.

Cooper now began quickly to gather enough money to go into the oil business. With his parents, he leased 2,000 acres of land in Palm Springs and announced plans to sink fifty-two oil wells seven miles east of the resort. Cooper also found time in 1932 to file suit in the U.S. Supreme Court for an injunction restraining the Sheffield Farms Co., Inc., from continuing to circulate an advertisement in which his name and picture were used, allegedly without authority. Cooper's suit charged that he was damaged because the ad pictured him as drinking milk, "to build up health and strength." Presumably the implication that he needed anything to build his health and strength was an affront.

Cooper continued to deny tales of his romance with the countess, saying, "She and her husband were very pleasant and hospitable when I was in Rome. I stayed at their villa as their guest for some time." Cooper was also fond of telling of his African safari, during which he was charged by a raging rhino.

After finishing *The Devil and the Deep,* Cooper heard he had lost out on the lead in *A Farewell to Arms.* It was announced that Fredric March would star opposite Claudette Colbert. Cooper was scheduled, instead, to play the role of Lieutenant Pinkerton in a nonmusical version of *Madame Butterfly* opposite Sylvia Sidney, but with negotiations for a new contract coming up, Coop convinced the studio he should get the lead in *A Farewell to Arms.*

Although he had used his clout to get the role, Cooper fearfully faced his first meeting with Helen Hayes, who was now scheduled to be his co-star. In her first film, the stage-trained Hayes had won an Academy Award for her role in *The Sin of Madelon Claudet.* The award, her stage background and her reputation as a lady awed Cooper.

What he didn't know was that Hayes was equally afraid of him, but for quite different reasons. She had followed the publicity about his love life and had an image of him as a lean and lecherous sophisticate. When they were introduced, they had nothing to say to each other. Sensing future problems with his actors, director Frank Borzage told them that the studio needed some preshooting publicity. He took them to a prop coach and called a still photographer. Borzage proceeded to spend several hours posing the two in love clinches until they became used to each other. It helped Borzage, because he soon discovered the potential difficulty of having the two play scenes standing up. Cooper towered over the diminutive Hayes, so much so that they looked rather bizarre together. Borzage decided to find reasons throughout the film why the two should have a minimum of scenes standing.

Borzage made a joke about the size problem while they were shooting the stills, and his two actors began to laugh in each other's arms. It didn't quite lead to a lasting friendship, but it did make Cooper and Hayes comfortable enough to do the film with no personality problems.

During the shooting of *A Farewell to Arms,* Marion Leslie interviewed Cooper for *Photoplay* and asked him about his apparently recent aggressive attitude toward Paramount in terms of his salary and roles. Cooper said that when he had gone to Europe he had felt

> sunk. Washed up. I had been working day and night. I was unhappy about the way things were going at the studio. My private affairs had reached a crisis.
>
> I shall never get into such a state, mentally, again. Life can never do anything like that to me again. I have learned something.
>
> In the first place, I shall never be dominated by other people again as I had allowed myself to be until that time. I had drifted, taken advice, let people get at me through my emotions, my sympathy, my affections. Perhaps through a sort of apathy, too, because I was not well . . . my attitude toward my work has changed. You are right. It isn't as important to me as it used to be. And therefore, I shall do better at it . . . I am no longer blinded by the glamour of pictures. I have learned that it is no use to have ideas unless you express them. And no one will have any respect for your ideas unless you are willing to fight for them.

Although Cooper would not actually meet Ernest Hemingway for four more years, *A Farewell to Arms* was the first step in an association with Hemingway that would eventually become a very close friendship. *A Farewell to Arms* received four Academy Award nominations, and Cooper's performance was accepted as a breakthrough from his previous roles. It was the most demanding role of his career to that point. Cooper's character is highly verbal, and he has a broad emotional range. In the course of the film, he moves from a self-assured, cocky officer to a childlike, babbling civilian. To mark this gradual change, Cooper begins the film standing erect; his hands are active; his eyelids are partially down. He is a man who knows how to protect himself. His change begins the first time he kisses Helen Hayes. When she slaps him, the fingers of his right hand move to his cheek. He touches the smarting cheek, lets his fingers dance away from the sting, tries not to show that he has been hurt both physically and emotionally, but that he has been is evident in his reaction.

Later, when confronted by a nurse who tells him he is a near-alcoholic who must return to the front, Cooper plays with an empty wine bottle, sticks his finger into it, avoids direct confrontation. In the second half of the film, as he grows more emotionally vulnerable, Cooper begins to slouch slightly. His eyes are wide and uncertain; his hands hang motionlessly at his sides, partly curled. The level of Cooper's voice also changes as the film progresses. Early in the film when he is in control and confident, his voice remains steady and low. By the end of the film, particularly in two scenes in which he is alone and worried about the potential death of his lover, he completely loses control of his voice level.

Martin Dickstein wrote in the *Brooklyn Daily Eagle* that "Gary Cooper, particularly in the closing scenes, is revealed as an actor with a greater emotional depth than he has ever displayed before."

At this point, Paramount agreed to loan Cooper to MGM, to appear with Joan Crawford in *Today We Live,* based on a William Faulkner short story, *Turnabout.* He was to play Bogard, an American fighter pilot who is the great love of the Crawford character's life. When shooting was scheduled to begin at Metro, however, Cooper simply did not show up. Emmanuel

Cohen, production head at Paramount, who had made the Cooper deal directly with Metro's Irving Thalberg, said he was surprised.

Cooper said nothing about why he hadn't shown up for shooting, but he did mention to a reporter that he had been promised a vacation he had not been granted, and he had also asked Paramount for permission to make *Secrets* opposite Mary Pickford but had been refused.

MGM and Paramount reported that Cooper was ill after he failed to show up the second day. By the third day, he was well but still not at work, and production costs were mounting. Acting as his own agent, Cooper told Paramount that he had learned they had obtained a bonus for his services to Metro. He wanted, he said, a share of the bonus, in addition to a salary increase of $200 a week.

Cooper got the bonus and salary jump, and he appeared on the fourth day. The director of the film was Howard Hawks, who would eventually direct Cooper in his first Academy Award performance as Sergeant York.

Although *Today We Live* was rather broadly panned when it appeared, Cooper once again was singled out for praise. The *New York Times* called his performance "restrained, sympathetic and quite believable." John S. Cohen, Jr. wrote, "Gary Cooper, who has really learned to act in the talkies, almost equals his performance in *A Farewell To Arms.*"

In his next film, Cooper was again teamed with Fay Wray. In *One Sunday Afternoon,* his new stature as an actor was accepted, and he was cast as a dentist, Biff Grimes, who marries the wrong girl and lives a quiet life of remorse. The film would be remade in 1941 as *The Strawberry Blonde,* with James Cagney as the dentist. Though the reviews of Cooper's performance were mixed, the film did well, and Cooper thought enough of his work to name his newly acquired bulldog Biff Grimes as a reminder of the role and the fact that many of the critics said his character had not been aggressive enough.

Meanwhile, his romance with the countess was coming to an end. It officially ended at a party given by Cedric Gibbons, the art director, for his niece Veronica Balfe. Miss Balfe was exactly the kind of society person Cooper was interested in at that point in his life. The stepdaughter of Paul Shields of the board of governors of the New York Stock Exchange, she was a full-fledged 1931 debutante. A recent graduate of the Bennett School for girls in Millbrook, New York, she had also attended the Todhunter School in New York City. She had come to Hollywood to try to break into movies under the name Sandra Shaw. As Sandra Shaw, she had appeared in one film, *Blood Money,* a strange crime film about a loan shark and a mad society girl, played by George Bancroft and Frances Dee, and directed by Rowland Brown. After seeing herself in a preview, Balfe had decided that acting was not to be her life's work.

At the party, she readily confessed to Cooper that she had loved him in *Morocco.* He was flattered and attracted. They dated for several weeks in spite of some concern from her family about the playboy image of Cooper, and on December 15, 1933, they were married in New York at the home of the bride's stepfather. Only six people attended the wedding, to minimize publicity.

According to *The New York Times* story following the wedding at the Shields' home at 778 Park Avenue, the wedding had originally been scheduled to take place at the Waldorf Astoria Hotel. But, according to the *Times,* "Apparently the plans of the couple were changed to avoid the throngs of admirers that have besieged Mr. Cooper during his recent appearances in public here."

The service was performed by the Reverend George A. Trowbridge of All Angels Church in New York. Shortly after the ceremony, the couple headed for Phoenix, Arizona, to spend the Christmas holidays with Cooper's parents.

What was not mentioned in the newspaper accounts was the fact that Veronica Cooper was a Catholic and Cooper a Protestant. The difference would become important in later years.

Cooper frequently said that the marriage saved him from his playboy life. Although the couple had originally said they would live in Beverly Hills, they rented a house in Van Nuys, discarded many of Cooper's African mementoes and got rid of the chimp and other reminders of the diFrasso episode.

At home Cooper became an avid gardener. He and his wife took up skeet shooting, swimming, skiing and eventually scuba diving. Rocky Cooper proved to be superior to her husband in each of the sports. In fact she became a national-caliber skeet shooter and won several championships.

At first the couple entertained few friends except for the Joel McCreas. Coop was content to make pictures, work on his garden and start a collection of guns which he enjoyed repairing. He also collected Mercedes-Benzes and other powerful foreign cars. "A Mercedes, I always figure, is the next best thing to a horse," he told a reporter.

SIX

ADVENTURES IN HOLLYWOOD: THE PARAMOUNT YEAR

Just before his marriage, Cooper had completed roles in both Design for Living and Alice in Wonderland. There had been talk that Cooper, after eight years with Paramount, would not sign a new contract and, after making one more film on his present one, would become an independent. The film was to be *Here Is My Heart,* which was never made. He was supposed to follow this with *Barbary Coast* starring Anna Sten, the Russian-born actress, who had specifically asked for Cooper. *Barbary Coast* would be made with Edward G. Robinson and George Raft, but not Cooper.

His role in *Alice in Wonderland* was very short, as most were, in this film filled with cameo performances. Cooper played the old White Knight, his face covered with makeup and his body heavily padded. The voice is the only thing that gives him away. The role itself is a comic cameo in which Cooper's character has trouble staying on his horse.

While he prepared for the role, Cooper read *Alice in Wonderland* and enjoyed it. "You know," he told Virginia Maxwell of *Photoplay,* "I get all mixed up about things sometimes. I try to figure out life's little ways, and when I get so baffled I don't know quite what to do, I pick up *Alice in Wonderland* and skim through it. Then I conclude that life is really just about as cockeyed as Alice found it."

Design for Living was shot in the summer of 1933 with Ernst Lubitsch directing. Lubitsch, the son of a Berlin tailor, was a good-natured, portly little man who chomped continuously on a cigar. He had begun his career in Germany as a stage comic and had moved into film roles and then to the directing of short comedies. He came to America to direct Mary Pickford in *Rosita* and stayed to earn a reputation as one of the most clever directors, if not the most clever, of sophisticated comedy. His eventual list of directing credits would include *The Love Parade, Trouble in Paradise, Ninotchka, To Be or Not To Be,* and *Heaven Can Wait.*

Design For Living was based on a Noel Coward play of moderate success. It dealt with a woman, Miriam Hopkins, who falls in love with two men, Cooper and Fredric March, at the same time. The Hopkins character moves from March's playwright character to Cooper's artist and eventually decides she cannot choose, so the three decide to live together. The play had distinct homosexual implications. The film did not.

Cooper, knowing he was getting a role his audience might have seen Alfred Lunt do on stage, decided to give it a change from his usual pacing. Comedy, he felt, should be done quickly, but rapid-fire dialogue was a bit alien to him. Lubitsch also told him to slow down, that he needed just as much Cooper screen time as March screen time. At this, according to Cooper, he got an idea and went to Paramount executives demanding that he get as much money as March.

With the picture already in progress and Cooper threatening to develop another illness, an agreement was reached to raise his salary. Cooper remembered later that it went to about $6,000 a week.

In the film, we first see Cooper asleep in a train compartment next to March when Hopkins enters. He smiles in his sleep, opens his eyes and begins a conversation in French with Hopkins. Though he had, indeed, learned some French both in school and in his European travels, he retained a Western twang when he spoke the language. While March then talks to Hopkins, Cooper, in the role of George Curtis, sulks with his arms folded.

Later in the film, the dialogue did get a bit beyond Cooper's image. "I don't want any competition," he tells Hopkins at one point, "it belittles me in my own eyes."

The rapid dialogue scene with March, in which they first

argue over Hopkins, is done in a relatively long take. In other words, the scene was played out, not broken into bits of dialogue and reaction. It is quite clear throughout the film that Cooper has mastered the dialogue, if not its delivery. Cooper constantly stuffs his huge hands in his pockets, plays with his fingernails, and continues to drop his "g's" though he is supposed to be a sophisticated artist.

Cooper did get to do several things he had not done before. He gets to play an artist, the profession he once aspired to, and even gets to do some drawing in the film. Since he did have experience as an artist, his movements seem perfectly natural and part of his background. He also gets to play his first major drunk scene, complete with the hiccups and raised left eyebrow he called upon for the many drunk scenes he played in later films. Strangely, the always somewhat inhibited Cooper found it relatively easy to play drunk scenes. The very playing of a drunk loosened him up.

While the film was being shot, Cooper's romantic off-screen image was put to use, and articles appeared relating the story of the film to Cooper's own life and his recently announced engagement to Rocky Balfe. *Photoplay* carried an interview with Cooper called "Can a Man Love Two Women?" and compared the woman loving two men in *Design for Living*. The interview was expectedly tame. About the film's supposition, Cooper said, "I believe two men could love the same woman, but not for a very long time. . . . Life is too drab a proposition to continue the gay, light manner such a situation would require."

In another 1933 interview, Cooper, who was described as having hair "whitening at the temples," had a much less sophisticated answer when asked what he would do if he had to choose between Hollywood and his ranch: "I'd most certainly take the ranch," he said. "But I'd want to take two things with me—my bathroom and my car."

The reviews of Cooper and the film were not kind, primarily because the film was compared unfavorably to the remembered theatrical performances. Removed by more than forty years from that memory, the film probably receives a better response now than it did when it was first released.

At the time, however, Richard Watts, Jr., in the *New York Herald Tribune* wrote, "You could hardly expect Mr. Cooper to be properly at home as a witty sophisticate, and I fear that he isn't."

For his next picture, Cooper was lent out to MGM again, this time to support Marion Davies in a Civil War spy tale, *Operator 13*. Operator 13 was Davies, not Cooper, and Cooper spent the picture, in which he played a Southern officer, pursuing the Northern spy.

Davies, born Marion Douras in 1898, was best known as the mistress of William Randolph Hearst and as the model for the downfallen opera singer in Orson Welles's *Citizen Kane*. Her career, to a great extent, was made possible through Hearst's influence and money. She starred in films for nineteen years and was a moderate success. In many ways, she was underrated as a performer, especially in comedy. Her association with Hearst and the knowledge of his backing were held against her. Davies also had a drinking problem which, like that of Susan Alexander in *Citizen Kane*, progressed as time passed.

Coop and Rocky became regular visitors to Hearst's massive estate at San Simeon. Apparently, Cooper would drink with Davies, but the results were different. Liquor put Cooper to sleep but made Davies thirstier. Hearst became quite fond of Cooper and enjoyed riding with him.

Of *Operator 13* the *London Daily Telegraph* wrote that the Southern officer was "entirely adequately played by Gary Cooper," but most of the reviews pointed out quite correctly that it was Miss Davies's picture.

Back at Paramount, Cooper was cast in *Now and Forever* with Carole Lombard and Shirley Temple. He played Temple's father. The mother, as in so many Temple films, is long dead.

Jerry Day (Cooper) has a plan to get $75,000 from his brother-in-law in exchange for legal custody of the girl, whom he hasn't seen since her birth. Lombard plays Cooper's girl friend, who leaves him in disgust when she learns of his plan. Learning, however, that the child is not happy in the home he has placed her in, Cooper schemes to get her out and into a better environment. The film was originally planned to have a tragic ending with Cooper's and Lombard's characters going off a cliff in a car. Instead, a happy ending with a family reconciliation was decided upon.

According to one account, Lombard got along with Cooper but found him a dilettante, effeminate in his mannerisms, and not what he appeared to be in film. Cooper's reviews were solidly affirmative, and Shirley Temple's budding career was pushed another step forward. For Cooper, perhaps the most important thing about the film was that it was directed by Henry Hathaway, who had directed the Zane Grey Westerns when Cooper was doing them. Hathaway and Cooper got along so well that Cooper's next two films were directed by Hathaway. Eventually, Hathaway would direct more Gary Cooper films than anyone else.

Coop's next film, *The Lives of a Bengal Lancer,* was a major undertaking for Paramount and Hathaway's first big picture. It won him an Academy Award nomination for directing. Set in India and shot in Hollywood, the film's sets were huge and impressive. They were retained after the picture and used, with minor alterations, for Cecil B. De Mille's film *The Crusades.*

Paramount had purchased the film rights to the Major Yeats-Brown book, *Lives of a Bengal Lancer,* in 1930. Difficulties came up soon after Paramount took a good look at what it had acquired. Yeats-Brown had written a book dealing heavily with polo and mysticism. By the time these elements were removed, there wasn't much left of the book to use for a film story. Yeats-Brown himself, Maxwell Anderson, Waldemar Young,

Grover James and a writer listed as Achmed Abdullah all contributed to scripts and rewrites.

While all this writing was going on and long before Hathaway was assigned to direct the picture, a crew of thirteen was sent to India to start shooting background. They shot 100,000 feet of film of the Khyber Pass, the Bengal Lancers, Indian cities and tribal camps near the Afghan border. For four years these reels of film lay unused in Paramount's film vaults. When an acceptable story was finally agreed upon by Paramount executives, the reels were taken out and drawn upon when shooting began. Footage shot in India was used as a guide to build the outdoor sets in California. The film was shot principally on a 3,200-acre ranch where eighty-five tents were set up to house cast and crew, each tent holding seven people each. Two stables were used to take care of the 300 horses used in the fifteen weeks of filming.

The movie was filled with action and would become a top box-office draw for Paramount. Cooper played Lieutenant McGregor, a Scotch-Canadian officer, complete with pencil-thin moustache and swagger stick, and not a single critic suggested that Cooper was ill-suited to the role of a British officer, though few would give him credit for the impersonation.

During the film, Cooper was reported to have devised the idea of placing a microphone by a rock and ricocheting a bullet past it to create the familiar "ping" sound of gunfire heard frequently from that time on. The filming also provided another instance of Cooper's ability to get into his character and lose himself. In one scene, Cooper and Franchot Tone are disguised as natives. The script called for this to be a deadly serious moment in the story, but Cooper was sure his character would not allow himself deadly seriousness at such a crucial moment. He knew, in fact, that McGregor would add a glance or a word to break the tension, and he told Hathaway. Hathaway agreed, and they did it Cooper's way. Cooper did his own riding and some rather dangerous stunts and received ample opportunity to appear in a variety of headdresses and costumes.

The reviews were outstanding. The *New York American* wrote, "Gangling Gary Cooper, every long inch an officer, stalks strikingly through both comic and tragic sequences." The *London Daily Telegraph* termed both Tone and Cooper "magnificent as the two subalterns." The film won six Academy Award nominations including Hathaway's and it received the award for best second-unit work.

The next picture for Cooper and Hathaway was as radically different as a film could be. In *Peter Ibbetson,* with Cooper in the title role of a nineteenth-century architect, Hathaway turned to a romantic fantasy. Based on an 1891 novel by George du Maurier, the tale had been filmed once before as a silent film with Wallace Reid. It had also been produced as a play and transformed into an opera by Deems Taylor.

In the film, which bears some resemblances to the later *Fountainhead,* in which Cooper played his only other architect, Ibbetson returns to his childhood home and looks at the garden of his youth and dreams. He then gets a commission from the local duke, who grows jealous of the architect's relationship with the duchess (Ann Harding). When Ibbetson and the duchess realize they are old childhood friends, their friendship turns to love, and the duke is killed when he attacks Ibbetson in a jealous rage. In prison, reality and fantasy begin to mix in Ibbetson's mind, and he fantasizes visits from the duchess, but the visits may be real. Eventually she dies, telling him that they will soon be together.

The budget was high and the cast was capable, but the genre was alien to American audiences and it did poorly. Reviews of Cooper's performance were mixed. The New York *Daily News* said, "He isn't the type to spend his adult life mooning over a lost love."

Cooper's next picture was *The Wedding Night,* directed by King Vidor. Vidor had already directed more than two dozen films including *The Big Parade, The Crowd, Hallelujah, Billy the Kid, Street Scene, The Champ* and *Our Daily Bread.* The Texas-born Vidor had started as a newsreel cameraman and worked his way through various Hollywood jobs till he became a producer-director.

Interviewed for this book, Vidor said, "I first met Cooper when I was doing a film called *The Wedding Night.* I was sure he was going to be awful in the picture. He couldn't remember his lines, and he looked awkward. To get him past his problem with lines, I had him remember no more than a sentence or two at a time. We shot all of his appearances in little pieces. Actually, he turned out looking good in the picture."

Why Cooper should have had particular difficulty with *The Wedding Night* is not difficult to understand. He was back on a heavy work schedule and was in the process of moving into a home he and Rocky had bought in Brentwood. The Brentwood property had soil problems, and Cooper devoted a lot of his energy to farming the three acres.

His next feature film, *Desire,* turned out to be a multiple reteaming. Marlene Dietrich was his co-star, though Cooper had vowed not to work with her again. The vow, however, had been with the assumption that Von Sternberg would always be her director. His seriousness had been underlined the previous year when he refused to co-star with Dietrich in the Von Sternberg-directed *Dishonored.* However, by 1935 Dietrich and Von Sternberg had parted company. The director of the film was Frank Borzage, who had done *A Farewell to Arms,* and Ernst Lubitsch was the producer.

Cooper played an American engineer vacationing in Europe who gets involved with a jewel thief, played by Dietrich. They fall in love, she reforms, and they end up together.

The film marked the first screen encounter of Cooper and the volatile Akim Tamiroff. When he saw their scenes, Cooper asked to work with the animated character actor again as soon as he could, and their next film together turned out to be *The General Died at Dawn.*

The year 1936 was a big one for Cooper. By the end of it, he would be in the list of the top ten money-making stars for the first time. This listing was an assessment of who brought the public in to see movies made by U.S. exhibitors. Cooper would subsequently make the list eighteen times, topping it in 1953.

After a two-week vacation with his wife in Bermuda in March, Cooper came back to work and found himself in the middle of a legal suit between Paramount and Sam Goldwyn. Goldwyn, who had lost the chance to get Cooper after *The Winning of Barbara Worth,* had convinced Cooper to come back to work for him at the end of his Paramount contract. Cooper reported that he was going back to work for Goldwyn for sentimental reasons—certainly uncharacteristic if true. Paramount contended that the negotiations were secret and unethical and sued Goldwyn for "stealing" the star's services "by means of false and fraudulent representations and statements." Paramount asked for $5,000,000 in punitive damages.

When the case got before the federal district court, the judge indicated that he favored the legal argument advanced by Paramount that Goldwyn or his representatives had influenced Cooper not to sign his new contract when his present one expired at the end of 1936. Sure that they would lose his services, Paramount plunged Cooper into four films in 1936, gave him what he wanted in them and hoped he would be convinced to change his mind.

The General Died at Dawn, originally called *Chinese Gold,* was based on a novel with that name written by Charles G. Booth. Clifford Odets, the playwright who had made his mark with such politically progressive plays as *The Adding Machine* and *Street Scene,* was hired to do the adaptation.

According to director Lewis Milestone, he came up with *The General Died at Dawn* when he went to see Ernst Lubitsch, who had been appointed head of production at Paramount. Milestone asked Lubitsch if he had any projects that might be suitable for him to direct, but Lubitsch said there was nothing at the moment. As Lubitsch was speaking, Milestone saw on the desk a thick manuscript titled *The General Died at Dawn.* Lubitsch told him that the script was junk, pulp, but he agreed to let Milestone take it and read it for possible ideas.

"It was easy reading," Milestone recalled, "because there were enough adventures in it to supply material for at least fifteen movies." According to Milestone, it was he, not Odets, who had the idea of setting up two forces, an American representing democracy and a Chinese general representing authoritarianism. After he had made that decision, he went to Lubitsch, told him what he wanted to do and got approval. Only then was Odets hired.

Odets created a tale about a soldier of fortune committed to helping the Chinese against a maniacal warlord, played by Akim Tamiroff. Cooper's O'Hara (named for novelist John O'-Hara, who actually appears in a small role in the film) spars with Tamiroff's General Yang throughout the film and romances Madeleine Carroll. At the end of the film, as Yang is about to execute him and his other prisoners, O'Hara convinces General Yang to let them live so they can tell the tale of the greatness of the general. He also convinces Yang to have his men execute each other to show the degree of their loyalty. In 1936, this final touch appeared ridiculous to critics. In 1979, following the Jonestown massacre, it can be seen as a chilling prophecy of blind obedience.

On August 23, 1937, following the release of the film, *The Daily Worker* carried an article on Odets identifying him as a well-known left-wing playwright. The article indicated that when asked if he ever tried to turn out screenplays with social content, Odets replied, "Well, I got away with some stuff in *The General Died at Dawn* and in the other two scripts that I did . . ."

Fifteen years later, when Odets testified before the House Un-American Activities Committee, he was asked about the *Daily Worker* interview: "I remember reading this from your hands a few weeks ago and saying that I thought the whole matter was nonsense because *The General Died at Dawn* is a picture that starred Gary Cooper and done by Paramount. There was nothing of any subversive nature in it."

In *The General Died at Dawn,* Cooper is first seen in a trench coat, walking down a street in China. Beneath his coat, he wears a flannel shirt and tie. He is clearly a working-class hero. O'Hara's mission is to deliver money to Shanghai. "The fate of this entire province is in your hands," he is told.

"I'll get through," O'Hara responds.

Forced to take the train, though he has been warned against it, O'Hara encounters Carroll. With a monkey named Sam perched comfortably on his shoulder, O'Hara entertains the lady. At one point, when he tells her that "Lots of things on the ground don't like me," he makes a casual finger-pointing gesture with his hand, implying the danger of guns. A few moments later O'Hara tries to kiss the woman. She backs away, and he hides his failure at the passionate moment by rubbing the thumb of his left hand caressingly across the monkey.

At this point, Cooper talks of having run away from an orphan asylum at fourteen, of selling papers. He "boxed for a while . . . dockworker . . . flyer . . . I've got a background of oppression myself. What's better than an American working for democracy?" The fictional background he had been given in this character was entirely alien to the real Gary Cooper but very much in keeping with his screen image.

Cooper's first scene with Tamiroff may well be the one that set the Russian in search of a new acting direction to upstage the American. Tamiroff has the bizarre character and the frightening lines, but Cooper is alive with gestures and a short, unexpected laugh of bravery. In a later scene, when Tamiroff's Yang is fishing, Cooper goes through their dialogue while shaving. A short time later, displaying the agility he still had from his stunt days, Cooper knocks out a light, turns the tables on his guards and, though he is shot, escapes.

"It's a dark year and a hard night," he says to his Chinese friend.

The Odets dialogue is every bit as allusive and unnatural as any Cooper had yet handled, but he managed to make it appear the normal talk of a romantic Irishman. "We could have worked to make ourselves a circle of light and warmth," he says at one point.

At the end of the film, when he convinces Yang to let the prisoners live, Cooper engages in some fast talk that a year or two earlier would have seemed foreign to his character, but now he was evolving into the Cooper who, when necessary, could be quick not only with guns but with words.

Paramount also got Cooper into an unbilled guest spot in *Hollywood Boulevard* as a man at a bar and scheduled him to appear in two more films. When he could get time at home, he told *Photoplay,* he and Rocky limited their social life. He set a curfew for himself of eleven-thirty. "And this isn't a health measure," Cooper said, "you just can't keep your eyes open after fourteen hours of physical work and fresh air."

SEVEN

DEEDS AND DE MILLE

Cooper obtained his independence, and though he continued to make films for Paramount and for Goldwyn, his first independent work was for Frank Capra at Columbia Pictures.

According to Capra, in an interview for this book, "Gary Cooper was not under contract [at the time he made *Mr. Deeds Goes to Town*]. He accepted the part before the script was written. Most unusual for stars. For me he was the ideal Mr. Deeds." Of course, Cooper could read Clarence Budington Kelland's story "Opera Hat," on which the film was based, but that was a long way from knowing what the character would be like in a film script.

When shooting began, Capra went on, "Cooper did not talk much about his part, but he thought about it a good deal. Gary carried his 'input' with him at all times—it was the integrity that was etched in his early-American face. A man with that face could never be taken for a crook or a greedy shyster. Honest he looked, and honest he was. A man's man, yes. But a woman's idol."

Although Cooper did not physically move as well as he had in previous pictures, Capra "saw no signs of decreasing health in him. In between scenes, he would often lie down on his back on the studio floor, put his head on a chair, pull his hat over his eyes and immediately fall asleep in spite of the hubbub around him."

Throughout filming, Capra found Cooper "very easy to work with because he was a great listener. He was friendly but very private and spoke very few words." Capra and Cooper did indeed become very good friends, in addition to being neighbors. "Our wives were very close," Capra said.

When asked if he ever had another choice for Longfellow Deeds, Capra responded, "Cooper *was* Longfellow Deeds. I can't imagine anyone playing the part any better. Who in Hollywood could play honest, humble, 'corn-tossed poet' Mr. Deeds? Only one actor: Gary Cooper. Tall, gaunt as Lincoln, cast in the frontier mold of Daniel Boone, Sam Houston, Kit Carson, this silent Montana cowpuncher embodied the true-blue virtues that won the West: durability, honesty and native intelligence."

By the time he came to direct *Mr. Deeds,* Capra was already a thirty-nine-year-old with fifteen years of directing credits and an Academy Award for *It Happened One Night.* Capra had begun as a writer for Hal Roach productions and then moved up to his first recognition as writer and director of silent comedian Harry Langdon's *The Strong Man, Long Pants* and *Tramp, Tramp, Tramp.* By 1936, Capra had directed more than two dozen features.

In *Mr. Deeds Goes to Town,* adapted by Capra's longtime writer Robert Riskin, Longfellow Deeds, a not very talkative young man from Mandrake Falls, inherits $20,000,000. Newspaper reporter Babe Bennett (Jean Arthur) is assigned to write a story about the simple millionaire and manages to get to him even though he has tried to keep away from the press. She does this by pretending she is an out-of-work typist. Deeds goes through a series of comic misadventures including getting drunk, punching a stuffed-shirt writer who ridicules him, riding on a fire engine out of sheer childish joy and feeding a horse on the street. Babe, who has fallen in love with Deeds, writes the stories of his exploits. When it is discovered that Deeds plans to give his money away to create farms for Depression-hit farmers, his lawyers, using Babe's stories, decide to have him sent to an asylum. At his sanity hearing, as witness after witness testifies that he is mad, Deeds sits silently in pain because he has discovered Babe's betrayal. When Babe confesses her love for him in court, Deeds defends himself, punches the crooked lawyer and stands up a hero of the people.

Cooper was thirty-five when the film was made, but, in the American tradition of cutting back on the years, the script says that he is twenty-eight. When he is first seen, Cooper has a number of the characteristics Capra had used on Harry Langdon to make him look like an overgrown child, though Langdon began his film career when he was over forty. Cooper's Deeds is wearing a bow tie and a jacket just a bit too short and tight for him, as if he has outgrown it but hasn't considered getting a new one.

Throughout the film, Cooper emphasizes the one-dimensional nature of Deeds by the way he carries himself. Deeds seldom turns his head to look at events or people. His head remains forward and his whole body turns to face people. Unlike many Cooper characters, Deeds is not a shy man. In fact, he is quite willing to assert himself with people. It is his simple interests and virtues that make him appear vulnerable, not his reluctance to speak.

The only people Deeds doesn't face directly are those he innately distrusts. When introduced to Jon Cedar (Douglass Dumbrille), the lawyer he knows from the start is not worthy of his trust, Deeds shakes the man's hand but won't look at his face. Throughout the film, Deeds uses his fingers to point and emphasize that he is in control of his body and not afraid to use it, not afraid to engage in the seemingly unsocial act of pointing for emphasis. At the same time that he acts with confidence, Cooper employs a series of eye blinks to indicate the childish nature of Deeds.

In a scene devoid of sexual implication, Deeds talks to Babe on the telephone. Throughout the conversation, Deeds moves his right hand restlessly, and his leg rocks back and forth in joy at talking to her. Deeds's struggle with his emotions is reinforced after the conversation with Babe in which he confirms his suspicion that she is a reporter. When he hangs up the phone, he holds back his tears and gives a small smile, but the smile won't work, and he tightens his lips to hold back his emotions, not because Deeds thinks it unmanly to cry but because he doesn't want to admit to himself what the woman has meant to him. It is a typically underplayed Cooper moment of emotion. Wordlessly and without broad gesture or sobbing, he conveys his character's rush of feeling.

In *Mr. Deeds,* Cooper, working with a highly sympathetic Frank Capra, created a character whose every movement and word suggests that he had lived a lifetime as Longfellow Deeds. When the Academy Awards were given, Cooper, who had been nominated, did not win, though Capra did, as best director. The Best Actor Oscar went to Paul Muni for *The Life of Louis Pasteur.* According to Capra, "My elation was tinged with disappointment. If ever anyone deserved Oscars for *Mr. Deeds,* it was Gary Cooper and it was Robert Riskin."

Writing in the *Philadelphia Evening Public Ledger,* Henry T. Murdock said, "Gary Cooper turns another corner in a career which has slowly developed him from a wooden-faced hero of horse-operas into a sensitive player with a reticent but wholly American wit." Thirty years later, in an article titled *Totem and Movies,* Sam Rhodie wrote, "Mr. Deeds and Babe Bennett were perfectly cast. Both ooze sincerity in a physical sense."

Cecil B. De Mille was fifty-five years old when he decided to make *The Plainsman,* which was based on a series of tales about Wild Bill Hickok by Frank J. Wistach and a fanciful biography, *The Prince of Pistoleers,* by Courtney Ryley Cooper and Grover Jones. De Mille was no stranger to Westerns. Since his first film, a Western called *Squaw Man* in 1916, De Mille had directed sixty films by 1936, including an early version of *The Virginian* and two remakes of his *Squaw Man.*

In later days, De Mille had many stories about Cooper and his relationship with him, some of which are highly suspect. For example, in 1951 De Mille wrote that the first time he planned to use Cooper (in *The Plainsman*), the late director

Sam Wood phoned him and said, "Don't let this boy's quiet manner disturb you. When Gary worked his first picture for me, I froze in my tracks. I was certain he was wrecking the picture." It is an interesting tale, and Wood did direct Cooper in three films, but the first of them was *The Pride of the Yankees,* five years after *The Plainsman* was finished.

In any case, De Mille reported that after the first day of shooting *The Plainsman,* there was concern over Cooper's performance: "It did seem," wrote De Mille, "that Gary's approach to Wild Bill Hickok, at least a forthright man, was on the quiet side, but Gary with no orders from the sidelines went about it with his own kind of authority. It was easy and effortless. Several on the sound stage that day were sure that what he was doing to Hickok would cause the great frontiersman to turn morose flipflops in his grave."

However, when De Mille saw the rushes, his concern ended. "It was all there," he reported, "a performance in remarkably low key, yet packing the wallop of a drop forge. Cooper, this gallant, kindly cherub, made the sparks fly in every scene with his special little dramatic tools—a flash of the eyes, a gesture or glance, the misleading air of relaxed casualness, the purposeful gawkiness."

Before the title *The Plainsman* was decided upon, the film was going under the working titles of *Buffalo Bill* and *This Breed of Men.* Since James Ellison played Buffalo Bill in the finished film and Ellison was never a major box-office draw, it is likely that Cooper was either considered for Buffalo Bill, which would have been in perfect keeping with his screen image, or another actor of greater box-office draw than Ellison was considered for the role. However, it is unlikely that Cooper, riding a crest of popularity, would have stood for the film being named for a character he did not play.

De Mille's supposedly cliché dialogue was a subject of Hollywood jokes for years. Howard Hawks, who had directed Cooper and would direct him to an Academy Award, had begun as De Mille's property man. Hawks, in an interview with Kevin

Brownlow in 1968, said that he once asked Gary Cooper how on earth he could "read those goddamn lines" De Mille gave him. "Well," Cooper supposedly replied, "when De Mille finishes talking to you, they don't seem so bad. But when you see the picture, then you kind of hang your head."

Whether true or not, Cooper certainly had no reason to hang his head for his delivery of the lines in any De Mille film. The lines indeed are at the folkloric level, but so is Cooper's presentation of Wild Bill Hickok, and actually the dialogue, like much of De Mille's work, has a kind of sardonic humor, which Cooper worked well with.

Cooper first appears in Union uniform on a dock peeling an apple. In fact, throughout this and other pictures, De Mille made better use of Cooper's hands than any other director with whom he worked, with the possible exception of William Wyler. Cooper also got to wear a variety of period costumes that he played around with, posed with and fitted into his character. De Mille was a master at visual detail, gadgetry and period objects, a clutter of authenticity his actors could play with and against. Few made as much use of these objects as Cooper. The apple is pared and eaten as Cooper talks to a boy on the dock. Cooper then shows him a watch with Calamity Jane's picture in it and shoots the boy's slingshot left-handed.

In a card game a short time later, Cooper goes through a variety of hand gestures and touches his nose with his right hand before he catches a cheater in the game and announces, "I'm calling the hand that's in your hat."

Throughout the film, Cooper as gunfighter Hickok keeps his hands active, touching, itchy, ready, regardless of the conversation. It appears automatic to the character, a man who can't be too far from his guns and knows the dangers he faces. The agility is demonstrated when Hickok goes to General Custer in Hays City to warn him about guns being run to the Indians. To make his point, Cooper throws a penknife into the map to show where the guns are being run.

Back at Buffalo Bill's cabin, Cooper talks to Mrs. Cody and

absently drops beans into a bird cage. When Mrs. Cody points out that birds don't eat beans, Hickok continues his conversation, but his hands vibrate for something to do to keep them moving. If one thinks this nervous use of hands is simply part of Cooper himself, one need only go back and look at Mr. Deeds, a man who keeps his hands still, an essentially slow, awkward man, a man radically different from Cooper's Wild Bill Hickok.

The absentminded gestures continue through the film. During a lull between Indian attacks in a siege, Hickok listens to his watch to be sure it still works, though his dialogue at the time is not about the watch but about a supposed betrayal by Calamity Jane. It is the casual action of a man who really owns that watch.

Continuing his tactic of underplaying when confronted with flamboyant actors, Cooper minimizes his dialogue and reactions with villain Charles Bickford. He grows tense and leaves the movement and action to Bickford, and the result is that the normally restless Hickok, by appearing still and cold in these scenes, draws attention to himself. He has changed. He is not the subconsciously nervous gunfighter. He is now the cold, righteous killer. His very difference draws attention in spite of Bickford's emotional responses.

The film's end is set up as if Hickok knows he will be murdered in the Deadwood Saloon. De Mille's dialogue might seem a mild, shared irony with the audience, a black joke, but Cooper plays it coldly, a man enjoying his last moments. "I got a feeling I'm gonna stay here," he says. And then later, not sadly or poignantly, but quite matter-of-factly, Hickok says, "What room is there gonna be for a two-gun plainsman?" It is not presented as the self-conscious statement of history that would appear in the adult Westerns fifteen years later, a statement of mourning at the passing of an era, the tragedy of a man who no longer has a place. Cooper's Hickok is a man who has lived out his legend and doesn't feel sorry for himself.

An essential point about most of Cooper's characters is that they do not feel sorry for themselves. They face what happens, hold back a tear if necessary, pull their lips into a thin line and face the threat. De Mille, however, couldn't let his film end with an image of his star dead in Jean Arthur's arms. Instead the film ends with a shot of Cooper on his horse riding toward the camera, a man who is dead, but a legend still alive.

The Plainsman marked the screen debut of Anthony Quinn in the small role of an Indian whom Hickok runs into on the trail after the defeat of Custer at the Little Big Horn. Later he would become De Mille's son-in-law and even direct a film under his guidance, but when he first appeared for his scene with Cooper, he had some problems. According to Quinn, he was supposed to be a Cheyenne singing a Cheyenne song. Since De Mille thought Quinn really was a Cheyenne, he simply told him to sing a real Cheyenne song. The Mexican-born Quinn tried but botched it badly. De Mille wanted him dismissed on the spot, but Cooper stepped in.

Quinn recalled, "And Gary—I'll always love him—said, 'Give the boy a chance. Maybe he's confused, it's his first picture, why don't you give him a chance?' "

"I don't want to waste your time, Gary," De Mille reportedly said.

"I don't mind," said Cooper. "I saw the boy in the makeup room and he seems like a nice kid."

The reviews of Cooper's performance were once again very good. The *New York Times,* for example, said Coop played Hickok "with considerable force, humor and salty flavor." The *London Times* wrote, "Cooper is sardonic, cynical, and immensely impressive." Certainly, Longfellow Deeds was neither sardonic nor cynical, quite the contrary. Thus Cooper's ability to mold his supposedly similar screen characters into different projections of heroism was recognized, but each time Cooper was to present a different hero it would be said that it was typical Cooper, though no two such presentations were ever alike.

EIGHT

A SOUL AT SEA

Cooper's next feature film, Souls at Sea, *1937, was origin-* ally planned as a giant spectacle to rival, it was hoped, the recent success of *Mutiny on the Bounty* with Charles Laughton and Clark Gable.

Cooper was set to star, but problems arose over who would co-star as the ne'er-do-well, rough-and-tumble and not too bright seaman who befriends Cooper. George Raft was origin- ally offered the part but turned it down. It was then given to Lloyd Nolan, and quickly withdrawn, when someone suggested that Nolan and Cooper looked too much alike. Perhaps it was the same Paramount executives who had thought Cooper and Cary Grant looked alike.

Director Henry Hathaway had an idea for who should play Powdah, the role Raft had vacated. At that time Cooper had an agent, Jack Moss, and Hathaway called him to get support for his choice, Anthony Quinn. According to Quinn, who was in the office with Hathaway when he called Moss, Hathaway said that the twenty-one-year-old Quinn would make it interesting, that Cooper's Nuggin character would "have someone young ideal- izing" him.

Cooper was in Moss's office at that moment, and since he remembered Quinn from *The Plainsman* and liked him, im- mediately agreed to test him. In the test the following day, Quinn gave a long speech from the film declaring his love and affection for Nuggin. "Gary's kindness to me during the filming of *The Plainsman* had endeared him to me forever," said Quinn. "So I found it very easy to tell the substitute [for Cooper] of my undying loyalty and affection."

When the test was over, Carole Lombard, who was friendly with Quinn, asked Hathaway how the test had gone. Hathaway said it had been great, and Lombard invited Quinn to her dressing room where she told him he would be a big star. She also urged him to push for co-star billing with Cooper. Quinn had no intention, he said, of demanding anything. He simply wanted the part, but unfortunately for him, at that point Raft had second thoughts about the role and went back to Hathaway saying he wanted the part. He got it.

Later Raft recalled, "Souls was a helluva good adventure movie about the slavery days. My hair was marcelled and I wore a ring in my ear—like some sailors did in those days. In one scene Coop and I are drinking rum together. Both of us were quiet actors. You know, we didn't like a lot of dialogue. Mainly we looked at each other." Finally, Cooper had the line, "You know I love you." The script had Raft respond, "I know I love you too."

Hathaway called out that the shot should be printed. "After we both stopped laughing," Raft recalls, "Coop jokingly told Hathaway, 'You can't put that in the movie. People are going to think Cooper and Raft are a couple of fags.' I guess he figured we were right because he cut it."

The cut scene was the one Quinn had tested and gotten the job with, and it was not the only thing cut from the film. When it was finished, *Souls at Sea* was scheduled to be shown at showcase prices at selected theaters. However, just before publicity was to begin for the epic movie, it was decided to cut it radically and release it with other Paramount productions for the year. Among the scenes cut was one at Queen Victoria's court—in fact, the cuts removed several dozen actors from the film, including Ward Bond.

Raft, who would receive his only Academy Award nomination for his role in *Souls at Sea*, was particularly appreciative of Cooper's work with him.

Years later he claimed that in 1931 he had possibly saved Cooper's life, though Cooper had never known about it. Raft, who had been raised in a tough neighborhood in New York and was friendly throughout much of his life with old friends who went into the rackets—including Bugsy Siegel—got a call one day from a man in New York. According to Raft, the man "wanted me to handle an emergency job. One of the big men in the rackets back east who'd been looking for his missing girl friend traced her to Hollywood."

The man told Raft the girl was crazy about a young actor named Gary Cooper. "Georgie," he said, "you'll find the girl and hustle her out of town. Otherwise this actor winds up on a slab." Raft then traced the girl through friends, went to her apartment, got her packed in a hurry, took her to the train station and got her on the first train east without telling Cooper.

Cooper's role in *Souls at Sea* is another major variation in his repertoire, different from either Deeds or Hickok. Nuggin, probably the most talkative character Cooper ever played, is a highly literate man who is given to quoting Shakespeare. In his first scene, for example, on deck of the slave ship *Blackbird* in 1842, he reads from *Hamlet:* "To die, to sleep no more . . . to sleep, perchance to dream . . ." He then tells Raft, who plays Powdah, that the slaves they carry are like Hamlet, unable to decide to live or die.

It soon becomes evident that Nuggin is not a slaver but a man dedicated to ruining slave runs by joining their crews and causing them to be caught in illegal transport. Through most of the film, he works as an undercover agent for the British government. The reason for his lifetime dedication to the end of slavery is never clearly explained on any personal basis. Nuggin's opposition seems to be on moral grounds. Following a scene in which he and Powdah have been hanged by their thumbs by the evil Lieutenant Tarryton (Henry Wilcoxin), Cooper launches an angry tirade in which he shouts that "the floor of the ocean is paved with the bones of slaves."

Shortly afterward, Nuggin and Powdah sing. Nuggin takes delight in the song and shows no signs of shyness or humility. In fact, many Cooper characteristics are dropped. There are no gulps, no awkward hands, no eyes averted from the lady, no hesitation when he speaks. What Cooper does play on is the slight secret smile, the hint that his thoughts and his life hold secrets of pain and knowledge. His self-confidence falters only once, when he helps the woman he loves down from a carriage —Cooper's foot gets stuck, and he trips awkwardly, in a stunt that would have made Buster Keaton proud.

Throughout the film, Cooper allows his character to be tender, to display love and emotion. In his longest scene alone in the film, Nuggin takes a flower Margaret (Frances Dee) has given him to his cabin on the ship they are sailing. He cups it in his hand, lifts it to his nose, smells it, places it gently in a glass of water, looks at it and smiles. In short, he plays a love scene with a flower, and there is nothing in the least awkward about it. Nuggin keeps evoking the image of flowers. In one scene he uses his hand and arm to emulate a sunflower, showing how the flower turns to the sun.

In the same scene, Cooper does something characteristic of all his screen characters and also in keeping with his and his father's sense of patriotism. He looks up in the sky at the American flag and says it is indeed something to "look up to."

As another example of Cooper's growing art, he has a scene with Raft in which Raft gives him important information about who is sailing with them. Cooper says nothing. His facial response is absolutely minimal, but it is quite clear what he is thinking. Raft responds that Cooper already must have the information, which is exactly what his knowing look has conveyed.

During a dinner scene on the boat, Nuggin tells a grim story of a wife who went mad on seeing slave horrors in Africa and put her head in boiling palm oil. His voice is tight, to match the muscles of his neck and face, and he gives the impression of a man who is restraining himself from violent action.

When an accidentally knocked-over kerosene lamp destroys the ship, Powdah decides to go down with the trapped girl he loves, but first he knocks out Nuggin, who falls into one of the few lifeboats. Cooper, by the way, is quite agile throughout the film, showing no signs of the strain that appeared to exist for him in *Mr. Deeds*. In a particularly grim scene, as the lifeboat appears to be ready to sink from the weight of too many people and they are unwilling to shift their weight out of fear, Nuggin acts quickly and begins to shoot people who are holding onto the boat.

The context of the film is a courtroom scene in which Nuggin is on trial for murdering people during the ship's abandonment. The head of the secret service of Britain steps forward to speak for Nuggin, who will not speak for himself because his mission has been secret. The entire courtroom sequence is a reversal of that in *Mr. Deeds* or other Cooper films. In this film, the talkative Nuggin never gets his moment in court. He has had his moments of articulation all through the film.

As frequently before, the reviews failed to notice the difference in Cooper's performance. The *New York Sun* simply stated that Cooper "plays his part with great restraint and subtlety and is always convincing."

The year was otherwise filled with personal activity for Coop. In July, his home was burglarized. An estimated $25,000 in jewelry and expensive table furnishings were taken. Apparently the burglars had cut a bathroom window screen when the Coopers were out and took a platinum bracelet, set with diamonds and rubies, valued at $5,000; a platinum ring set with an eight-carat ruby, $5,000; a cluster-set diamond ring, $1,000; a pair of diamond-and-ruby-studded clips, $3,000; a diamond cigarette case, $800; a gem-set compact, $300; and a pair of diamond earrings, $850.

But the Coopers were concerned about other things. Rocky was pregnant. On September 14, she went to the hospital. Coincidentally, Frank Capra's wife went to the hospital on the same day to have her baby. Capra remembers that "Like a Mutt and Jeff team, tall Gary and I paced the maternity halls, gave passing nurses anxious pleading looks. They ignored us. Heman Coop became unglued. He had a room next to Rocky's, but he cowered in the halls and fire escapes where he could chain-smoke."

The Capra baby came first, a girl, Lulu. "Like two idiots," Capra recalled, "Gary and I gitchy-cooed at little Lulu through the baby window. The next day, Rocky gave birth to her beautiful baby girl, Maria. I helped Gary gitchy-coo at little Maria." According to Capra, Maria and Lulu have remained good friends to the present.

Shortly after the birth of Maria, Cooper told *Photoplay*, "Before the baby came, it seemed hard to believe that somebody was coming along, walking right into the picture where there hadn't been anybody before. . . . That youngster is not going to have just dresses and dolls. Maria's going to be an all-around girl. She's going to see life from every angle. She's going to have athletics and education, friends and solitude."

Indeed, as Maria grew up, the Coopers did provide her with an education and an athletic background, and a loving childhood. When she grew to adulthood, Maria Cooper married pianist Byron Janis. In 1979, Mrs. Janis said, "My parents were totally committed to giving me a normal childhood. As a consequence, I've never wanted to be an actress."

Accompanying her husband on concert tours, Maria sketches constantly, much as her father did as a young man. "I'm never without it [the sketch pad]," she told the *New York Daily News,* "but I prefer the scenes around my mother's home in Southampton. I adore seascapes."

Her sketches sell from $200 to $1,800, and she confided to the *Daily News* that she did once have the equivalent of the experience of stage fright. "It happened once," she said, "in Paris— the first time I saw my work on a gallery wall."

Back in 1937, Cooper delivered to *Photoplay* a monologue on his newborn child that was worthy of Mr. Deeds: "The first thing any child should learn is democracy," he said. "The youngster should know she isn't elected to be a big shot and that other people are human beings too. I know spoiled brats who by accident of birth have been born into money. If the parents haven't been careful those youngsters have an idea that they've been personally responsible for their good fortune. I've known youngsters like that—they don't go places."

If Cooper's thoughts turned somewhat to money, he had reasons. In January of 1937, he complained publicly that the government was taking one-third of his income in taxes. "We're actually working for the government," he told the *New York Times*. Those who might have felt a bit sorry for Cooper's loss of income during these Depression years probably lost their feelings of sorrow at the end of 1937 when *The New York Times* announced that the nation's highest-paid entertainer was Gary Cooper, who had earned $370,214 in 1937.

In one sense, it is ironic that Cooper, so often the spokesman for the little man in film, the man who suffered from the Depression and poverty, never himself suffered a moment of poverty in his life. Certainly there is no great virtue in being poor, and it would be foolish to imply that Cooper was somehow derelict in his responsibilities because he didn't suffer financially. The point is that this lack never affected his ability to enact the role of someone who did suffer. In private, however, he remained a strong Republican, antagonistic toward Roosevelt and the New Deal, and he was always willing to speak out against the president as he spoke out against no other individual. Cooper would in fact ultimately buy his own radio time to campaign against Roosevelt during the war, when Roosevelt's popularity was at an all-time high. It was a decision of integrity for Cooper, though he knew the possible consequences to his screen image and knew that the prevailing attitude in Hollywood was for support of the Democratic administration.

In quick succession, Cooper did three films in 1938: *The Adventures of Marco Polo* and *The Cowboy and the Lady* for Goldwyn and *Bluebeard's Eighth Wife* for Paramount.

Marco Polo, Cooper's first Goldwyn film, proved to be somewhat of a financial disaster. John Cromwell, who had directed Cooper in *The Texan,* began the film but quit after five days.

He was replaced by Archie Mayo. The film was a big-budget feature designed to take advantage of Cooper's services, and perhaps the project was on a larger scale than Mayo had ever handled—certainly it was filled with problems. Sigrid Gurie, announced as a discovery from Norway, proved to be from Brooklyn, which somewhat undermined the publicity campaign. In addition, the film was filled with well-known actors from other studios impersonating the Chinese in the court of Kublai Khan. In *The General Died at Dawn,* the choice of actors and makeup helped give the illusion of Chinese character. In fact, only two primary actors who were not Chinese played Chinese parts in *The General Died at Dawn,* Akim Tamiroff and Dudley Digges. In *Marco Polo,* the list of Chinese impersonators included Alan Hale, Binnie Barnes, Lana Turner, Stanley Fields, Harold Huber, H. B. Warner and Ward Bond, and Basil Rathbone played an evil Babylonian.

In this, his second biographical film—*The Plainsman* had been the first—Cooper plays Polo, about whom very little was actually known, as a cunning and dedicated fellow, a man extremely popular with the ladies of the court of Venice and the daughter of the Khan. It appears to be one of the few films he made in which Cooper could not determine what he wanted his character to be, a dandy or a shy young explorer. It was the role most distant from Cooper in historical time and most lacking in research material about the character he played and the cultural background.

The *Illustrated London News* said Cooper "preserves his invincible sincerity against heavy odds." The *New York Sun* wrote that "In spite of its elaborate settings and the presence of Gary Cooper, *The Adventures of Marco Polo* never quite lives up to its promise."

Bluebeard's Eighth Wife, a comedy directed by Ernst Lubitsch for Paramount, also had some problems for Cooper. In the film, based on a play by Alfred Savoir, Cooper plays a wealthy American, a man with many ex-wives and millions of dollars. He falls in love with Nicole (Claudette Colbert), daughter of a poor aristocrat. Convinced by her father (Edward Everett Horton), she agrees to marry the American, but does so only for his money. She succeeds in getting him to divorce her and gets a sizeable settlement, but then she realizes she loves him and starts pursuing him. He hides from her in a sanatorium near Paris. She buys the place, has him put in a straitjacket and confronts him. He realizes that she is at least his equal, and the two are reunited.

Cooper drew upon the knowledge of European wealth he acquired during his days in European society and played Michael Brandon as a man comfortable with his money, a man who eats in the European style with his left hand, sits straight, is well groomed and at ease ordering people about. Brandon can comfortably put his hands in the pockets of his tuxedo and has no embarrassment in staring directly at whatever he wants or whoever he is addressing. The role was another kind of opposite from Longfellow Deeds and a far cry from his previous Western roles.

Cooper's reviews were generally good, though F. S. Nugent in the *New York Times* wrote that the film "has the dickens of a time trying to pass off Gary Cooper as a multi-marrying millionaire." Strangely, the role was much closer to his actual private self than almost any other he had played, but by 1938 he had become so identified with the underdog image that his portrayal of wealth—to which he was actually accustomed—did not seem right to Nugent or, apparently, to much of the American public. The *New York Herald Tribune* echoed the *Times* and said, "Cooper is not altogether at ease in the role of a cosmopolitan banker." In fact he was at ease in the role, but his public image was at odds with it.

With two box-office problems behind him, Cooper and Sam Goldwyn decided to head back to a Western image. A story was prepared by Leo McCarey and Frank R. Adams, and Merle Oberon was cast opposite Cooper's cowboy Stretch. Walter Brennan became his sidekick, Sugar. When *The Cowboy and the Lady* was released, the *Brooklyn Eagle* would voice the opinion of most of the press and public: "Gary Cooper, the long-legged Montana boy who was ill at ease as Marco Polo and as a modern Bluebeard earlier this year, got back into chaps and Stetson to play *The Cowboy and the Lady* for Samuel Goldwyn. That gave all of us, including Mr. Goldwyn, something to be thankful for."

In the film, Mary Smith (Oberon) and her uncle are picked up in a nightclub raid. Her father is a senator running for the presidency, and, to protect his reputation, he sends her to his Florida estate where she joins her maid and cook on a blind date with three rodeo cowboys. She is paired with Cooper's Stretch. She tells him she is a poor girl supporting a family, and he believes her. They fall in love and are married the next day. The rodeo circuit doesn't suit her, so she goes back to Florida with the understanding that she will join him at the end of the rodeo season at his Montana ranch.

The senator, learning of the marriage and afraid it will affect his political chances, hurries the nomination. Stretch dashes back to Florida and discovers his wife's identity. At a big party for the senator, he is ridiculed by the rich guests for his cowboy manners. In a characteristic Cooper speech, he puts down the wealthy throng with simple eloquence and leaves.

When the senator attempts to have the marriage annulled, his daughter faints, and he is made to realize that he is standing in the way of her happiness. He withdraws from the presidential race and joins his daughter in a trip to Montana so she can reunite with Stretch.

NINE

LEGIONNAIRE, DOCTOR, AND COWBOY

*In 1938, Paramount engaged William Wellman, who had di-*rected *Wings,* to handle the remake of *Beau Geste.* Since Cooper had been in *Beau Sabreur,* the sequel to the earlier Paramount silent version, he was immediately considered to play Beau, the title character, even though Beau is English.

There is a story that, during the making of *Beau Geste,* Cooper's ability to fall asleep anywhere almost got him killed. Beau is shot near the end of the film and Robert Preston, playing his brother, carries the body to Beau's bunk, drenches the room in oil and sets it on fire to give Beau the Viking funeral he always wanted.

Wellman warned Cooper not to fall asleep while he was playing dead. Then, when the burning scene was being set up, extra precautions had to be taken and extra cameras had to be used because the shot could be done only once. After the set had been destroyed by fire, the only way to reshoot would be to rebuild. Supposedly, the setting-up took so long that Cooper, lying in the bunk with his Foreign Legion uniform on, fell soundly asleep. After the fire was started and the cameras were rolling, Preston looked around for Cooper, didn't see him and realized where he was. Rushing into the burning set, Preston woke Coop and led him out through the smoke.

Because of the desert shooting and the all-male cast and crew, Cooper couldn't bring his wife and daughter to Buttercup Valley, nineteen miles east of Yuma. However, Rocky and the baby did go to Phoenix, where Maria got sick. Wanting to know about the baby's condition, Cooper decided to find a phone, and the nearest one was in Yuma. With a sandstorm blocking the roads, Cooper hitched up a camel and rode to an open highway where he could hitchhike the rest of the way to Yuma. One can only wonder at the reaction of the surprised motorist who came upon Gary Cooper and a camel on a highway in the middle of the desert.

The role of Beau is one of a handful with which Cooper has continued to be identified. It was his last film under contract for Paramount, and Paramount made a major effort to promote the film, in addition to allowing a large budget for the building of the fort and the hiring of an outstanding supporting cast including Brian Donlevy, Ray Milland, Robert Preston, Susan Hayward, Broderick Crawford, J. Carrol Nash and Albert Dekker.

The mystique of Cooper in the role of Beau has become so powerful that in 1977, when comedian Marty Feldman made *The Last Remake of Beau Geste,* he acquired the rights to footage from the film and achieved an amazing—and for some, a poignant—effect. By careful cutting, Feldman managed to play a scene with Cooper, who had been dead almost seventeen years.

The praise for Cooper's performance in *Beau Geste* was almost universal. No one commented on the surprising fact that Beau, as a child played by Donald O'Connor, has a heavy British accent, but when he becomes Gary Cooper the accent has disappeared. Nor did anyone seem to notice that Cooper appears in remarkably few scenes in the film. An examination of the film simply in terms of screen time indicates that *Beau Geste* is the Gary Cooper film in which Cooper appears the least. He does not even show up on the screen until twenty minutes have passed. Cooper's character has no love interest in the film. It has been remarked, incorrectly, that Susan Hayward plays opposite him in the film, but it is the character Milland plays, John Geste, who is in love with and loved by Hayward's Isobel.

It can surely be argued that not only Brian Donlevy but

Albert Dekker, who plays a mutinous legionnaire, had "better" roles than Cooper, and as far as screen time is concerned, both Milland and Preston have as much as Cooper. On the other hand, one might argue that, though Cooper's appearance in the film is limited, he has the opportunity to make the most of his scenes. In fact, this is not the case. In a few scenes—at the start of the film when he and Preston chase a mouse with a battle-ax or when the brothers are talking at night when they first meet at the isolated desert training center—Cooper does have the opportunity to be at the center of the action and dialogue, but these are not major scenes in terms of the story. Cooper doesn't even get a chance to do a major death scene. His last words in the film are, "Lovely sound, but a little late," in reference to the bugles of the rescuing troop of legionaires who have not come in time to save Beau's life. In fact, his speech is only a transition to several more plot resolutions in the film, including the death of Preston's character.

It is quite likely that audiences and critics have tended, because of their fond memories of a favorite action picture and a favorite actor, to confuse their reception to the picture with the image of Cooper. Surely in his scenes Cooper employs his acting talents to fit the character. For example, after a long siege by the Arabs, Cooper is shown leaning back, eating a piece of bread. His cap is back and he looks weary. His brow is furrowed, and his eyelids are partially down, as his shoulders slope slightly forward. Without a word, he is the image of the overworked, overtired man who accepts his lot in life. At other points, Cooper gets to display the traits of Beau the hero. When a mutiny is announced against the evil Markoff, Beau won't join it and makes a small speech of pride, pointing his thumb at himself to emphasize his commitment to the law.

There is no sign of physical rigidity in Cooper's performance, though apparently he had recently had some problems with his hip and recurring pains from injuries. However, the film does not make the same kinds of physical demands on him as did *Lives of a Bengal Lancer* or *The Plainsman*.

Beau Geste did fall into a growing category of Cooper films in which he was not simply alone, but responsible for and to a small group. This tended to be the case more and more with the Westerns and the action films in foreign locations. In the contemporary, urban-setting films, Cooper played characters who were more individual and disdained social responsibility.

There is one interesting point in the film, in which a direct reference is made to Cooper's physical description. A note mentions that Cooper's eyes are a blue like that of the Blue Water Diamond that is stolen. Although the film is in black and white, it is interesting that Cooper's description was so well known to film-goers that such a reference point could be incorporated and understood.

Cooper's major recollection in an interview shortly after it was made was that the film was tough because the sand kept getting in his sinuses.

In her review of the film for the *New York Daily Mirror,* Bland Johaneson made a particularly appropriate observation. "The men dote upon Mr. Cooper for his stature, his taciturnity, his gaunt countenance. The apotheosis of the manly, he is flawlessly fitted for the strong, silent boyish heroics of Beau Geste. That he no longer looks quite boyish enough to play the grateful ward of a patrician lady is a captious criticism."

Cooper had changed. He was thirty-eight years old when the film was released, and he was not the smooth-faced boy of a few years earlier. He was fast becoming the craggy figure that his later film image made so well known.

In 1939, Cooper apparently had the opportunity to play the role of the Ringo Kid in John Ford's *Stagecoach.* According to Frank Capra, Rocky Cooper told him that the *Stagecoach* script had been sent to her husband. "Gary was on the fence about it," Rocky Cooper said. "I read it and advised him to turn it down. *Stagecoach!* It made a star out of John Wayne, and we turned it down."

It was also in 1939 that Cooper casually told Hedda Hopper,

among others, that he had been offered the lead in *Gone With The Wind* but had turned it down. "I turned it down like a cold potato," he said. "I'm still thankful that I didn't try it. Imagine what a spot I'd have been in if I'd loused up a picture like *Gone With The Wind.* Shouldn't we do just what we can do best and leave the rest to the other fellows?"

In his published memos, David O. Selznick later confirmed that Cooper had been his primary choice for the lead in *Gone With The Wind.* Cooper was considered for the role as far back as 1936, when Ronald Colman had also been considered as a possibility. Later Errol Flynn became a prime choice. According to a 1937 Selznick memo, "One of our strongest possibilities for the lead in *Gone With The Wind* is Errol Flynn." Gable was also in the running and high on the list, but in 1938, just before shooting actually began, Selznick was in the final stages of getting approval from Goldwyn for the release of Cooper to make *Gone With The Wind.* The deal with Goldwyn was necessary because with the Paramount contract coming to an end, Goldwyn had the right to Cooper's services.

According to Selznick's memos, it was not Cooper's humility that stopped the negotiations—in fact, they had been going on for several years. The difficulty was getting Goldwyn's approval. In a telegram to United Artists, which was originally to have handled distribution, Selznick stated his regrets about the film. This was after he had agreed to do it at MGM with MGM star Clark Gable in the lead. In the telegram, Selznick said: "The only regret I have about the deal is that you [George Schaefer of United Artists] and I will not be associated in handling of this picture. I cannot help but feel that the picture would have been made by now and would have been released through United Artists had we been able to secure the long sought cooperation on Gary Cooper." Selznick's wording is "cooperation *on*" Cooper, not "by Cooper."

Though Cooper did have a great deal of humility concerning his ability as an actor, he had tried roles far more ambitious than that of Rhett Butler in *Gone With The Wind.* Of course, now that the film has been established firmly in the public mind with Gable, it is a bit difficult to imagine Cooper in it, but Cooper would surely have altered the character and made it his own. Rhett Butler would, for example, have probably been far easier for him to deal with than Marco Polo had been.

So, instead of *Gone With The Wind,* Cooper moved over to Goldwyn and made *The Real Glory.* The film is about a small outpost of American officers in the Philippines who battle rampaging Moro tribesmen in the period just following the Spanish-American War. Directed by Henry Hathaway, who had also handled *Bengal Lancer,* the film resembled *Lancer,* the recently completed *Beau Geste* and *The General Died at Dawn* in a number of ways. Once again Cooper played a soldier sent to do battle against foreigners in the foreigners' land.

The colonial viewpoint was justified by the explanation that the foreign land has two forces, the weak nationals who have to be protected and the evil natives who want to take over the country, to rape, murder and molest. Only the white presence, in the form of Cooper and a few loyal companions—in this case David Niven and Broderick Crawford—stand in the way of the evil hordes and true democracy, or at least democracy with a strong guiding hand from the English or Americans. The political sentiments were in concert with Cooper's own views, and they would emerge again the next year in *Northwest Mounted Police.*

Though *The Real Glory* has been given far less attention and recognition than *Beau Geste,* Cooper's role is much longer and stronger in *The Real Glory.* It was his portrayal of the army doctor in *The Real Glory* that caused Graham Greene to make his observation about Cooper's ability to make the very life of the character his own.

The film credits begin with the words, "Samuel Goldwyn Presents Gary Cooper in *The Real Glory.*" After an introduction to demonstrate the evils of the Moros, Cooper is presented in a way that would become characteristic of his status. He is first seen from behind, on a boat coming to the jungle outpost;

his frame rather than his face identifies him. He then rolls a cigarette in his huge hand and, in a tracking shot, joins Niven and Crawford in a discussion of old times.

Once in his dispensary, Cooper (Dr. Bill Canavan) handles the experimental rats, hypodermic needles and bottles of medicine as if he is totally familiar with them. Throughout the film, the act of his being a doctor is always in the background, never foregrounded. At the fore is Bill Canavan's view of himself as a soldier.

Cooper's screen time in *The Real Glory* is extensive, as are his opportunities to display his acting skill. Not only does he display agility when he catches an assassin or is attacked on a rope bridge; he also gets ample opportunity to create with his hands and body. In a throwaway gesture, Canavan indicates his ability to dance with a deft, twisting motion of his hand. The hand duplicates the movements he knows his body can make. He does in fact dance later in the film.

In a public moment before the village, Canavan makes an impassioned speech for self-rule, as he holds a captive Moro on the end of a rope. "This is your country," he shouts. "You've got to protect it." Later in the film, after Canavan has spent days fighting a cholera epidemic, Cooper sits, hat tilted back, brow furrowed and loose, an extension of the battle-weary man in *Beau Geste*. But this time he is not a man tired from battling men; the tiredness in Canavan is that of a man who has used his mind and mental skills. It is a man not only weary of body, but weary of mind as well. And this difference is quite evident in Cooper's portrayal.

The film proved to be a box-office bonanza for Goldwyn, though there was no particular appreciation of Cooper's performance. *Life* said the film was "less of a personal triumph for Gary Cooper than for the professional stunt men, headless dummies and repaint experts." *Life* reacted against the violence in the film and pointed out that Goldwyn had even prepared a more violent version for distribution in South America.

The *New York Daily Mirror* said that Cooper displayed "his

usual calm valor, and he has a pleasant cast to support him."
The *Daily Worker,* although not interested in Cooper's performance, did suggest that "In times like these, we question the
wisdom of rattling the bones in Yankee imperialism's closet. To
show the Moros as bloodthirsty savages is neither fair to them
nor to history."

However, with war in Europe and threatening the United
States, such films and attitudes bolstered an American feeling
of superiority and control, a calling on history—albeit a distorted history—to support and sustain the country in a time of
crisis. It was nothing peculiar to the United States or to this
time. The English, French, Japanese and Russians in time of
crisis would often manipulate historical memories to support
the nation's image of itself. In this case, Americans doing battle
in a strange land against strange foreigners is presented as
something they can respond to and handle with ingenuity and
courage.

At the end of 1939, Cooper went on tour to promote *The Real
Glory* but spent little time talking about the picture. B. R.
Crisler, who interviewed him for the *New York Times* in September of 1939, indicated that he was more interested in talking about "baby lobsters, little places in Paris, and precisely
how such and such a dish should be eaten." When the talk
turned to Alfred Hitchcock during lunch, Cooper's comment
was "damn good soup." "The conversation at lunch," wrote
Crisler, "was by no means highbrow."

The next month, a by-lined article by Joel McCrea appeared
in *Photoplay.* McCrea, who was perhaps Cooper's closest friend,
had agreed to do a piece on Cooper. The two actors had met a
few years earlier at a party given by Buddy Rogers and Mary
Pickford. They had gotten along well, and Cooper had taken to
calling McCrea "McFee."

McCrea said that, during the filming of *The Real Glory,* he
had pointed out to Cooper a Los Angeles newspaper headline
that said, "Goldwyn Trying to Trade Cooper Plus Script for
Tyrone Power." McCrea thought Cooper should deny the story,

but Cooper made it clear that his policy was not to get embroiled in responding to things that were not true. To do so would simply prolong public interest and speculation. Actually, that was also Cooper's policy about things that were true. His relationships with women and his disputes over salary were generally treated by Coop as if they had not taken place.

According to McCrea, Cooper had convinced him to join the Screen Actors' Guild, not because the two of them needed the organization but because Cooper felt a lot of other people did. McCrea also remarked on Cooper's ability to relax and tune out distractions. Once at a concert in the Hollywood Bowl that McCrea and his wife, Frances Dee, and Cooper and his wife attended, a rude autograph-seeker popped up behind Cooper and asked him for an autograph. Cooper, who had a slight hearing problem, simply looked forward and listened to the concert. The autograph-seeker grew louder, but Cooper didn't respond.

"And after the concert was over," McCrea recalled, "he rose and rubbed his hands together that way he has when he is pleased. 'Fine program, wasn't it?' he said. Sure, he meant it. As far as he was concerned, nothing had happened to mar his evening. Not a thing."

McCrea also referred to Cooper's seldom-seen but rather bizarre sense of humor. He said that Cooper, when deep-sea fishing, liked to tie pieces of meat to each end of a piece of string. He would then throw them overboard and "chuckle quietly to himself as he watches the squabbling of a couple of outraged sea gulls who have gobbled them up and are, therefore, 'tied' together." McCrea was careful to add that the string was never strong enough that the gulls would have a serious problem.

Particularly interesting in McCrea's account of the difficult-to-fathom Cooper is the statement that Cooper "never kicks. He never mentions, even to me, any sort of problem or difficulty he may have encountered. He never discusses anything personal with anybody."

It is unlikely that Cooper even discussed personal matters with his own family. Part of the image of manliness he developed was that one does not bring his troubles to others, that one handles things alone. Certainly this led to his image as a strong, silent American, and, in truth, he was a private, relatively silent man, though he denied this and pointed out that his friends and family would confirm that he often spoke at length.

Because he was so reticent, it was not until late in his life that the public had any idea of the physical problems Cooper had suffered. To a great extent, the strong, silent American was not nearly as strong as the image he projected, but he would never in his life knowingly betray the image of himself he had nurtured.

In his next Goldwyn picture, *The Westerner,* Cooper was directed by William Wyler. Wyler had begun his career directing Westerns at Universal in 1926. By 1940, he had become known as the director who could get the best performances in Hollywood. His four films before *The Westerner* were *Dodsworth* with Walter Huston, *Dead End* with Humphrey Bogart and Joel McCrea, *Jezebel,* for which Bette Davis won an Academy Award, and *Wuthering Heights. The Westerner* was Wyler's return to the Western after ten years.

When Cooper and his friend Walter Brennan were assigned to the picture, Brennan, according to the legend, immediately balked. "When I read the script of *The Westerner,"* Brennan told Hedda Hopper seven years afterward, "I saw immediately that despite the fact that Gary was the star of the picture, my part was better. I went to him and said, 'Did you know that this is my picture, not yours?'" According to Brennan, Coop replied, "Sure, go ahead and take it."

Cooper himself would say later, "I couldn't figure out for the life of me why they needed me for this picture. I had a very minor part. It didn't require any special effort. All the character had to do was exchange a few shots with the judge in the dramatic moment of the picture." This had been the generally accepted view of the picture since it was made. It was reinforced by the fact that Brennan won one of his three Academy Awards for best supporting actor for his role as Judge Roy Bean in *The Westerner*. However, the film does not really support this assessment.

Director Wyler remembers the film as one in which he decided to improvise a bit in the rehearsals and let the two friends, Brennan and Cooper, work toward achieving something of their real relationship. "I got all kinds of ideas," Wyler recalled, "and these two actors carried them out marvelously. Cooper was a very subtle and fine comedian once he understood the humor of a scene." Wyler's view is close to what actually happens in the film. Cooper plays Cole Hardin, a rambling cowboy who has to become a male Scheherezade to keep a story going for Judge Roy Bean, who wants to hang him as a horse thief. Hardin weaves a comic series of tales about his respect for Lillie Langtry, the actress with whom Bean is in love from a distance. The relationship of the two characters, which is the real heart of the film, gradually develops from indifference to antagonism to friendship to love. As with other Cooper relationships, his character's conviction of what is right and moral comes in conflict with his friendship, and he must face the comic, emotional Bean and, with great regret, destroy him. In every one of his scenes, Brennan's reactions are totally dependent upon Cooper's setting him up, playing with him. Bean's humor depends on Hardin's ability to convince him of the elaborate comic lies he is told.

Cooper also has at least one major comic scene in which Brennan doesn't appear. Hardin, in need of a lock of hair to convince Judge Bean that he not only knows Lillie Langtry but has a memento, goes to Jane-Ellen (Doris Davenport in her only major film role) and pretends to be a love-smitten, shy cowboy who wants a lock of her hair to remember her by. The scene, in which Cooper actually pulls out a huge scissors, is played straight-faced by Cooper as a joke between him and the audience. Hardin is a magnificent teller of tall tales. Later, when Brennan finally insists on seeing the lock of hair, Cooper, sitting with his knees up against a rock, goes through an elaborate opening of the package containing the hair and looks longingly at it, while Brennan's Bean almost salivates in anticipation.

A more subtle example of Cooper's performance in the film occurs one morning after Bean and Hardin have been drinking. Through their waking-up conversation, Cooper puts his head in a bucket of water, searches in vain for a clean part of the rotating towel in Bean's room and finally cleans his face on his jacket. These background activities help to establish the aura of authenticity throughout the film.

Wyler had few restrictions on his budget for the film. The largest herd of cattle ever seen in the movies up to that time appeared in one scene. The herd of seven thousand was photographed as it crossed the Mexican border in Arizona. Shooting in Goldwyn City, Arizona, near Tucson, Wyler had eight and a half miles of road constructed to cross a mountain range and meander through the desert, and the company remained on location for four weeks. To build the background of authenticity of the late 1800s, the Goldwyn production crew found copies of old periodicals, including *The New York Clipper, The Volcano* and *The National Stage and Sport* to appear in various scenes.

While *The Westerner* was in progress, the U.S. Treasury Department boosted Cooper's notoriety by announcing that, for the year 1939, with an income of $482,819, he was the top individual taxpayer in the United States. Following the picture, taxpayer Cooper agreed to go on a promotional tour to help insure the popularity of the film and his continuing salary.

Hollywood columnist Sheilah Graham went on the publicity tour to Dallas in 1940 for the premiere of the film. Two planes were rented to fly the entourage of fifty people. The trip took overnight and berths were provided. Cooper went in one plane serving as host, while Bob Hope served the same function in the other plane. Graham chose to go on the Cooper plane.

Graham, who was romantically involved with writer F. Scott Fitzgerald at the time, remembers the flight: "We were all talking and enjoying ourselves and Gary was flirting outrageously with me and the champagne was flowing and I was somewhat flushed with excitement when I felt the pink glow turning green. In a few minutes I would throw up. . . . Gary took me in his arms as though I weighed two pounds (I was much thinner then) and placed me on a top berth. He was very solicitous. 'Shall I rub your tummy?' 'No,' I implored with a whisper. It would have been disastrous even with Gary doing the rubbing."

Later, at a big suite in the Adolphus Hotel in Dallas, Graham found Cooper waiting for her in the bedroom. "I had obviously overplayed my adoration," Graham reported. "Gary, who never made the first move with a woman, took my hands, drew me close (what ecstasy), and stood there looking down at me while I looked up at him. But only for a few seconds, then I felt a giggle coming and I broke away."

So, nothing came of the moment described by Graham. It is, however, one in a string of tales linking Cooper romantically with a number of women he encountered, but about whom he never spoke publicly.

Frank (Gary) Cooper, his older brother Arthur and Dorothy Barton (Adams) in Dunstable, England, 1911.

Clara Bow and Cooper in *Children of Divorce.*

Lupe Velez's hairdresser prepares Cooper for scene in *Wolf Son*

Jean Arthur, Frank Capra and Cooper on the set of *Mr. Deeds Goes to Town.*

Franchot Tone and Cooper prepare for a scene in *Lives of a Bengal Lancer.*

William Wellman (left), Cooper and J. Carrol Nash take a break during the shooting of *Beau Geste*.

Cooper and his friend and double Slim Talbot in costume for *The Adventures of Marco Polo*.

Sergeant Alvin York admires photograph of Cooper as *Sergeant York*.

James Daley, Ralph Bellamy and Cooper in scene from *The Court-Martial of Billy Mitchell*.

Phyllis Thaxter
and Cooper in
Springfield Rifle.

Cooper in *Friendly Persuasion.*

Cooper in *The Wreck of the Mary Deare*.

Cooper and John Dehner in *Man of the West*.

Cooper and
Deborah Ker
The Naked E

Dorothy McC
and Cooper i
*Friendly
Persuasion.*

TEN

ACADEMY AWARD: SERGEANT YORK

Cooper's next film, Northwest Mounted Police, *was Cecil* B. De Mille's first film in Technicolor. It was also Cooper's first color film, or nearly so. In 1930 *Paramount on Parade* in which Cooper had a small guest shot, had been in color.

In *Northwest Mounted Police,* Cooper plays Dusty Rivers, a Texas Ranger who wanders into Canada in search of a criminal he is chasing. The time is 1885, and Dusty Rivers gets involved in the final crushing of the second revolt of Canadian insurgent leader Louis Riel. In the film Riel, played by Francis McDonald, and his henchmen, played by Akim Tamiroff and George Bancroft, are presented in much the same light as the Moros in *The Real Glory.* Although historical assessments of Riel's role in Canadian history have since been radically revised in his favor, at the time of *Northwest Mounted Police,* De Mille's depiction was still the popular one. In it, Riel and his men are little better than bloodthirsty savages—or worse, rabid revolutionaries. As in *The Plainsman* and the later *Unconquered,* for De Mille, Cooper's character would run afoul of cunning evil white men who join forces with savage, not-very-bright Indians.

Cooper's love interest in the film is again Madeleine Carroll. For the scenes with her, Cooper takes a great deal from his role as Cole Hardin in *The Westerner.* Rivers is not a shy man, nor is he particularly humble about his abilities. Rivers, who stands tall, his height never denied, is direct and self-confident.

As in *Beau Geste,* Robert Preston again appears as an impetuous younger brother. In this case, however, he is not Cooper's brother, but in a bit of unusual casting, he plays the younger brother of Preston Foster, who actually was Robert Preston's older brother.

As always, De Mille provided Cooper props galore to work with and play against. When captured by the Indians, Cooper gets to play an entire scene with his hands tied to a wooden bar across his shoulders. The lanky figure clearly alludes to the crucifixion. In fact the allusion, after Indian capture, exists in *The Plainsman* and later in *Unconquered.* In all three films, Cooper's character is prepared to sacrifice himself for the good of others, but in all three films he escapes from the Indians through his own resources or the help of others. The hero of De Mille's American West is not a religious sacrificial figure; he is a resourceful, moral man, who will fight to the end.

The New York Times, in reviewing the film, said of Cooper, "He is himself, even in a De Mille film." What Cooper himself was or even the specificity of his image remains a rather complex matter, but the *Times* comment was a consensus concept that remained with him.

The film was a great financial success for Paramount and De Mille, and earned five Academy Award nominations. The only Oscar for the film went to Anne Bauchens, who was to edit all of De Mille's sound films.

Cooper's next picture was his first for Warner Brothers and his second for director-producer Frank Capra. Capra and his writer Robert Riskin had been looking for a film idea that would let them work with Cooper again. They found a story by Richard Connell and Robert Presnell in an old issue of *Century* magazine and got excited about it as a possible project.

"For the part of 'John Doe'—a lanky hobo, an ex–bush league pitcher with a glass arm—I had but one choice: Gary Cooper," Capra said. "I wouldn't have made the picture without him." A primary problem, however, was that at the time Capra had no screenplay, just the story, but Cooper read the story and accepted the role in *Meet John Doe* without a script.

In the film, Ann Mitchell (Barbara Stanwyck) is a reporter

not unlike Jean Arthur's Babe in *Mr. Deeds*. After losing her job, Ann writes a fictional letter about a man who claims he is so upset by the fraud and inhumanity in the world that he will kill himself on Christmas Eve. The story becomes a national favorite and gets Ann her job back, but the paper has to produce the John Doe who supposedly wrote the letter. She finds him in the form of Long John Willoughby (Cooper), a hobo and former minor league baseball player with a bum arm. Although warned by his companion the Colonel (Walter Brennan) not to be taken in by Ann, Willoughby agrees to become Doe both because of the opportunities it will give him and because he believes he can help others by doing so. Doe becomes a national figure, and the newspaper's publisher D. B. Norton (Edward Arnold) decides to use him to further his own ambitions. Norton sets up a third political party and plans a public convention, at which Doe will nominate him for the presidency. Seeing Norton as a potential selfish dictator, Doe decides to denounce the publisher at the convention instead of nominating him. Norton, however, cuts Doe's speech off and denounces him as a fake. Totally disillusioned now, Doe decides to do what the fictional Doe had planned—kill himself at midnight on Christmas Eve. Ann, however, finds him about to jump from a building and convinces him not to die, but to live and fight against Norton.

It was another role in which Cooper could stand up for "the little people." It becomes a bit confusing when given close inspection just what the villain represents. At one level, the tale may be seen as a warning against Hitler and Mussolini, who were gobbling up countries in Europe and Africa and threatening the United States. Norton is, however, such a blatantly selfish and evil character that there is less a clash of ideas and ideals than a struggle against pure evil.

It was not the moral or political level of the film, however, that caused reaction, but Cooper's performance. Again, his scenes with Brennan show a comradeship that is totally sustained. The Colonel is a cynic who can't be taken in but wants to save John. Even in their most sentimental scenes together —including one in which they play a harmonica duet—the aura is retained by the willingness of the two men to look at each other with affection and the way in which they operate together physically. In another scene, for example, Cooper talks to Brennan while the former throws a ball to remind him of his baseball days. Cooper's John is loose-limbed and comfortable, an especially difficult acting task since Cooper had never played baseball in his life and had to be taught at the age of thirty-nine how to throw a ball. The problem would be magnified a year later when he would play one of the most renowned baseball players in history, Lou Gehrig.

In an interview with Marian Rhea on the last day of shooting *Meet John Doe,* Cooper commented on his character in the film. Long John Willoughby "thought the most important thing in the world was to get his pitching arm back so he could get rich and famous," said Cooper. "Then he met up with a hobo that everyone called the Colonel (that's my friend Walt Brennan in the picture), and the Colonel taught John things. He was a hobo from choice. He called people who were trying their darndest to make money so they could buy things—radios, fine houses, cars, country-club members and such—'helots.' 'They're slaves to things,' he'd say. Seemed as though if everyone could stop wanting so many things—Hitler and Mussolini and all the rest —the world would suddenly find itself with a weight rolled off its shoulders.

"Guess there's a law in there somewhere," Cooper added. "When human beings accumulate more than they really need, they start losing their souls. Seems to me time for friendships like John's and the Colonel's, time to sit by a stream and talk along is a pretty fine thing. But no one has very much of it these days. Everybody is too busy chasing after things."

Since Cooper himself was quite wealthy at the time and since he was and had for years been working almost nonstop, one wonders how he reconciled his role and his life. At one level, Cooper never considered himself a rich man, as strange as that sounds. He always compared himself to friends who, through wise investments, had parleyed their earnings into millions. Cooper would point to his friends Bing Crosby (whose son Gary was named for Cooper) and Bob Hope as real millionaires. Cooper always considered himself a man who lived reasonably on his salary. Thus, in his own mind, he was not out of touch with the roles in which he played the little man pitted against the evil so frequently related to the upper classes and to money.

Andrew Sarris, in his book *The American Cinema,* goes so far as to say that, "With *Meet John Doe,* Frank Capra crossed the thin line between populist sentimentality and populist demagoguery. Capra's political films . . . had always implied a belief in the tyranny of the majority, but John Doe embodies in Gary Cooper a barefoot fascist, suspicious of all ideas and all doctrines, but believing in the innate conformism of the common man."

The *New York Herald Tribune*'s Howard Barnes said Cooper "is great in this motion picture." The *Baltimore Sun* wrote that Cooper "is so right in every respect as this country's Everyman that it is hard to imagine anyone else in Hollywood filling the bill." It seems odd amidst such praise, even if deserved, that no critic pointed out that both Spencer Tracy and Jimmy Stewart had played related roles in their careers. Cooper is Doe because Cooper got the role and made it his, but it is quite likely that Tracy, Stewart and even a few others would have molded a different and quite effective John Doe.

A week before *Meet John Doe* was released, Gary Cooper had made the cover of *Time* magazine for the first and only time. According to *Time,* the Coopers were then living "in an elaborate white Georgian mansion in Los Angeles' smart Brentwood section. They are surrounded by three and a half acres, a swimming pool, tennis court, dogs, ducks, chickens, a vegetable garden and a citrus grove that Coop cultivates with a small tractor. . . . At home their social life consists largely of tennis, bridge or backgammon with cinema people including such special friends as Tyrone Power and Annabella, the Fred MacMurrays, the Robert Taylors, the Joel McCreas." *Time* further reported that Cooper was "daft" about guns, his favorite being a .22 Hornet with a German telescopic sight, with which he and his wife went hunting for coyotes and bobcats in the mountains near Malibu.

Cooper was still under contract to Goldwyn, but Goldwyn had no suitable work ready for him. Meanwhile, Jesse Lasky, a pioneer in American film, did have a project. Although he had been relegated to the second or third rank of producers, Lasky was persistent. In 1919, shortly after World War I, he had stood in a crowd on Fifth Avenue in New York watching the parade to honor war hero Alvin York. France's Marshall Foch had publicly told York, "What you did was the greatest deed accomplished by any Allied soldier." York was a ready-made potential endorsement for products and causes, but he refused to let his name be used for advertising testimonials and also refused to make stage appearances. "Uncle Sam's uniform, it ain't for sale," York told Lasky, who approached him with the idea of a movie of his life.

Lasky approached York again in the early 1930s when York the farmer, like a lot of Americans, was having trouble making a living, but York again refused. However, when Lasky approached York in 1940, he had an argument that York accepted. It was York's patriotic duty, said Lasky, to allow his life to be filmed as an inspiration to others in the approaching war.

York agreed but laid down several conditions. First, the money he would be paid would not be disclosed and would not go to him but to a Bible school he wanted constructed. Second, no cigarette-smoking actress could be chosen to play his wife. And, finally, no one but Gary Cooper could play him in the film.

Lasky paid York with his own money in "a do-or-die effort to make a comeback," as Arthur Marx described it in his biography of Goldwyn. After other studios had turned the picture down, Jack Warner agreed to do it if Lasky could get what York wanted, Gary Cooper.

Lasky and Goldwyn had been brothers-in-law and had a long-standing enmity, but Lasky, a shy man, had no choice but to approach Goldwyn. Assuming he wouldn't succeed, Lasky went to Goldwyn and told him how much he needed the loan of Cooper to Warner Brothers. To Lasky's surprise, Goldwyn agreed. Goldwyn's reason was that he was engaged in a lawsuit against United Artists and was making no films, though he had to pay Cooper several hundred thousand dollars a year whether the actor worked or not. The loan was not a favor to Lasky but a way of saving money. Lasky told Warner, who couldn't believe that Goldwyn had made no conditions, so he called Goldwyn to find out what was going on. Seeing his advantage, Goldwyn suddenly insisted that in return for Cooper, Goldwyn should get Warner's top star, Bette Davis, for one picture.

Warner's policy was never to loan out Bette Davis, so he refused the deal, thus unsettling Goldwyn's plan. Hal Wallis, Warner's production head, finally persuaded him to go for the deal with Goldwyn, pointing out that without Cooper there would be no York film, and the film had every sign of being a major financial success. Warner gave in, and Bette Davis went to Goldwyn, where she made *The Little Foxes* under William Wyler's direction.

According to Cooper, it was Wallis who showed him the *Sergeant York* script. Cooper was reluctant to take the role, but Warner Brothers brought York out to talk to the actor. Cooper was still not sure. He went to New York, where Lasky "accidentally" ran into him. Lasky told him the part was waiting for him. For two days, Cooper kept running into Lasky and finally asked the producer what was going on. Lasky told him the entire tale and how much he had staked on the film. Cooper agreed to do it.

To prepare for the role, Cooper went to Tennessee and learned as much as he could about York, who was—like Cooper himself—a rather difficult man to understand. York in his youth had been an extreme pacifist, had fought against induction into the army and had gone reluctantly. A strict fundamentalist throughout his life, York didn't smoke, drink or swear. Then one day, October 8, 1918, this young, almost illiterate man went wild during the Battle of the Argonne. He shot an unknown number of Germans and attacked a German machine-gun nest alone; shortly afterward he single-handedly captured 132 Germans.

Howard Hawks, who directed Cooper in *Sergeant York,* remembered Cooper as a man for whom "things would happen that wouldn't be visible to the eye. . . . You'd watch him do a scene. You'd wonder whether you had it. And I'd go home worrying about it. And come look the next day at the rushes—and there was more there than I wanted in the first place."

Hedda Hopper visited the set of *Sergeant York* and commented on the way Cooper's presence tended to keep everyone relaxed. "I watched him doing a scene with a dog in *Sergeant York,"* she said. "It was the highly dramatic one in which Cooper, after spending all night on a cliff, was supposed to have reached the decision to go against his antiwar beliefs and become a soldier.

"The dog and the actor were supposed to stand up simultaneously and face the rising sun. But . . . the dog couldn't stay awake. During each take, when the actor arose, the dog was fast asleep." The dog's trainer finally had to call the dog to wake up in a shot with the sound not rolling.

Dickie Moore, who played York's little brother, also remembered Cooper in the film. Moore, who eventually quit films and became a successful public relations man in New York, was fifteen when *Sergeant York* was made. Cooper "taught me how to throw a knife, how to fire a rifle," Moore recalled. "Basically, he oriented me to the things I'm most interested in today and probably will be for the rest of my life. I don't hunt. I don't kill things, but I'm very fond of animals." Moore remembered Cooper taking time to give him detailed advice on the first rifle he bought.

For his performance in *Sergeant York,* Cooper would win the New York Drama Critics' award as best actor. He would also win his first Academy Award. In 1950, Cooper told the *Saturday Evening Post* that the role of Alvin York had been the one he liked best. It was also the role in which Cooper's father liked his son best.

According to Cooper, "Sergeant York and I had quite a few things in common even before I played him on the screen. We both were raised in the mountains—Tennessee for him, Montana for me—and learned to ride and shoot as a natural part of growing up. Physically, I looked pretty much as he did when he became the outstanding hero of the first World War. And I managed to pick up a fair Tennessee dialect."

Cooper admitted that while he could shoot, he was no marksman like York. False perspective had to be employed in some of the scenes so 80-yard targets looked as if they were 200 yards away, and the eighty-yard targets, in turn, were brought up to 30 yards. "The directorial touch I liked best," Cooper recalled, "came in the turkey shoot when York licked his thumb and wet the gun sight to make it stand out clearly. I've never heard of anyone having any success with this method off the screen, but in the movie it looked very effective."

Cooper's York is a naive man torn between what he considers to be his duty to his community and God and what he is told is his duty to his country and morality. The pulls in both direction are great, but ultimately York convinces himself that God really wants him to fulfill his obligation to the army. In a sense, the issue is quite similar to that of *Meet John Doe,* but the solution is not quite so clear. The issue is never stated so that the Germans are clearly evil (as Edward Arnold's Norton had been in *Doe*), but York feels that one must act out of a sense of loyalty and obligation. Ultimately he is an American and must place his faith in his country, even if it means giving up his principles.

Once he has given up his position of leadership and strength within his Tennessee community, York, in the film, finds himself in a community of soldiers not unlike those in *The Real Glory* and *Bengal Lancer.* They are men who are loyal to each other and respect each other, recognizing that risking one's life is essential to proving oneself a man. The theme is one Howard Hawks had dealt with before and would continue to deal with in films from *The Dawn Patrol* to *El Dorado*.

Seldom, however, would Hawks have a character as resolute as Cooper's Alvin York, a man who, once he has committed himself, cannot be swayed from his task. Cooper's character actually goes full circle. From the comic killing of turkeys in the early part of the film to the comic killing of Germans toward the end, York takes things as they come, with no remorse or conscience once he has come to his decision. The point is made explicit when Cooper uses his turkey call and wets the sights of his gun to shoot Germans just as he had in shooting the turkeys.

As for his performance, Cooper does manage early in the film to give the physical impression through his slumping body and languid movements of an undisciplined, free man, a man for whom the restrictions of the army would be devastating. His accent, however, is not nearly as authentic as Cooper assumed. In fact, Cooper always had enormous difficulty with accents, most notably in *The Virginian* and *Sergeant York*. Certainly part of the recognition for his portayal rests with the climate of the times—with the memory and resurrection of York as a national figure at a time when a new war needed to be rationalized. Also related may have been the fact that Cooper had been overlooked by the Academy the previous year in spite of broad critical support for his performance in *Meet John Doe*.

ELEVEN

BASEBALL AND PAPA HEMINGWAY

Cooper's range as an actor may have been limited, but it was a broad limitation. His next feature for Goldwyn was *The Professor and the Burlesque Queen,* the title of which would be changed to *Ball of Fire* on release later in 1941.

In the film, written by Charles Brackett and Billy Wilder and directed by Howard Hawks, Cooper plays Professor Bertram Potts, who is writing a section of an encyclopedia dealing with slang. While both Alvin York and Potts are essentially shy human beings, York was minimally educated and Potts must be articulate and literate. York was presented by Cooper as a physically agile man, a farmer used to working with his hands who has trouble expressing himself in words. Potts is highly articulate but awkward, stumbling, and physically incapable. Potts's shirt is too large; his pants are slightly wrinkled. However, Potts's hands are light, delicate, in contrast with York's firm-gripping ones. Watch Cooper in *Ball of Fire* pick up his coat or tip his hat to the girls at the burlesque show, or watch him hold Barbara Stanwyck's bare foot when she intrudes on the small community of scholars of which Cooper is a part. Cooper lets his neck bend slightly through the film, implying the scholar who has spent years looking at books instead of sitting straight in the saddle, and his Potts is a character who can quote from *Richard III* when the occassion arises.

Howard Barnes in the *New York Herald Tribune* called Cooper's portrayal "strange" but added that "he handles it with great skill and comic emphasis." The film, which was extremely popular, was remade seven years later, with Hawks

again directing but starring Danny Kaye in the Cooper role.
The Hawks/Kaye version, *A Song is Born,* was not quite the
financial success of *Ball of Fire.*

Although Cooper's performance is unusual, it was Barbara
Stanwyck, recast opposite Cooper because of *Meet John Doe,*
who earned an Academy Award nomination for the film.

The film, which opens with "once upon a time" on the screen,
is in some ways a version of *Snow White and the Seven Dwarfs,*
with Cooper as the world's tallest dwarf. In the film, burlesque
stripper Sugarpuss O'Shea (Stanwyck) agrees to move in with
Potts and seven other professors working on an encyclopedia.
Supposedly she will help Potts in his work on slang. She in turn
will have a hideout from the police, who are after her.

The professors—played by Oscar Homolka, Henry Travers,
S. Z. Sakall, Tully Marshall, Leonid Kinskey, Richard Haydn,
Aubrey Mather and Cooper—are disrupted by the presence of
this female. There is even an evil witch in the form of Joe Lilac
(Dana Andrews), a gangster who Sugarpuss is supposed to
marry. However, she has fallen for Potts. The professors and
the gangsters, who include Dan Duryea as Duke Pastrami,
clash, and Sugarpuss and Potts live happily ever after.

An important event in Cooper's life also took place in 1941.
He met Ernest Hemingway. According to Hemingway's friend
and biographer, A.E. Hotchner, "the two men first met in Idaho
in the early thirties." However, Cooper never reported such a
meeting. It is possible that the two met briefly in 1932 but it is
not likely, as Hotchner says, that they "had been good friends
from the time they first met."

According to Teet Carle, who was involved in publicity work
for Paramount in 1941, it was Cecil B. De Mille who brought
the two men together. "I had seen the Cooper-Hemingway
friendship begin," said Carle. "I sat at a luncheon table, to
cover the event as a publicist, when Cecil B. De Mille got the
star and novelist together in advance of making *For Whom the
Bell Tolls*. At the time, De Mille was to produce and direct

filmization of that best-seller. Gary had starred in *The Plains-man* and *Northwest Mounted Police* for C. B. and liked him. . . ." Cooper would star in *For Whom the Bell Tolls* two years later, but it would no longer be a De Mille project. De Mille would make instead *Reap the Wild Wind.*

In November of 1941, Cooper went hunting with Hemingway in Sun Valley, Idaho. Along with Cooper were his wife and the four-year-old Maria plus Hemingway and his third wife, Martha Gellhorn. Howard Hawks, his twelve-year-old son and Hawks's fiancé, Nancy Gross, were also in the party as was Leland Hayward and his wife, Margaret Sullavan. Hemingway also brought his three sons by previous marriages.

According to Hotchner, Hemingway and Cooper "respected each other's hunting skills and knowledge of the outdoors, and they were always completely honest with one another." At least they appeared to be so to others. Without getting into their minds, it is difficult to judge their level of mutual honesty or the degree to which they were honest with themselves about their motives and emotions. "They shared rough jokes," Hotchner wrote in his biography of Hemingway, "swapped philandering secrets and enjoyed their mutual disdain for the encroaching years."

The disdain would become quite important as the ends of these two very public men's lives came near. Cooper and Hemingway did not meet often from 1941 on, but they did maintain a distinct respect and affection for each other. It is quite easy to see why Hemingway admired Cooper. Cooper was a man who had physical and emotional problems throughout his life, yet chose to suffer stoically. Cooper was not a man of great verbal skill, and he tended to speak sparingly. He liked the outdoors, liked and was liked by people. In many ways, he was a typical Hemingway hero. Unlike Hemingway heroes, Cooper had never suffered the experiences of war or poverty. Still it was not the actual experience but the effect of these experiences that intrigued Hemingway about his heroes, and it was the same attitude, the calm acceptance, the dryness of Cooper that must have appealed to him.

Cooper, as the years passed, became more and more of a figure apart. As actors arose who spoke faster, moved faster, drew their characters in broad emotional strokes, Cooper continued to move slowly, talk slowly and quietly and control his emotions. In fact, Cooper grew even slower as time passed. It began to appear as if many of the other, younger actors were racing in one direction while Cooper was walking resolutely in another. The contrast, as his career went on, was striking. More and more he began to appear a figure bigger than life, an American monument. And more and more, as his career drew to a close, Cooper's character became a man alone. It was these characteristics, both in Cooper's private life and screen character, that must have appealed to Hemingway.

Cooper's next film was not a Hemingway tale but a tragic baseball tale, *The Pride of the Yankees,* which was indeed the story of a man of great strength who loses that strength and accepts his tragedy stoically.

Cooper had illness on his mind while working on *Pride of the Yankees.* A year earlier, he had sent his father on a trip around the world. The elder Cooper had been officially retired at the age of sixty-nine in 1935, but had kept a law office open at Cahuenga and Hollywood boulevards in Los Angeles, where his friends, including Bing Crosby's father, used to drop in. Judge Cooper had returned from his world trip just after *Sergeant York* had been finished and had been hit by a car not far from his office. Although he recovered and lived to the age of eighty-one, he never fully regained his strength and was susceptible to various illnesses.

When Cooper agreed to do *The Pride of the Yankees,* his father was still suffering from the accident. Judge Cooper wanted his son to appear in the film, based on the life of Lou Gehrig, the iron-man first baseman of the New York Yankees who had set a record of 2,130 consecutive games played. Gehrig had died in June of 1941 at the age of thirty-seven, and plans had begun almost immediatedly to film his life from a story written for this purpose by Paul Gallico.

There were two primary problems with Cooper's playing the role, and he almost didn't get it. First, Cooper was forty years old and looked it, and there was some question as to whether he could handle the proposed early scenes in the film when Gehrig was a baseball and football player at Columbia University. Second, Cooper could not play baseball. He had not played the game as a boy and didn't even know how to throw a ball. He had done a little throwing when he played John Willoughby, the would-be pitcher in *Meet John Doe,* but even that couldn't carry him because Gehrig was left-handed and had thrown left-handed.

After it was agreed that Cooper would play Gehrig, the problem of age was handled adeptly by cameraman Rudolph Mate, who would go on to be a highly respected director. Mate decided to light Cooper from below during the early part of the film to remove the wrinkles in the actor's face. As the historical time passed, Mate reduced and finally removed the special lighting.

The problem of playing baseball was not as easily solved. Lefty O'Doul, a former player who later became a major league manager, was hired to work with Cooper. He soon decided that there was no way Cooper could throw left-handed and convince anyone that he was a pro.

It was decided to let Cooper throw right-handed but to employ a photographic trick. Two Yankee uniforms were made for Cooper. One of the uniforms had the Yankee name reversed. In the shots in which Cooper threw the ball with his right hand, the editor simply reversed the negative. It was like looking into a mirror, but there was no clue to the reversal because of the reversed lettering.

But the problems didn't end here. Cooper couldn't even throw right-handed. He had taken so many falls in early films and sustained so many injuries that he couldn't raise his arm over his head. O'Doul continued to work with Cooper, who, he said, "threw the ball like an old woman tossing a hot biscuit."

Eventually they got the actor to the point that he could give a reasonable semblance of throwing, though it was painful for him to do so.

In the film, Walter Brennan again appears as a best friend to Cooper's character. This time he is Sam Blake, a sports reporter who helps nurture Gehrig's career. Dan Duryea appears as a cynical rival reporter who finds it difficult to accept Gehrig's greatness. In a major role in the film, Babe Ruth plays himself and is impressive in doing so. Ruth had appeared in silent films and in guest spots before this and displayed a distinct talent for acting. Former Yankees Robert Meusel, Bill Dickey and Mark Koenig also played themselves in the film, with Mate's technique of lighting from below to cut down their years.

Gehrig is presented as a young boy (Douglas Croft) who idolizes rookie Babe Ruth and wants to be a ball player. However, his immigrant mother wants him to be an engineer like "Uncle Otto." Gehrig (now Cooper) goes to Columbia and works as a waiter in the fraternity where his mother is a cook. The fraternity invites him to join, but a few of the members harbor prejudices against the son of a cook joining them. They ridicule Cooper at a dance, eavesdropping when he is played up to by Myra (Virginia Gilmore). In the party scene, the forty-year-old Cooper appears every bit the clumsy young man, his arms folded awkwardly. When he asks Myra to dance, his face goes through seven changes of expression, each a slight, frightened variation on the former. Later, alone in his room, Cooper with a foolish grin dances quite gracefully with his coat to simulate his dancing with Myra.

When it becomes clear the next day that he has been made a fool, Gehrig drops the tray with which he has been serving and leaps across the table at his chief tormenter. Throughout the film, Cooper's physical problems are handled by cuts to doubles and matching shots so that he doesn't have to do any extended physical activity in a single take. The one exception is a particularly skillful tripping on a row of bats the first time he steps out to bat as a Yankee.

Perhaps the most remarkable thing about Cooper's performance in the film is his evolution of Gehrig's character. There are no massive changes in the character, but he gradually grows more confident, able, for example, to stand up to his rather domineering mother in a confrontation between wife and mother and later able to take the news of his coming death.

Cooper has one comic scene in which the Yankees convince him, as a joke, to take a bite out of Babe Ruth's new straw hat. Ruth catches him with a mouthful of straw, and Cooper's silly look is a comic highlight in an essentially tragic film.

Cooper plays Gehrig not as a college-educated, soft-spoken, intelligent man who became a leader of his team and the sport, which he was, but as a naive American who does his job, helps his family, feels deeply and quietly for other people and takes great pride in his job.

A contrast is drawn between Babe Ruth's outgoing, publicity-seeking good nature and Gehrig's quiet determination. In one scene at a hospital, Ruth tells a sick boy that he will hit a home run for him in the World Series game that day. The reporters take note. Gehrig talks to the boy quietly and the boy urges him to hit two home runs. "I'll hit two homers for you if you hit one for me . . . We can both do it," Gehrig tells the boy.

Word of Gehrig's promise leaks out and is announced on the radio. Gehrig hits the first home run. It goes down to the end of the game with one more at bat, and it is clear that Gehrig will get an intentional walk. Gehrig, however, goes for a purposely bad pitch and hits the homer.

Ruth, for all his good nature, had during the twenties and early thirties represented one pole of American heroism, the man who defied convention and succeeded. Ruth smoked, drank, overate, chased women, spent his money foolishly and was an image for a nation breaking loose in the Jazz Age. Like Jack Dempsey, he was the good-hearted bad man who could fly in the face of traditional morality and not only get away with it but triumph.

Gehrig, although appreciated as a player and recognized for his achievements, always lived under Ruth's shadow. Gehrig was essentially a quiet family man, a decent man who did not have an inflated image of himself, who believed in traditional American ideas of morality and democracy. The Jazz Age image, the new morality, was in the news, but the majority of the nation still clung to the traditional image. It may have been a myth. It may have been a conviction to build a nation on, but it was believed by many. Cooper's Gehrig time and again demonstrated the value of that belief. He was the decent, capable, often-naive man who triumphed in his chosen field—and used his triumph to help other people in some way. Never did he buckle under to the pressures of so-called progress. Cooper's character remained an old-fashioned man, a man of the past who would not compromise his values.

Cooper brings Gehrig alive through little touches: the tasting of pancake syrup with his finger when he talks to his wife about leaving baseball, the slight look of bewilderment quickly masked when he loses control and falls off his locker-room stool. As the disease progresses and Gehrig supposedly has less control of his body, Cooper gradually changes. His arms hang limply at his sides, not in affectation, but not moving with the ease of the prediseased Gehrig. His face ages, thanks both to lighting and the very slight lowering of his brow in the later scenes to increase the look of weariness.

The climax of the film, the inevitable public speech, became the most famous of all such speeches by Cooper's characters. It is in fact the very speech Gehrig made to the Yankee Stadium crowd in his last public appearance. Cooper's Gehrig delivers the thanks to his teammates and fans, holding back emotion but projecting real pride. When he delivers the key line about being "the luckiest man on earth," his voice trembles with emotion but an emotion he will not, out of pride, allow to surface fully.

In later years, that speech was the one Cooper would recite publicly without clear embarrassment. When he began touring military bases two years later, he was asked to give the speech and had no trouble memorizing it. It became his standard presentation for servicemen and one that always brought tears and roars of applause.

Of his performance as Gehrig, Archer Winsten of the *New York Post* wrote, "Gary Cooper, though entirely lacking the physical equipment of a Gehrig, manages the technical aspects of baseball in a manner which should not be too distracting except to a critical expert. On the other hand, his projection of the mental and spiritual side of the man is brilliant." *The New York Times* noted that Cooper's "performance grows, as the character grows, from shy gawky undergraduate to modest, unassuming hero of millions."

The film received eight Academy Award nominations, including Cooper's third. Cooper, however, lost out to James Cagney, who won the Oscar for *Yankee Doodle Dandy.*

TWELVE

GARY COOPER, PRODUCER: GIVING ORDERS IS HARD TO DO

Ernest Hemingway's novel For Whom the Bell Tolls *was* published in 1940 and purchased shortly after by Paramount for Cecil B. De Mille for a record $150,000. When De Mille left the project, it was assigned by Paramount to Sam Wood. De Mille and Hemingway's choice to play Robert Jordan had been Cooper from the start. In fact, Hemingway suggested that he had Cooper in mind when he wrote the novel.

Cast opposite Cooper as Maria was Vera Zorina, who had cut her hair short for the role. Cooper, Zorina and a cast including Akim Tamiroff, Katina Paxinou and Arturo de Cordova moved with the crew into the Sierra Nevada mountains at the end of 1942. From the start of shooting, Sam Wood was worried. Even though Cooper was a celebrated actor, Wood feared his underplaying. Viewing the rushes made him feel better about Cooper, but he began to worry about Zorina. After three weeks of shooting, Wood and the Paramount executives decided to replace her with Ingrid Bergman.

Dudley Nichols's screenplay deemphasized the Spanish Civil War and played up the growing romance between Jordan and Maria and their conflict with the guerrilla leader (Tamiroff) and his woman, Pilar (Paxinou). In fact, the Hemingway politics were submerged in a triangle worthy of Arthur Miller.

By the time the film was shot and edited, it was two hours and forty minutes long. When the film was reissued in the 1950's, an hour was removed and remains missing from the prints in general circulation.

In the film, Cooper plays a soldier of fortune dedicated to

helping the fight against the Fascists. The character is similar to the one Cooper played in *The General Died at Dawn.* In *For Whom the Bell Tolls,* however, Jordan does not save himself by any last-minute double-talk. Instead, he sends Maria away, blows up the crucial bridge and holds the pass with machine-gun fire, knowing that he will die for the cause.

For his role, Coop earned his fourth Academy Award nomination. Tamiroff was also nominated, but the only acting award for the film went to Katina Paxinou as best supporting actress.

According to Paul Anthony writing in *Photoplay* in 1961, Hemingway had disliked the previous film versions of his works. He supposedly had called the filmed version of *The Sun Also Rises* "the silliest damn thing I ever saw." Of *The Killers,* Hemingway is reported to have said, "Get me to the bathroom —I'm going to be sick." Although he thought Cooper had done a good job in *A Farewell to Arms,* Hemingway hated the happy ending the studio had tacked on. Only *For Whom the Bell Tolls* pleased him. According to Anthony, his comment to Coop was, "You played Robert Jordan just the way I saw him, tough and determined. Thank you."

Recalling her association with Cooper in an interview for this book, Ingrid Bergman said, "I first met Gary Cooper in Nevada where *For Whom the Bell Tolls* was being shot. I was replacing another actress who had worked on the film for a short time, and I was very scared, very frightened. Gary Cooper was a famous actor. When I did begin to work, I found him to be an extremely kind, very simple person who kept to himself and didn't join in much with the others. One of the things I liked about him from the very start was his size. He is the tallest leading man I have worked with, and working with him was one of the few times when I did not have to slouch over for a leading man.

"As an actor, I think he was extremely good. I remember one time I was standing next to him and he started talking very quietly. I couldn't make out what he was saying. I asked him to repeat what he had said, and he told me that he hadn't been speaking. He had been rehearsing his lines. It had sounded so natural that I couldn't tell then or in the film when he was acting. You never noticed that he was working. He spoke quietly, never tried to do an interpretation like an Alec Guinness. Instead he did little things with his face and his hands, little things you didn't even know were there until you saw the rushes and realized how tremendously effective he was.

"Although I never got to be a really close friend to Gary Cooper, my daughter Pia and his daughter Maria did play together quite a bit. He did get along extremely well with our director Sam Wood, and while we were making *For Whom the Bell Tolls,* we read a novel, *Saratoga Trunk.* I wanted very much to do it, to change my type, to put on a dark wig and makeup and play this emotional woman. The three of us agreed to make *Saratoga Trunk* as soon as we could. I also remember we discussed the possibility of Gary and I doing *The African Queen,* but, as you know, we did not."

In October, 1943, Cooper agreed to go on a two-month, 23,000-mile trip to the South Pacific to help entertain servicemen. He toured with a USO camp show that included actresses Phyllis Brooks and Una Merkel and accordionist Andy Arcari. Merkel later remembered, "Gary had never been on the stage in his life; he did some of Jack Benny's material. I asked if I could do the song Celeste Holm did in *Oklahoma,* 'I'm Just a Girl Who Cain't Say No.' Then all four of us—Gary, Phyllis Brooks, Andy Arcari and me—did 'Pistol Packin' Mama.' We were the first white women to go to New Guinea. Some of the men had been there two years, and they didn't even have female nurses."

When he returned from the tour, Cooper described the show: "Well, I'd open the show with a few Benny and Hope gags and then introduce the girls. Neither is a blues singer, but Una and Phyllis gave out like a Dinah Shore. Then we'd do some comedy skits, Andy would play the accordion—and how he kept it from being ruined by rain I'll never know—and I gave the Lou Gehrig farewell speech . . . I didn't remember it, but when they kept asking for it, I sat down and wrote it out as well as I could recall it. Then I'd recite it for them, and they seemed to appreciate it. Then I'd give them some words of appreciation from the folks back home." When he returned to the United States, he continued to visit servicemen's hospitals all over the country.

Shortly after his return from the Pacific, Elsa Maxwell, an old friend, visited him and watched him stare intently at Maria as she played. When asked why by Maxwell, he replied, "You know I've never been a great fellow for hoarding things, Elsa. Life's so blamed short. . . . But I'm hoarding her . . . I always want to be able to remember her at every age."

The trip to the Pacific, the stage appearances and what he saw greatly affected Cooper's interest in war propaganda. Cooper told newspaper interviewers that the troops "resent propaganda pictures that show the enemy as a stupid dope— the same thing applies to radio—the boys tune out the obvious morale junk in favor of Radio Tokyo which gives them entertainment without commercials."

As a result of his trip to the Pacific, Cooper suffered an amoebic infection a year later. According to Cooper's physician, Dr. Leland Hawkins, the infection was aggravated by an attack of influenza. The problem eventually sent him to the hospital and joined the many recurrent illnesses that plagued Cooper for the last fifteen years of his life.

Cooper also became quite active politically for the first time in his life. He was so opposed to the reelection of Franklin D. Roosevelt that he purchased radio time on November 1, 1944, to support Dewey and attack the president. On the show, Cooper spoke emphatically, saying, "I've been for Mr. Roosevelt before—but not this time. There have been too many broken promises to suit me—and too much double-talk."

After referring to his visit with troops in New Guinea and Australia, Cooper added: "And now that I'm back, I keep asking myself whether I would like to have a man in charge of getting jobs for everyone after the war that was unable to get jobs for pretty near everybody before the war."

The speech opposed the prevailing Hollywood position in support of the President. Radio shows in support of Roosevelt always boasted a long list of top stars. The Cooper statement for Dewey stood almost alone.

It is not surprising that Cooper's next picture was *The Story of Dr. Wassell,* the tale of a World War II hero. The idea for the film was that of Cecil B. De Mille, who had heard President Roosevelt in a radio talk in April, 1942, tell about the exploits of a Dr. Corydon Wassell, a plain Arkansas country doctor who went as a medical missionary to China, later joined the U.S. Naval Reserve and was put in charge of wounded men from the badly damaged cruisers *Marblehead* and *Houston.* In Java, just ahead of the Japanese, Wassell had hidden his wounded in an inland hospital. When 60,000 Japanese invaded Java, Wassell was ordered to evacuate all his wounded who could walk and abandon those who could not. Wassell disobeyed and got all the men to the coast. When a ship's captain refused to take the wounded, Wassell stayed behind with them and led them back through the jungle. Eight men and Wassell made it, got on a crowded Dutch steamer, the last Allied ship to leave Java, and headed home. Wassell expected to be greeted with a court-martial when he got home, but got the Navy Cross instead.

After registering the film title, De Mille had sought out Wassell, gotten his story and gone right to work. De Mille added a love interest for Wassell, Madeleine Day (played by Laraine Day). In keeping with the wartime position of cooperation and mutual support, the apparent heartlessness of the navy was underplayed, and each barrier to Wassell's securing safety for his men was the result of nature or the Japanese. The story for the film was credited both to Wassell and novelist James Hilton, who was best known for the romantic *Lost Horizon,* and *The Story of Dr. Wassell* is indeed a rather fanciful account.

Cooper, once again as in *The Real Glory,* plays a military physician, and once again he makes the profession a part of his being, whether he is looking through a microscope or deftly bandaging a wounded man while he carries on a conversation with a nurse on how to take care of a man whose arm has been shattered.

Primary criticism of the film was directed at the fact that Cooper's Wassell is presented almost as a saint. He hasn't a single defect and won't even utter an angry word. Regardless of the pressure of bombs or advancing Japanese or the responsibility he has for the wounded men, Cooper's Wassell proceeds stoically with De Mille's highly stylized dialogue. But this time the dialogue was in the mouth of a contemporary figure, and both De Mille and Cooper were at their most comfortable when dealing with the past and not the present.

The *New York Times*'s Bosley Crowther wrote, "Cooper's performance as the good doctor is familiarly shy. Except for an occasional 'Good gravy!' and a startled look, you'd hardly know he was pressed." *Time* wrote, "*Dr. Wassell* is a big, bright, brassy specious show in which Gary Cooper . . . goes through some highly Technicolored, highly ordinary motions."

Following the release of *Dr. Wassell,* Cooper announced that he was through with biographies. His portrayals of York, Gehrig and Wassell, Marco Polo and Wild Bill Hickok were enough. He was in fact afraid that he might be typecast and ruin his career—a curious attitude for a man who kept coming back to Westerns and would forever be identified with them. "I want to appear in some comedies for a change," Cooper told Edwin Schallert of the *Los Angeles Times.* However, he said, the men in the armed services needed "good American entertainment and, especially, I think, light entertainment or inspiring pictures like *Wassell.*"

It was 1944, and Cooper decided to insure that his next picture would be a comedy. He would do this by starting his own production company. Cooper's anti-Roosevelt speech and position may also have cooled him as a property for producers. In any case, International Pictures, Inc., was formed with William Goetz as president and Cooper the principal stockholder. Nunnally Johnson was brought into the firm to handle day-to-day production and write the first picture. Cooper announced his intention of becoming a producer with the statement to *The New York Times* in August, 1944, that, "Directors and producers don't pay much attention to suggestions from actors. If I'm a producer, too, maybe they'll listen to me."

Joining Coop, Goetz and Johnson was Leo Spitz, a former RKO president. The idea was for International Pictures to make two films a year and release them through RKO. For the first of these films, Johnson adapted a short story, "The Little Accident," by Floyd Dell and Thomas Mitchell. The production company hired Cooper's friend Sam Wood to direct and Teresa Wright to star with Coop.

Cooper was quite pleased with the proposed project, which was retitled *Casanova Brown*. He said, "I think Casanova Brown should be just about right. It's more on the order of a Lubitsch picture." In fact, the film has none of the wittiness and sophistication of the Lubitsch films. It is a rather straightforward romantic comedy with touches of *His Woman,* which Cooper made with Claudette Colbert in 1931.

In the film, Cooper plays English teacher Brown, whose former wife Isabel (Wright)—the marriage was annulled—announces that he is to become a father. After the baby is born, Isabel tells Brown that she plans to put the baby up for adoption. Brown kidnaps the baby and tries to care for it in a hotel. He plans to marry the hotel chambermaid so he can adopt the baby. However, the real mother has a change of heart, shows up and reconciles with Brown.

Reviews were mixed. Crowther wrote in *The New York Times* that "Cooper's somewhat obvious and ridiculous clowning over the baby takes on a silly complexion . . . All in all, there is so much endeavor with so little subject in this film that one is exposed to the impression that anything went for a laugh." However, Alton Cook in the *New York World-Telegram* said the film did just what Cooper wanted it to do: "His work in this picture belongs with his best, right up with *Mr. Deeds.*"

According to Cooper, he and Johnson had thought the film

scenes were very funny when they were written, but, said Cooper, "The public just wouldn't believe it. The character they knew as Gary Cooper would never be that dumb, and the fact that the picture made money was no consolation."

Casanova Brown did have one historical distinction. Prints of the film were rushed overseas so that on August 8, 1944, at sixteen spots along the Normandy front, men could take time out from war to watch the world premiere of *Casanova Brown*. The film was the first premiere to be celebrated on the soil of liberated France.

Cooper credited Nunnally Johnson with urging him to become producer of his next film, *Along Came Jones*. Johnson, who came to film after a successful career as a short story writer, had a long string of credits as a screenwriter when he went into partnership with Coop. Among his film credits were *The Grapes of Wrath*, *Tobacco Road* and *Jesse James*. He would later write *The Gunfighter*, *The Woman in the Window*, *The Dark Mirror*, *The Desert Fox* and *The Dirty Dozen*, in addition to writing films that he himself produced and directed, including *The Man in the Gray Flannel Suit* and *The Three Faces of Eve*.

Johnson adapted *Along Came Jones* from a novel by Alan LeMay. Stuart Heisler, who had been editor on Cooper's *The Wedding Night* almost a dozen years earlier, was named director, and Loretta Young was hired for the love interest. For Cooper's sidekick George, William Demarest was chosen, and the villain was Dan Duryea. Duryea was chosen not only because of his ability as an actor and his friendship with both Cooper and Johnson, but because the story required that the villain be someone who physically resembled Cooper. The script called for some confusion of identity.

Cooper was moved into a producer's office at the Goldwyn Studio that had been specially designed for him. It included a lemon-colored rug, white walls, bottle-green chairs and a tomato-red couch. Then came the time for Cooper to make some of those producer's decisions he had longed for.

Johnson recalled what he called Cooper's "acid test" as a producer shortly after the film was released:

> That day the designer brought Mr. Cooper his sketches for Miss Young's wardrobe, a series of garments suited to a simple ranch maid. A man of few words—of none, if he can get away with it—Mr. Cooper was about to initial the drawings when he remembered the obligations of his new role.
> "How much?" he asked.
> "They'll average $175 apiece," the designer replied.
> After some thought: "Supposed to be cheap store dresses, aren't they?"
> "Yes, sir."
> "Kind that cost about $7.50?"
> "Yes, sir."
> "Then why don't we just go out and buy them?"

According to Johnson and others, it was then explained to Cooper that the dresses made by the designer would be special wrinkle-resistant garments that would not wilt or show wear and have to be changed frequently. According to Cooper, however, his decision to buy cheaper dresses was heeded.

Involved in the job of producer, Cooper sometimes forgot that he was also a very expensive actor and was late in getting to the set on several occasions. He eventually got a bicycle to speed the move from his office to the sound stage. During one of his hurried flights on two wheels, he ran into a thin chain that had been hung across the studio street. The chain shot him off the bicycle, and he landed on the back of his head.

While serving as producer, Cooper also picked up the nickname "Pincus," which he disliked and which only his closest friends dared use.

In the film, Cooper plays Melody Jones, an extremely mild-mannered cowboy who sings endless verses of "Old Joe Clark" and who is mistaken for killer Monte Jarrad (Duryea). Their initials are even the same on their saddles. After a series of comic misadventures of mistaken identity, Jones is about to be killed by Jarrad when the gunman's girl, Loretta Young, shoots

Jarrad and saves Jones. The ending is a somewhat comic fore-shadowing of the conclusion of *High Noon*.

Duryea's villainy was an important step in his career. When Duryea's small son Peter finally saw the picture, he stood up during the crucial scene and shouted, "Don't you dare shoot my daddy. I don't care if he is bad."

Just before his death, Cooper told a reporter, "I plead guilty to a picture several years ago called *Along Came Jones,* a West-ern in which the cowboy couldn't hit his hat while he was wearing it. The hero wasn't too bad, I'll say that; he had won third place as a bronc rider in a rodeo. But he was all thumbs when it came to shooting, and we played that up for laughs."

Cooper then said the picture had made money but when Cecil B. De Mille saw it, he "raked me over the coals for it." De Mille thought it was a terrible blow to Cooper's image to play a man who couldn't handle a gun, kept getting lost and let himself be taken advantage of by a woman. Cooper, he said, was an institu-tion, and you don't do that to institutions. "Never play any-thing that lets the public down, your public," De Mille is re-ported to have said. "If you kid a Western, if you kid a hero, you are doing yourself damage. People who come to see you—they want to see a fellow who can do no wrong and can come through in tough spots."

In spite of De Mille's warning and Cooper's misgivings about the role, *Along Came Jones* is probably the tour de force of Cooper's career, the single Western in which he stood back and looked at his own character and questioned the use of a gun and the need for it. It is almost as if the Cooper persona is divided in half: the gentle, well-meaning inept man, Jones, and the gunfighter who reacts to violence with violence. There is even a scene in which the two men exchange clothes and comment on their similarities and differences. When Jones faces Jarrad, he confronts the very idea that the one who triumphs is the one with the fastest gun. Sometimes the man with the fastest gun is not a good guy. The king is not always benevolent.

Cooper's co-directors of International Pictures persuaded

him to go on an extended publicity trip with the film. In Tulsa, he was trapped by a group of teenage autograph seekers. A young girl touched his sleeve, squealed and fainted. Cooper caught her, carried her to a chair and tried to revive her. Although he was due at a theater, he waited to be sure she was all right and all through the day kept asking about the girl's condition.

"What did I do to bring that on?" he asked his publicity man.

Moving on to Texas, Cooper was made an honorary member of the Texas Rangers, an honor that had been given to only two others before him. So moved was Coop by the act that he came near to breaking down in his acceptance speech.

Although the film did well and the reviews were affirmative, only the *New York Daily News* really saw *Along Came Jones* as a major film for Cooper: "Not since his beloved *Mr. Deeds* has he been able to expand on all the charm, befuddled naivete and droll humor at his command."

Following *Along Came Jones,* Cooper decided to give up producing. He had had enough and didn't think he had done as good a job as he might have. One associate recalled that Cooper was incapable of being firm. One of his friends early in the film told Cooper that he had to stay on Johnson, prod him, be sure the script was getting done, and if it wasn't, Cooper was advised to be firm and demanding.

Cooper called Johnson in front of the others and said, "Hello Nunnally. This is Coop. How are you? How's your wife? How's the story getting along?"

"Fine," Johnson replied.

"Gee, that's great," said Cooper. "Keep up the good work."

When he turned to his friends in the room after hanging up, Cooper solemnly said, "It's fun to bawl writers out."

"I guess being a producer has given me a better appreciation of details," he said when he finished his tour for the film. "Angles which one is not aware of as an actor, such as selecting sets, making them and providing budgets for all the various departments, become not an awareness but a headache."

Cooper's partners kept International going for several years and then merged with Universal Pictures to become Universal International, now the largest studio in the world.

Before his next picture, Cooper took some time off to work on his guns and be with his family. A reporter visiting the Cooper home in Brentwood was escorted into the living room, where she noted a "distinct Chinese influence in this avocado-green room with the painted dark green floors and the huge fireplace. But very much from our part of the world is the grand piano in the corner, with the music to 'Don't Fence Me In' on the stand and beside it a report card with the name 'Maria Cooper' on it. All the spaces for marks were filled with chubby little 'A's." Cooper told the reporter that Maria, then eight, was also pretty good at playing the piano, particularly boogie-woogie.

On days when they weren't home, the Coopers liked to go to the beach with their boxer Arno. When time and weather permitted, the family would also go to Sun Valley for skiing.

The next Gary Cooper film released, in 1945, was made before *Along Came Jones. Saratoga Trunk,* based on an Edna Ferber novel, had actually been shot immediately after *For Whom the Bell Tolls.* The co-stars, Cooper and Ingrid Bergman, were the same, as was the director, Sam Wood. The film had been shot between February and May, 1943, and had been shown several times to Armed Forces units before its official release.

Saratoga Trunk was made for Warner Brothers with producer Hal Wallis, who had been largely responsible for getting *Sergeant York* made. Second-unit director on *Saratoga Trunk* was a young Warner Brothers fledgling director named Don Siegel. Siegel, who would later direct such films as *Invasion of the Body Snatchers, Dirty Harry, Charlie Varrick* and *Escape from Alcatraz,* was the studio's resident expert on action sequences. As second-unit director, he would be given full charge of all the scenes involving fights, chases and various action.

Siegel had done some second-unit work on *Sergeant York,* but none had involved Cooper.

In an interview for this book, Siegel recalled Cooper and *Saratoga Trunk:* "Cooper was a very private person. I was never able, really, to get friendly with this man. Then I discovered that he couldn't fight. Physically, he was not a fighter. He was almost feminine in the way he would throw punches. On the other hand, his face was very good, so I got in close to his face during the fight shots, so that his face would show what his body was supposedly doing. He could look very determined. I was, however, very disappointed that he couldn't fight. He did what he was told to do and did it with little trouble."

The suggestion of effeminate behavior or even bisexuality followed Cooper throughout his career, especially during his early years in Hollywood. Whether there was ever any homosexual behavior or not, at any level and at any time, is impossible to prove and is in fact irrelevant to his career. What is important is that Cooper's portrayals did contain elements that were usually associated with femininity. His characters were sensitive and his movements were delicate. This incorporation of the feminine with his manly image of strength may well have been a factor in his fame. There had been and have been many heroic American film stars whose portrayals are dependent on an assumed masculine invulnerability. Cooper's fragile heroism brought together the myth of American manliness and the tempering of emotionalism. There was no absurdity assumed or masculinity questioned in the Cooper character's clear love for his male friends in such films as *Souls at Sea, The Westerner* and *Vera Cruz.* It was no threat to his character's masculinity to display emotion, to be openly moved. Cooper's characters made no effort to hide their masculine/feminine nature, a nature all people have but few can come to terms with. Ironically, it may well have been Cooper's ability to accept the feminine that made him such a popular male hero.

In the film, Cooper plays Colonel Clint Maroon, who gets embroiled with fortune hunter Clio Dulaine (Bergman). Maroon, a Texas cowboy, gets involved in saving the Saratoga Trunk Line for Bartholomew Van Steed (John Warburton) and other owners, only to find after doing so that Clio is about to marry the wealthy Van Steed. When he staggers to the engagement party, Clio throws herself at him, forsaking the wealthy Van Steed.

Reviews were mixed. Howard Barnes in the *New York Herald Tribune* thought Cooper was "perfect as the backwoodsman who tries unsuccessfully not to become entangled with the scheming spitfire." Bosley Crowther in the *New York Times,* however, didn't like the film, though he labeled Cooper "pleasantly roguish."

After *Along Came Jones,* Coop made *Cloak and Dagger,* directed by Fritz Lang and released by Warner Brothers. It costarred Lilli Palmer in her American film debut. Lang, who began his career in Germany as a director of serials and spy tales, had a considerable reputation both for his German-made films, including *Dr. Mabuse, Destiny, Metropolis* and *M,* and his American-made films, including *Fury, You Only Live Once, The Ministry of Fear, The Woman in the Window* and *Scarlet Street.*

For *Cloak and Dagger,* Lang had returned to the spy tale with Cooper as physics professor Alvah Jesper, drafted into the OSS just before World War II to go into Europe and rescue an atomic scientist. Lang later claimed that he had made the film for one reason and that reason was nullified by the studio when it edited the film. According to Lang, Cooper's character was based on the late J. Robert Oppenheimer, whom Lang had met.

The film as released showed Cooper getting on an airplane and rescuing the atomic scientist at the end. Lang, however, had gone beyond this to shoot what he thought was the essence of the film, a more pessimistic ending involving Jesper's return to Germany. Lang's version of the film, which was shot but never seen, ends with Cooper walking out of a captured Nazi cave where atomic research had been under way. He meets a paratrooper sitting in the high grass.

"Nice weather, isn't it, professor?" the paratrooper asks.

Jesper responds, "Yes," looks around and adds, "This is Year One of the atomic age, and God help us Americans if we think we can keep the secret of the atomic bomb for ourselves."

That was in 1945, when the United States had a monopoly on the bomb.

Lang said he was never given any reason why his ending was removed from the film.

Lilli Palmer, in her autobiography *Change Lobsters and Dance,* remembered *Cloak and Dagger* well. As a girl of fourteen she had seen Coop in *Morocco* and had become a fan. In fact, she used to fantasize conversations with him. When she finally met him just before they were to do a test for *Cloak and Dagger,* he gave her a friendly wink and said, "Hi, kid." She found Cooper to be radically different from others with whom she had worked. He never strained. He appeared to have no nerves.

"Cooper," she wrote, "could deliver a long speech on camera while rummaging in his pocket for a cigarette, continue talking while he fussed with the matches, pause for a moment of what looked like intense concentration, pick up where he left off, put the matches away, rub his nose, and go on talking as if the camera didn't exist." When she tried to praise his work, Coop replied, "It's a cinch. I just learn my lines and try not to bump into the furniture."

Palmer also found that the forty-five-year-old Cooper was quite different from the image of her childhood. He moved slowly, spoke deliberately, tired quickly and would fall asleep wherever he happened to be. By this time he also had a distinct hearing problem.

Palmer found him quite friendly and enjoyed working with him, though their heights were so different that she had to stand on a box in their scenes together. Her problem was with Lang. Lang remained unapproachable. She tried talking to him in German, but it didn't help. She found the director particularly curt and difficult when Cooper wasn't present. Lang's verbal attack finally got to be too much for her after she accidentally shot herself in the leg with a blank during one scene, and Palmer walked off the set.

At a party that night, Tyrone Power asked her why Coop had not come to her aid when Lang got abusive. She had no answer. After a three-day walkout, she returned to the picture, and Lang pointedly disappeared during her rehearsals and spoke little to her for the rest of the shooting.

When the film was over, and Lang had given her a polite goodbye, Cooper appeared outside her dressing room, swinging an imaginary golf club. "Hey, kid," he said, hitting an imaginary ball, "say, that business with Lang, you know—I probably should have . . . uh, but you see, I'm . . . not much good at that sort of thing, I never seem to find the right words. I need a script. Know what I mean?"

THIRTEEN

"I'M NO DANGED RED": THE RED SCARE AND PATRICIA NEAL

In 1947, the forty-six-year-old Cooper made his fourth and final film for Cecil B. De Mille. In addition to Cooper, Paulette Goddard, who had appeared in *Northwest Mounted Police,* starred in *Unconquered.* The villains were Howard DaSilva as Martin Garth and Boris Karloff as Guyasuta, Chief of the Senecas. De Mille's daughter Katherine played a sympathetic Indian in love with Garth, while Henry Wilcoxin, De Mille's friend and assistant who had been the villain in *Souls at Sea,* played a British officer. Also in the cast as a snivelling villain was Porter Hall, who had appeared in related roles in both *The Plainsman* and *The General Died at Dawn.* He had also appeared in *Souls at Sea* as the prosecutor who tries to convict Cooper of murder. Hall made a career out of being the little coward in dozens of films. In fact, Cooper's career was so extensive that it is rare to find a film actor over the age of forty-five who did not have some experience with him.

Unconquered was the biggest film Cooper had yet appeared in. With a $5,000,000 budget, it was a radical change from the two films he had produced for International Pictures. In the film, Abigail Hale (Goddard), an English girl, is sentenced to slavery in North America early in the 1760s. Although she has committed no crime, she is put up for auction and bought by Captain Christopher Holden (Cooper), a Virginia militiaman. Holden does not really want her but wants to thwart the lusting Garth (DaSilva), who is plotting with the Indians against the colonists. Holden gives Hale her freedom, but Garth bribes an official to tear up the freedom papers as soon as Holden leaves. Hale is then made a slave, while Garth plots with the Indians, and Holden does his best to thwart them. In his efforts to stop Garth, Holden acts independently and is court-martialed and sentenced to death for desertion.

Although Cooper's character deserts to rescue a woman and gets into all kinds of difficulties, including capture by Indians, the desertion greatly upset Cooper's father. Cooper tried to persuade his father that the character was not being dishonor-able, but the judge was reluctant to accept his son's explana-tion. It took an extended visit by De Mille to convince the judge that Holden's desertion was not only honorable but actually resulted in the saving of the colonies.

Cooper's performance in *Unconquered* is one of the most distinctive of his career, thanks in great part to De Mille's playing on his abilities and image. In his first appearance, Cooper is seen throwing a knife at a target while he engages in the bidding with DaSilva for Goddard. Since Cooper could actu-ally throw a knife and would frequently whittle and play with one on his films, De Mille simply incorporated this into the character.

Cooper's first words in the film after DaSilva has made a bid on the slave are, "and sixpence," to indicate that whatever the villain bids, he will bid just a bit higher. That in fact is the position Cooper's Holden takes throughout the film. He bids just a bit higher and gambles just a bit more. For De Mille the outcome of history is to a great extent a result of heroic gam-bling.

Throughout the film, De Mille provides period props for Cooper to respond to: an arrow to point to a map, a tankard of ale to grasp tightly in his knuckle-whitening hand when he is angry at DaSilva, some dry corn kernels to sift through his fingers. In his key scene, Cooper convinces the Indians that he has a magic box he can control. The magic box is a compass, and he controls it by loading Karloff with metal so the compass will point at him. Cooper plays the scene as a man who appears outwardly confident but makes it quite evident through the tension in his face that he is pulling a dangerous trick.

Unconquered gave Cooper the opportunity to move, use his body, whether confronting a group of men in a tavern, burying corpses or escaping from prison. It is evident in De Mille's films that he does not believe in letting people simply have scenes in which they talk. He finds it essential that they act, engage in their lives as the crucial conversations take place. Not only was Cooper particularly adept at this, it was one of the things he felt most comfortable doing. The union of word and act to define the character was a key to Cooper's confidence. His awkwardness in performances, especially in some of the comedies, arises when he is not playing a character who is defined by his actions as well as his words. This may well account for why Cooper appeared much more confident and capable in films directed by De Mille, Wyler and Hathaway than he did in films by Lubitsch or Wood.

Once again, the De Mille/Cooper film came under attack for its lack of respect for the facts of history. It was the constant cry against a director who really had no interest in history. His primary interest was the fantasy that arises from assumptions about history and heroism. De Mille did not want to deal with naturalistic, troubled and uncertain people. He wanted to and did deal with decisive, mythic figures from Moses to Wild Bill Hickok. Cooper so represented the mythic American figure that De Mille naturally gravitated toward him when dealing with American subjects.

Following *Unconquered,* Cooper appeared in a brief guest shot as himself in *Variety Girl,* the tale of a couple of Hollywood visitors who get into the Paramount lot. Cooper, in full cowboy costume, is seen briefly on a merry-go-round horse.

In October, 1947, Cooper was suddenly thrust into the headlines of the nation's newspapers for a reason other than his acting career or personal life. He was summoned before the House Committee on Un-American Activities, which was conducting an inquiry into the degree of Communist infiltration in the film industry. Cooper testified as a friendly witness along with Ronald Reagan, George Murphy and Robert Montgomery.

A committee was formed to oppose the House committee's inquiry. This Committee for the First Amendment held a press conference and said that the House committee was stifling "the free spirit of creativeness" and was violating the constitutional right of free expression by investigating individual political beliefs. Spokesmen for the Committee for the First Amendment were John Garfield and dancer Paul Draper. Also on the committee were Paulette Goddard, Henry Fonda, Gregory Peck, Van Heflin, Myrna Loy, Burgess Meredith and playwrights George S. Kaufman and Moss Hart.

In August of that year, *La Tribuna,* Rio de Janeiro's Communist newspaper, had carried a 1,500-word article on its front page describing in some detail Gary Cooper's appearance at a Philadelphia meeting of 90,000 Communists assembled, according to the article, "beneath the red flag flying from the tower of the Philadelphia Communist Federation."

La Tribuna even quoted Cooper's address to the gathering. "To be a Communist today is the highest of honors," they reported Cooper as saying. "To be a Communist means having sun and light in one's spirit. It means living and striving. . . . The time has come to do away with the kings of petroleum, of coal, of coffee, of sugar, and of lemonade, of doing away with these Al Capones of the yellow gloves. No more shall there be the shameful spectacle of young Bob being forced to leave good and pretty Jane to go and die without knowing why."

This story appeared in spite of the fact that there was no Communist Federation building in Philadelphia and the estimated Communist population of Philadelphia was no more than 2,300. When the editor of the *Philadelphia Bulletin* called Cooper, he responded, "That's a hot one. I'm no danged Red, never have been a Red, don't like the Reds, and never will be a Red." In fact, Cooper had not been in Philadelphia for at least eight years.

Even the Communist Party in Philadelphia realized the

story was ridiculous and announced that it had been planted by the fascists. Nonetheless, the House Un-American Activities Committee wanted to ask Cooper about that and other things.

Three days before Cooper testified, Sam Wood had appeared before the House committee. He announced that he was a member of the Motion Picture Alliance for the Preservation of American Ideals. Among the founders were Wood, Gary Cooper, Clark Gable, Robert Taylor, Victor Fleming, Clarence Brown and Ginger Rogers. Wood told the committee that the Alliance had been formed in 1944 "in self defense. We felt that there was a definite effort by the Communist Party members, or Party travelers, to take over the unions and the guilds of Hollywood, and if they had the unions and guilds controlled they would have the plum in their lap, and they would move on to use it for Communist propaganda."

The afternoon that Cooper testified, right before Leo McCarey, with whom he would make his next picture, the committee was disposed in his favor. His political position was well known, and his broadcast of 1944 supporting Dewey had made it clear that his politics were essentially conservative. When he began his testimony, Cooper had to be told to speak up. He then launched into his testimony.

> Committee: During the time you have been in Hollywood, have you ever observed any communistic influence in Hollywood or in the motion picture industry?
> Cooper: I believe I have noticed some.
> Committee: What do you believe the principal medium is that they use–Hollywood or the industry–to inject propaganda?
> Cooper: Well, I believe it is done through word of mouth—
> Committee: Will you speak louder, please, Mr. Cooper?
> Cooper: I believe it is done through word of mouth and through the medium of pamphleting—and writers, I suppose.
> Committee: By word of mouth, what do you mean, Mr. Cooper?
> Cooper: Well, I mean sort of social gatherings.
> Committee: That has been your observation?

Cooper: That has been my only observation, yes.

Committee: Can you tell us some of the statements that you may have heard at these gatherings that you believe are communistic?

Cooper: Well, I have heard quite a few, I think, from time to time over the years. Well, I have heard tossed around such statements as "Don't you think the Constitution of the United States is about 150 years out of date?" and—oh, I don't know—I have heard people mention, that, well, "Perhaps this would be a more efficient Government without a Congress"—which statements I think are very un-American.

Committee: Have you ever observed any communistic information in any scripts?

Cooper: Well, I have turned down quite a few scripts because I thought they were tinged with communistic ideas.

Committee: Can you name any of those scripts?

Cooper: No; I can't recall any of those scripts to mind.

Committee: Can you tell us—

Cooper: The titles.

Committee: Just a minute. Mr. Cooper, you haven't got that bad a memory, have you? You must be able to remember some of those scripts you turned down because you thought they were Communist scripts.

Cooper: Well, I can't actually give you a title to any of them, no.

Committee: Will you think it over, then, and supply the committee with a list of those scripts?

Cooper: I don't think I could, because most of the scripts I read at night, and if they don't look good to me I don't finish them or if I do finish them I send them back as soon as possible to the author.

Cooper's memory was quite good, and it is likely that his records and memory could have been combined to come up with some of the elusive titles if he had so chosen. After all, he had memorized film speeches which he could construct years later. Cooper did say he had turned down one script because "the leading character . . . was a man whose life ambition was to organize an army in the United States, an army of soldiers who would never fight to defend their country." He went on to testify that the Communist Party had never attempted to use him:

Apparently, they know I am not very sympathetic to communism. Several years ago, when communism was more of a social chit-chatter in parties for offices, and so on, when communism didn't have the implications that it has now, discussion of communism was more open and I remember hearing statements from some folks to the effect that the communistic system had a great many features that were desirable, one of which would be desirable to us in the motion-picture business in that it offered the actors and artists—in other words, the creative people—a special place in Government where we would be somewhat immune from the ordinary leveling of income. And as I remember, some actor's name was mentioned to me who had a house in Moscow which was very large—he had three cars and stuff, with his house being quite a bit larger than my house in Beverly Hills at the time—and it looked to me like a pretty phony come-on to use in the picture business. From that time on, I could never take any of this pinko mouthing very seriously, because I didn't feel it was on the level.

The committee then read into the record an Italian pamphlet recounting the supposed Communist Party rally at which Cooper was supposed to have spoken in Philadelphia. Cooper denied it, and the committee told him that they believed him. They then read into the record what the Committee described as a pamphlet distributed by the Yugoslavian Communist Party. The pamphlet said that Cooper, Tyrone Power and Alan Ladd had been imprisoned because they had been denounced as leftists, while actor Buster Crabbe had been shot and killed. Cooper responded to the pamphlet that Crabbe was alive and "a very healthy specimen of American manhood."

Cooper's testimony continued along the same vein for another half-hour, during which he said he had never been asked to join the Communist Party. When asked if he thought that Congress should pass legislation to outlaw the Communist Party in the United States, Cooper responded, "I think it would be a good idea." But, after adding that he had never read Karl Marx and didn't know the basis of communism "beyond what I have picked up from hearsay," he amended his comment and said, "I couldn't possibly answer that question."

In his 1978 autobiography, director Edward Dmytryk, who had to suffer at the hands of the committee, wrote that he thought the questionable script Cooper had referred to was *Jubal Troop*. Since the original novel and the film that was finally done have nothing to do with a man who raises an army that refuses to fight, it is difficult to understand what Cooper meant. There is a peaceful Quakerlike group in the film that remains essentially passive, but the lead in the film, which Cooper would undoubtably have played, was a decisive man of action in no way involved in issues related even obliquely to political ideas. *Jubal Troop* was supposed to have been directed by Sam Wood with Cooper after they finished *Casanova Brown*. The project was dropped. Later the film would be made with Glenn Ford in the lead and Delmer Daves directing.

Commenting on Cooper's House testimony, Dmytryk wrote, "Cooper was no idiot. He was a good and simple man, the ideal embodiment of a great American myth. Politics was a puzzle to him, and the stale smell of a crowded committee room in Washington was no match for the heady air of hunting season in the Montana wilds. . . . He just shouldn't have been sitting there 'yupping' and 'noping' before a man who wasn't fit to shine his shoes."

One thing that Dmytryk points out and Cooper's testimony quoted above confirms is that Cooper, for all his cooperation with the committee, did not yield to them a single name nor a solid lead to any script that might be investigated. He did gulp and have trouble keeping his voice up, a sharp contrast to the many screen appearances of Cooper at trials, but he yielded nothing. He can be accused of being naive in his testimony, or he can be given credit for a Cooper performance, but the fact remains that, while others gave names, Cooper, for all his rather simplistic rhetoric on communism, rhetoric in which he almost certainly believed, did not turn over to the committee anything they could use.

Cooper had been working on *Good Sam* when called to testify. During the shooting, it was announced that he had signed a secret deal with Warner Brothers under terms of which he would apparently make one film annually for the studio and receive both a salary and a percentage of the film. According to *Hollywood Reporter*, that was the deal he had made with Paramount on *Unconquered*, and it had given him more than $450,000. When reporters tried to question Cooper about the Warner deal, his attorneys, who had handled the negotiations, announced that the actor was on a hunting trip.

Good Sam was directed and produced by Leo McCarey. McCarey's list of credits when he came to the film included *Duck Soup, Ruggles of Red Gap, The Awful Truth, Going My Way* and *The Bells of St. Mary's*. Co-starring with Cooper was Ann Sheridan. As Sam Clayton, Cooper plays a man who is almost too good, is, in fact, a comic projection of the ever-helpful Cooper hero. Sam, who works in a department store, lends his car to a neighbor, who destroys it. He lends the money he has saved for a new house to a young couple so they can buy a business. Sam gives away everything to anyone in need. When money he has raised for charity is stolen from him and he is responsible, no one comes forth to pay him back or help. Sam goes on a drunk, gives his clothes to a bum and is escorted home by a Salvation Army–like band. His friends come to his aid, and he is finally rewarded by being made a vice-president of the store where he works.

Cooper's Sam is a remarkable straight man for the series of freeloaders he encounters. When he philosophically asks his ne'er-do-well brother-in-law Claude why Claude thinks he was put on earth, Claude responds glumly, "Sometimes, I think I'm just here for contrast."

Throughout the film, jokes are made about Cooper's size contrasted with his lack of aggression. Cooper gets to play jacks and look ridiculous in a chef's costume, a carnival barker's suit —with which he wears a false moustache—and a drunk's rags.

In one scene, in which he has to tell his wife Lu (Ann Sheridan) that he has lent their money to the young couple, Cooper sits on a bed, avoids looking at her and starts to play with the bedspread. Gradually he starts to pick at the spread as he comes closer to revealing what he has done.

In his drunk scene, Cooper sings not one but two songs, "I've Been Redeemed" and "Let Me Call You Sweetheart." He twiddles his tie in imitation of comedian Hugh Herbert and generally turns in what is probably his most overt comic role. In other comedies he had been a man caught up by circumstance. The dialogue and situations were comic, but there was nothing inherently comic in the character. Sam—the film was remade a decade later with Jack Lemmon as Sam—however, is a comic character, a big guy who can't say no, who gets pushed around by others, who is tongue-tied not because he is nervous but because he has trouble expressing himself.

The film did not do well critically. *Time* said that Cooper "does a beautiful job" but qualified this by saying that the picture had an "air of haggard and ill-concealed desperation." *Cue* magazine wrote that "Cooper is by now a grown man, and his boyish bashfulness, sheepish grins, trembling lip and fluttering eyelids are actor's tricks he can surely do without." *The New Yorker* commented that by the end of the picture Cooper "looked pretty tired . . . and I can't say that I blamed him."

Following the making of *Good Sam,* Cooper, Rocky and Maria, who was then ten and going to Marymount School, went in for what was then a Hollywood fad, painting. They evicted their dog Arno and another boxer, Gretel, from a large doghouse and set up a painting studio for the family.

Coop's paintings were primarily marine scenes and landscapes. One landscape was of Rocky's mother's home at Southampton, Long Island. One visitor suggested the picture "has a sharp definition suggesting Grant Wood." Inside the house in the library hung a French landscape by Pierre Bonnard. In other rooms were paintings by Bonnard, Georgia O'Keeffe and Max Weber, the Coopers' favorite American painter.

Cooper was never particularly taken by abstract painting or literature. "My taste in art and literature is rather ordinary," he remarked. "I don't try to pretend I know anything. I don't place myself above other people. I'm the average guy in taste and intelligence. If there's any reason for what you call my success, that's it."

When he met Pablo Picasso a few years later in France, Coop said, "You're a hell of a guy, but I really don't get those pictures."

"That doesn't matter," Picasso said. "If you really want to do something for me, get me one of those hats you wear in the movies."

Cooper sent him the hat, and Picasso responded with a painting.

The next Cooper movie was one of the most important in his life, primarily because of its effect on his personal life. *The Fountainhead* was written by Ayn Rand from her highly successful novel of the same name. King Vidor, who had directed *The Wedding Night* with Cooper, was named director.

In an interview for this book, Vidor remembered that he had had problems with Cooper's ability to memorize lines for *The Wedding Night*, but by *Fountainhead* he had learned to memorize well. And he had some rather long speeches in the picture. We did something that helped him a great deal. We recorded his speeches on records before the film, and he learned the speeches by listening to the records over and over again.

"We were good friends, though we hadn't seen a great deal of each other socially, but we talked a lot while we were on *The Fountainhead*. We would drink together, and he would talk quite a bit, particularly about cars, automobile driving and guns.

"I remember the day we drove up to Fresno to do our location shooting for *The Fountainhead*. We met Patricia Neal there that night. It was the first time they had met. They went for each other right away. After dinner we never saw the two of them again except when we were shooting."

Patricia Neal was twenty-two years old when she met Gary

Cooper. He was forty-seven, and the Cooper/Neal relationship would, shortly after the film was finished, cause the major turmoil in Cooper's marriage. Later in 1948, he moved out of his house and into the Bel Air Hotel.

Back on the film, however, there were some professional problems: "I had some reservations at first about Cooper playing the lead in *The Fountainhead*," recalls Vidor. "I really didn't think he was right. The character in the book is quite aggressive and hard, but Cooper gave the role a quiet strength he had. He didn't have to do a lot of hard talking, and I think he gave the character a quiet determination that comes through forcefully in the film. I also think his performance and Patricia Neal's had an extra dimension because of their relationship—and that helped."

Cooper, himself, was always uneasy about his performance in *The Fountainhead*. His typical comment in interviews was, "Boy, did I louse that one up." He felt that, among other things, he had played his final courtroom scene in the movie too low-keyed, that it needed a forcefulness he didn't give it.

Ayn Rand's original novel, from which she did the screenplay, is 754 pages long. Rand, who was born in Russia in 1905, was violently anticommunist. Fearing that America would become a victim of collectivism, she set forth her rather unusual philosophy in a series of novels starting with *The Fountainhead* and culminating in *Atlas Shrugged*.

Both the novel and screenplay emphasize the same point, that people should not work for the common good but for themselves. Concessions to the needs of others is weakness. Hero Howard Roark is an architect who designs buildings for his own aesthetic reasons and doesn't care in the least if they are functional or if others like them. Roark designs a vast housing complex, letting an old friend take the credit providing the complex is not altered from his plans. When the complex is altered, Roark blows it up in the belief that it is his right to do so. The *Banner,* a newspaper published by Gail Wynand (Raymond Massey), supports Roark but eventually has to knuckle under to pressure. Roark defends himself in court, arguing the value of selfishness, and he convinces the jury, which lets him go. Wynand shoots himself, while Roark designs a new building and finally gets Dominique Francon (Patricia Neal), a jaded heiress who loves him but has thought he was dooming himself.

Kevin McGann, in an article on the film and the book in *The Modern American Novel and the Movies,* compared the Rand-Vidor film with Capra's *Mr. Deeds* and *Meet John Doe:*

> In the Capra films the hero's determination at first comes from nonconformity expressed as boyish innocence and naivete . . . whereas in the Rand-Vidor film, from the beginning, it comes from manly strength and hard-nosed conception of Self. Unlike Capra's hero—one of the "folk," vulnerable and sensitive, likely to get hurt—Roark begins as a rock and ends as a rock. The most striking difference between the politics of Frank Capra and Ayn Rand is in their conception of the public, and the fundamental argument is over the nature of human nature. For Capra, consonant with his conservative populism, the films end with jubilant social salvation, a conclusion that is anathema to Rand.

The Vidor film is one of the most noteworthy of American films. It is one of the most antinaturalist films imaginable. The sets are large, artificial and elongated by art director Edward Carrere in keeping with the tradition of German Expressionism, which had flourished more than two decades earlier.

There is almost no attempt in the film to make the dialogue or scenes conform to the prevailing American goal of "realism." The characters are nearly allegorical, and their speeches are monologues on human behavior rather than human statements. Symbolism is overt with no apologies. When Dominique dreams about Roark, whom she has seen working in her father's rock quarry, she writhes to the image of him operating a jackhammer. In fact, she later encourages him to rape her.

The above is not said in an effort to denigrate the film. On the contrary, the very decision to ignore so-called realism makes the film a strange and courageous effort, rather like a building by Howard Roark.

The Fountainhead is a film that not only opposes realism, it is against democratic decision-making and in favor of selfishness. Gary Cooper, so often the spokesman for American democracy, is here a man who devotes his life to self-interest.

In the film, Cooper's Roark is first seen going from architectural office to architectural office. We see only his familiar back in shadows. Later in the film, Cooper does become Roark. In one scene, Cooper carries on a conversation with a fellow architect. Roark wants the conversation ended, and he absently looks at his watch, but there is no watch. He has pawned it. Roark is a proud man but one who cares nothing about the opinion of others. He does not even try to hide the fact that his watch is missing.

Throughout the first part of the film, in all their scenes together, Neal is shown physically above Cooper, on a hill or a horse, standing while he sits. Only when she becomes sexually vulnerable does she appear in a lower position on the screen.

Dominique tries to get Roark to give up architecture so he won't be destroyed by the world, which fears and rejects his independence. He refuses and she marries Wynand. In an expressionist coincidence of the first magnitude, Roark happens to be looking out of an office window when he sees Wynand and Dominique come out of the St. Charles Hotel after their marriage ceremony.

In the film, Coop as Roark gets to do some architectural drawings.

Perhaps his most impressive scene takes place when he is approached by a humiliated old friend, Peter Keating (Kent Smith), an architect without ideas, who begs him to ghost design the Courtland Housing Project. "My purpose is my work. My work is done my way," Roark says firmly. When Peter agrees, Roark turns away in subdued triumph and, with his back turned, rises slightly on his toes. The move conveys the inability of a proud man to conceal his joy and triumph, and it is done with the slightest of gestures.

During his defense of himself at the trial, Cooper addresses the jury with his hands in his pockets, says things like "There is no such thing as a collective brain," and "I do not recognize anyone's right to one minute of my life." He utters a comment about being "the individual against the collective" and refuses to concede that he will accept any responsibility for anyone but himself. The jury quickly finds him not guilty.

The film ends with a final rejection of naturalistic style. Dominique is riding up a construction elevator to Roark. Roark stands triumphantly at the top of his under-construction skyscraper, hands on hips, at the top of the world.

A baffled public and critics had trouble deciding what to make of the film, as did Cooper. One thing Cooper was apparently trying to do was alter his screen image, which he would gradually do, but this role was more than a slight alteration; it was a massive assault.

Vidor, who had also liked Neal's work in the film, wanted to work with Cooper again a few years later. "I was doing *War and Peace* for Dino De Laurentiis [in 1955]," said Vidor. "I sent a telegram to De Laurentiis suggesting that I direct *Don Quixote* for him and that we consider Gary Cooper for it. I think he would have been excellent. De Laurentis liked the idea and said he would do it only if Cooper agreed to be Don Quixote. I sent Cooper a telegram immediately and got one back soon after saying he didn't think he was right for it. We never discussed it further."

Following *The Fountainhead,* Cooper and Neal continued being seen together. Though he didn't talk about the change in his life, Cooper didn't deny it as it became more and more public.

Now that he was officially a Warner Brothers star, Cooper appeared in another guest spot in a Warner Brothers picture as himself. The film was *It's a Great Feeling,* starring Dennis Morgan, Doris Day and Jack Carson. In the film, Cooper, wearing a cowboy hat, has a soda with Morgan. They then look at a scene from *The Fountainhead.*

For his next Warner Brothers film, Cooper returned to the

military adventure. *Task Force* was written and directed by Delmer Daves, a former actor and writer, who had directed and written *Destination Tokyo, Pride of the Marines, Dark Passage* and four other films before being assigned *Task Force.*

Most of the film is presented as a flashback told by retiring admiral Jonathan Scott (Cooper), who recalls his naval life from 1921 to World War II and the survival of his ship, the USS *Saratoga,* after a kamikaze attack. World War II color footage was incorporated in the action-filled film, and Cooper was supported by Jane Wyatt, Walter Brennan (again as Cooper's buddy), Julie London and Jack Holt.

In the course of filming a battle scene aboard the aircraft carrier USS *Antietam,* Cooper and several cast members came close to getting killed. During gunnery practice on the carrier, a robot target plane was struck by shells from the ship. Catching fire and going out of control, the flaming plane headed for the deck, where Cooper and other members of the cast and crew were standing. Coop and the others dived for cover. The plane skimmed over the spot on the deck where they had been standing and toppled into the sea right behind the ship.

Shooting on the *Antietam* lasted for five weeks with shooting stops up and down the Pacific coast. During filming, Cooper came near another mishap. He was riding in a naval barge that broke down as it skirted the rocky edge of a breakwater in Long Beach Harbor. The barge was temporarily lost in December fog. Taking on water, it continued to drift close to the jagged rocks until another naval ship came to the rescue. Cooper was hospitalized with a sore throat and a cold. A few days later, the sore throat was a strep condition, and he was running a temperature of 103.

Cooper's performance in *Task Force* drew praise. Howard Barnes in the *New York Herald Tribune* wrote that "Cooper and the documentary shots are the chief mainstays of the production. The star plays a stubborn advocate of air power on the high seas with commanding persuasion. His characterization is rigidly correct but extremely sympathetic."

When asked about his performance by Hedda Hopper, Cooper replied, "The main thing I remember about that film is that it interfered with my fall hunting." Cooper then claimed he had made the film for money and that, in spite of the fact that he was getting more than $300,000 a picture, his expenses, including a newly acquired seventeen-acre home in Colorado, kept demanding more.

In spite of his relationship with Patricia Neal, Cooper took his family to their recently purchased Aspen, Colorado, home in March of 1949. A *Life* reporter visited the home, and the magazine carried a photograph of it. It was far from a mansion —in fact it was a burned-out, somewhat ramshackle and not very large wooden house nearly in ruins. It was, however, a convenient point of departure for skiing and hunting.

Shortly after his return from Aspen, it was announced that Cooper and Robert L. Lippert had formed a new company, Mayflower Productions, in which, the *New York Times* reported, "They are equal stockholders." The goal was to make pictures for distribution by Lippert Pictures. "Cooper will not appear in the films, which will be made on small budgets, and his name will not be used to exploit them, according to his representatives," the *Times* reported.

Cooper also announced that he had purchased the rights to a book, *The Girl on the Via Flaminia.* The acquisition had been made when the book was still in galley form, and Cooper had an offer almost immediately to buy it at a substantial profit for the rights. His original goal was to produce the film version with Ingrid Bergman as the star, but he eventually sold the film rights to the book to Leland Hayward and Anatole Litvak.

His next project for Warner Brothers was *Bright Leaf,* directed by Warner's top director Michael Curtiz and co-starring both Lauren Bacall and Patricia Neal. In the tale, Cooper plays Brant Royle, who has been driven out of his hometown by a tobacco baron because he paid too much attention to the tobacco man's daughter (Neal). Royle then meets John Barton (Jeff Corey), who has invented a cigarette-making machine.

Royle uses the discovery to become rich and drive out competition, including the tobacco baron (Donald Crisp).

To save her father, the Neal character marries Brant, who gradually realizes that she has used him. When she dies in a fire, Brant rides off, leaving his old love Sonia (Bacall), but indicating that he will be back some day.

Jeff Corey, who would become one of Hollywood's top character actors and a highly respected acting teacher, recalled that he got the role in *Bright Leaf* by doing a screen test in competition with eight other actors. According to Corey, Cooper explained that he had been away from the cameras for quite some time on vacation and apologized for his stiffness in the scene they rehearsed.

"I, in turn, overwhelmed that he was even doing a test with me, found myself assuring him that he was very good indeed, and that he needn't worry about it," said Corey. "Coop felt compelled to reply, 'I only have one or two tricks at best, and that's not enough, is it?' "

Cooper spent a great deal of time with Corey, and one day Corey mentioned that he had just finished a ten-week run in the Actor's Lab production of *Abe Lincoln in Illinois,* playing the title role. Corey discussed his approach to Lincoln.

"Cooper offered some astonishing information," Corey recalled. "He not only knew a great deal about the play, but told me with some reluctance that Robert E. Sherwood had written it for him. When the finished play was submitted to him [Cooper], he admired it enormously but felt he didn't have the experience to cope with so massive a role. It had tortured him to refuse it, he said. But he may have been right to turn it down. His effectiveness on film may not have translated to the stage."

The following year, 1951, Patricia Neal, Cooper's friend Akim Tamiroff and Arthur Kennedy attended Michael Chekov's acting classes at the Stage Society of Los Angeles. Cooper joined them. He participated in some improvisations based on the play-within-a-play in *Hamlet.*

Later, when Corey taught his first acting classes, Cooper

asked if he could sit in on some sessions. Corey readily agreed and urged him to participate and make suggestions. Cooper rarely participated, though he sat among the students, absorbed and attentive.

"There was that reticence," recalled Corey, "a visible reluctance to commit himself fully." Corey saw Cooper as a paradox, a man with a voice that could be tentative and unequivocal at the same time, a man who could appear brave but modest, worried but capable in a pinch, heroic and uncertain.

FOURTEEN

HIGH NOON: A MAN IN PAIN

In the fall of 1950, the Los Angeles Times *paid a visit to* the Coopers at home and took a picture of Coop, Rocky and Maria, then thirteen, in the den-workshop. Coop was working on a shotgun with several other guns propped up against the wall. Maria sat with a tennis racket in her hand, and Rocky sat behind her. Cooper talked about his interest in sports, and the reporter commented that the actor was "not a naturally robust man."

By March of 1951, Louella Parsons was reporting that the sixteen-year Cooper marriage was in danger. Although he was not making a picture at the time, Coop remained in Hollywood for Christmas, while his wife and daughter went to New York. Cooper assured Parsons that he was looking forward to going to New York to be with his family, though he admitted that there was a problem.

In May, Rocky Cooper's attorney said that she and the actor had officially separated. The attorney, Graham Sterling, said he did not know whether she planned to seek a divorce, but the strong speculation was that, being Catholic, she would not do so.

Meanwhile, Coop was working. In 1950, he finished *Dallas* with Stuart Heilser, who had directed *Along Came Jones,* again in charge. Ruth Roman played opposite Coop's Blayde "Reb" Hollister. In the film, Hollister, a former Confederate officer, goes to Dallas to get revenge against the men who killed his family. Hollister shoots, one by one, the three brothers he has sought. This is interrupted by Hollister himself being shot, which requires that he be nursed by Roman, with whom he falls in love.

Bosley Crowther in The *New York Times* remarked of the film, "There is something about the sadness that appears in Mr. Cooper's eyes, something about the slowness and the weariness of his walk, something about his manner that is not necessarily in the script which reminds the middle-aged observer that Mr. Cooper has been at it a long time."

In 1951 he went to Twentieth Century Fox to make *U.S.S. Teakettle,* the title of which was changed after release to *You're In The Navy Now.* In the film, Coop exchanged his cowboy clothes for almost-as-familiar naval dress and went back to director Henry Hathaway. The film was a comedy about an inept crew of ninety-day wonders who have trouble keeping their World War II patrol craft going with a steam turbine engine. Cooper, as Lieutenant John Harkness, is the skipper with no more experience than his men.

The seldom-seen film had a supporting cast that included Eddie Albert, John McIntyre, Jane Greer, Ed Begley, Charles Bronson, Jack Warden and Lee Marvin. The picture did very poorly at the box office, which resulted in the change of title, though the change didn't help. The film's failure was strange because it had uniformly excellent reviews. The *New York Times* called it "the best comedy of the year." The *New York Herald Tribune* praised Cooper's performance as one "that would make any audience identify itself with his frustration."

You're In The Navy Now was publicized as Cooper's first film for Twentieth Century Fox, which technically it was not. He had appeared as a stunt man and extra in several Tom Mix silent films for the studio in 1925.

Cooper went back to Warner, where he was under contract, to do another guest shot, this time in *Starlift,* a tale about movie stars and Air Force men during the Korean War. Cooper, appearing as himself, did a comic scene for the airmen at a special show. The comic Western sketch within the film featured Cooper, Frank Lovejoy, Phil Harris and Virginia Gibson, all of whom sang, "Look Out, Stranger, I'm a Texas Ranger." The *New York Herald Tribune* remarked that Cooper looked "patently uneasy."

From *Starlift,* Cooper went to Metro-Goldwyn-Mayer to appear in *It's A Big Country,* an eight-part tale about different parts of the country. Cooper, as a cowboy called Texas, appeared in a brief comic episode directed by Clarence Brown. Texas gives a comic monologue in which he pretends to be very humble about Texas but is actually bragging. The impressive cast included Ethel Barrymore, Gene Kelly, Fredric March and William Powell. Cooper was given praise for his small role, but his string of guest shots and medium-budget films presented a distinct threat to the career of the forty-nine-year-old actor. However, Warner Brothers did not seem to have any bigger plans for him.

His next picture was *Distant Drums,* in which Coop in cowboy attire fought the Seminole Indians in Florida. Besides Cooper, there wasn't a single big name co-star or supporting actor in the film. The director, however, was Raoul Walsh, who had begun his film career as an assistant to D. W. Griffith and had appeared in *The Birth of a Nation* as John Wilkes Booth. He had begun directing in 1915, earning a reputation as a man who could work quickly and who loved to deal in action. When he came to *Distant Drums,* Walsh had already directed an incredible total of ninety films, including the Douglas Fairbanks version of *The Thief of Bagdad,* the silent version of *What Price Glory?,* the original *Sadie Thompson, In Old Arizona, The Roaring Twenties, They Drive by Night, High Sierra* and *White Heat.*

Distant Drums was filmed in the Florida Everglades in color. "The fauna of the Everglades did not take to the camera crews," Walsh recalled in his autobiography. "I had to hire some local talent to clear out the snakes, mostly unfriendly rattlers and moccasins.

"Cooper complained," Walsh continued, "that he had donated a gallon of his best blood to the mosquitoes and leeches.

He brought back a rattler skin, which he claimed he had torn from its original owner in a fit of berserk rage."

The film was action-filled and popular, but Warner Brothers did not give it the publicity campaign or budget of previous Cooper films, and the reviews tended to see it as standard Walsh and Cooper fare.

If there was some doubt about Cooper's career in 1951, his health and personal life were in even worse shape. In August, Dr. Arnold Stevens operated on Cooper for a hernia in St. John's Hospital in Santa Monica. Cooper remained in the hospital for a week.

When *Distant Drums* came out, several publications including *Modern Screen* reported that before the film, Cooper and Patricia Neal had vacationed together in Havana. Throughout the filming of *Distant Drums,* reporters who called him in Florida were told that Cooper was out in the swamps working and couldn't be reached.

In an interview with the author, Patricia Neal said, "I fell desperately in love with Gary, and he was in love with me. I'm sure he was. I'm also sure I was not the first woman he had after his marriage. When I met him, I knew about some of his political beliefs and I didn't like what he did before I met him, but if you meet somebody and you love their looks, their politics don't mean anything. I know I was very important in his life even though he had a lovely marriage."

Following the filming of *The Fountainhead,* Neal, who had been living with her mother and younger brother, rented a townhouse near Twentieth Century Fox from Rudolph Valentino's widow so she could be alone with Cooper. They remained together for more than three years, from 1948 to 1952. According to Neal, their appearance together in *Bright Leaf* was not something they planned. It was simply an act of casting.

"When we did *Bright Leaf,"* she recalls, "I desperately wanted to play the role that went to Lauren Bacall. I would have given a tremendous performance, but they wouldn't even test me for the role. Gary could have helped, but he wouldn't fight for anybody. He didn't have the fight in him that I had in me, and I think he admired it in me. He was always very secure and avoided fights, but I think his doing *High Noon* in spite of the House Un-American pressure on Carl Foreman had something to do with me. That time he had the courage to go out and say, 'I'll stick with him.' "

Neal recalled that Cooper "adored people with money. That was what had happened with the Countess diFrasso. When he met Rocky, he knew her stepfather was rich, rich, rich and he wanted to marry her and, in fact, they were very happy. When you met him, he pretended not to care about money, but he loved it. He loved to live well, and he did live well: fabulous suits, ties, shirts and shoes which he had made for himself. He was the best dresser I've ever known.

"He was also one of the best actors." His ability to relax, or even sleep, according to Neal was a way of dealing with nervousness. "He was nervous even though he didn't appear to be."

"I was really in love with him," she said. "Eventually after three years, we had to break up, and I lost a lot of weight. I almost had a nervous breakdown. My heart was broken."

In the years that followed, Neal encountered Cooper several times, once at a party shortly after they stopped seeing each other, another time when they accidentally ran into each other in New York City and had a drink together and a final time when she met him in London while he was shooting *The Wreck of the Mary Deare*. She remembers him as a gentle and kind man. "He was," she concluded, "a lovely man."

In late summer 1951, Cooper made a promotional trip for *Distant Drums* and announced that he and Walsh were planning an independent company to "make several short stories—preferably Ernest Hemingway stories—abroad." Cooper thought they might make the films in England, though he admitted that they had not yet acquired any stories, and in the end the Walsh/Cooper venture never came to pass.

Cooper was still not feeling well and showing it. When he began making *High Noon,* he was living in a hotel and suffering from various ailments. In December, he was back in the hospital for minor surgery. By February of 1952, Cooper had an ulcer on top of his back ailment, hernia, and assorted pains.

Although he would talk to reporters during this time about his family and admitted his marital problems, he always refused to mention Patricia Neal, though there was certainly no secret about their relationship by this time. In his 1956 autobiographical story for the *Saturday Evening Post,* Cooper does not even mention Neal's name, nor does he mention his dates during this period with Kay Topping, who would later become Mrs. Clark Gable. He said his reason for the separation from his wife was that he did not feel right about himself.

Contributing to his ulcer was undoubtedly the public statement by his wife that Cooper could have a divorce if he wanted one: "I told Gary last July I would get a divorce any time he wanted it." Meanwhile, she was dating airline executive Robert Six, but later in 1952, when the Coopers were talking about reconciliation, Neal left Hollywood.

Meanwhile, back in Hollywood, Cooper had completed *High Noon,* which would move his career upward again and would be considered by many the single most important film in his career. However, no one knew or thought the film was destined for big things when it was first conceived.

Carl Foreman, who wrote *High Noon,* had been a writer for Monogram in the early 1940s and then for Republic. His big break came in 1949 when he wrote *Champion* and followed it with the scripts for *Home of the Brave, Young Man With a Horn, The Men* and *Cyrano de Bergerac.* Foreman was also co-producer on *High Noon,* but his problems with the House Un-American Activities Committee in 1951 kept getting in the way of his functioning as producer and eventually led to his blacklisting and his departure for England, where he had to write under pseudonyms. His screenwriting on *The Bridge on the River Kwai* was uncredited. In 1958 he joined Columbia Pictures as a producer and writer and was responsible for *The Mouse That Roared, The Guns of Navarone* and *The Victors,* which he also directed.

Stanley Kramer, producer of *High Noon,* had produced *The Champion, Home of the Brave, The Men* and *Cyrano de Bergerac.* Director Fred Zinnemann, an Austrian who had come to the United States in 1930, had to his credit such films as *The Seventh Cross, The Search* and *The Men.*

Cooper was not Kramer's first choice to play Marshal Will Kane in *High Noon.* In fact, he was fairly far down the line below Marlon Brando and Montgomery Clift. Charlton Heston was also offered the role. The chief financial backer of the film, however, a Salinas lettuce tycoon, wanted Cooper. The backer threatened to pull his money out and Kramer couldn't change his mind about using Cooper, so the script had been sent to Coop. Later Cooper said he took the film, even though he was ill and emotionally troubled, because it represented what his father had taught him, that law enforcement was everyone's job.

In an interview for this book, Fred Zinnemann gave his recollections of Cooper and *High Noon:* "His recurring hip problem bothered him on one or two occasions. It made it difficult for him to do the fight with Lloyd Bridges, but it didn't stop him from working very hard and very long hours under some trying conditions. If I remember correctly, we made the entire film in thirty-one shooting days. Not once were we delayed or held up by him for whatever reason. For most of the time he seemed to be in good health, and it was only two or three months after shooting had been completed that he became ill.

"He did in fact look quite haggard and drawn, which was exactly what I wanted for the character, even though this was in contrast to the unwritten law, then still in force, that the leading man must always look dashing and romantic. If I remember correctly, we used a minimum of makeup for

Coop, which was perhaps a bit of a novelty in those days.

"For me," continued Zinnemann, "the theme of *High Noon* was and is the victory of a man over his own fears, which *happened* to be portrayed by Western characters against a Western background. I had no political construction in mind; the problem of man's conscience was what interested me.

"Cooper seemed absolutely right for the part. It seemed completely natural for him to be superimposed on Will Kane."

According to Zinnemann, *High Noon* "is the one picture I directed which more than any other was a team effort. There was a marvelous script by Carl Foreman, a brilliant job of cutting by Elmo Williams, an inspired musical score by Dimitri Tiomkin, a solid contribution by Stanley Kramer. And Gary Cooper was the personification of the honor-bound man. He was in himself a very noble figure, very humble at the same time, and very inarticulate. And very unaware of himself."

In a 1979 interview in *American Film,* Carl Foreman claimed that he and Zinnemann had made the film apart from the Kramer company. According to Foreman, "neither Kramer nor anyone around him had any use for the film from the beginning. We had very little money to work with, even for a tight script that ran only 110 pages. . . . Having so little money made it necessary for Fred and me to work very closely together—which was a wonderful experience, despite the difficulties, and Gary Cooper and the rest of the cast were heartwarmingly enthusiastic and cooperative."

Foreman decried the rumor that much of the film shot for *High Noon* had been unusable and the film had been saved in the editing room. After calling this a "vicious libel against Fred Zinnemann," Foreman recounted two scenes in the script that had not been shot to indicate how little footage had actually been filmed. The two scenes involved a deputy who was on his way back to town to stand by the marshal. Foreman and Zinnemann thought that if they showed two scenes of the deputy on the way back it might add a dimension of suspense. They decided not to shoot the scenes because they wanted the action concentrated in the town and because they decided the scenes weren't necessary.

Foreman added that he had done a seminar at the American Film Institute in which the film was compared to the script he had written, and, with the exception of the two scenes not shot, "it's remarkable how little fancy editing had to be done in comparison with practically any film made," said Foreman.

In the film, Coop's first line is the same as the first line he had ever uttered in film back in 1928 in *Shopworn Angel*—"I do." Kane is marrying Amy (Grace Kelly) on a Sunday morning. It is just past 10:30 when the tale begins, and it ends a few minutes after noon. The length of the story and the length of the film almost coincide. The film is filled with reminders of the passing of time, time that brings Marshal Kane closer to having to face Frank Miller (Ian MacDonald) when he gets off the noon train in Hadleyville and seeks his revenge against Kane, who sent him to prison. Clocks in the background show the time and tick ominously. People refer to meetings in five minutes. One by one the people whom Kane assumes he can count on in his battle against Miller and his gang (played by Lee Van Cleef, Robert Wilke and Sheb Wooley) find reasons or excuses to stay out of the coming fight. Only the town drunk comes forth, but Kane turns him down, realizing he is more of a liability than an asset.

At one point Kane, alone in his office, puts his head down on his desk, possibly to weep, and then wearily pulls himself up again. In the final confrontation with Miller and his gang, Kane does stand alone until the last moment, when Amy saves his life by shooting Frank Miller. Kane then throws down his badge in a sign of contempt for the town and rides out with his bride.

For his performance in *High Noon,* Cooper would win his second Academy Award. Yet it is a performance in which he does less with the character than he had done with almost any of his major roles before. His walk is stiff and pained. His arms remain at his sides through most of the film. He hasn't a single extended speech. What audiences apparently responded to was the look that Zinnemann had captured and that Cooper, with years of experience, had played on. They also responded to the simple story of a man who is not supported by his community in a time of mortal crisis and who triumphs alone through courage and determination.

Will Kane and Gary Cooper were tired, sick men of fifty-one. Cooper's performance is basically put together in relatively short takes and scenes. This was exactly what Zinnemann wanted and what he got, and it was interpreted by a public that loved Cooper as a supreme performance.

Cooper later said that when *High Noon* was finished, he was "acted out," and that pained weariness is exactly what is seen on the screen. Perhaps for the first time, he had truly become the character he portrayed, for Gary Cooper and Will Kane were the same persona. Kane's pain came from his fear and his betrayal by others. Cooper's was a result of illness and domestic and career worries.

When the twenty-fifth Academy Award night took place, Cooper was not in the audience. He was vacationing and still trying to recuperate. He had bumped into John Wayne shortly before the awards and asked Wayne to pick up the Oscar for him if he won. He had no doubt that he wouldn't win.

In his acceptance speech for Cooper, Wayne said: "Ladies and gentlemen, I'm glad to see that they're giving this to a man who is not only most deserving, but has conducted himself throughout his years in our business in a manner that we can all be proud of. Coop and I have been friends hunting and fishing for more years than I like to remember. He's one of the nicest fellows I know; I don't know anybody nicer. And our kinship goes further than that friendship because we both fell off of horses in pictures together.

"Now that I'm through being such a good sport spouting all this good-sportsmanship, I'm going back and find my business manager and agent, producer and three name writers and find out why I didn't get *High Noon* instead of Cooper."

Commenting on the film in a famous article in his book *The Immediate Experience,* Robert Warshow wrote that, "In *High Noon* we find Gary Cooper still the upholder of order that he was in *The Virginian,* but twenty-four years older, stooped, slower moving, awkward, his face lined, the flesh sagging, a less beautiful and weaker figure, but with the suggestion of a greater depth that belongs automatically to age."

In 1961, Cooper told *McCall's,* "I hate to disappoint a lot of customers, but *High Noon* wasn't new or especially genuine. There was nothing especially Western about it. It was a story about a phase of life, more current today, I suspect, than years ago—namely, how tough it is for a man to buck the apathy of the crowd even when he is trying to do something for their own protection. . . . I suppose incidents like that happen in real life, but it's hard to believe that any man in the West was so completely alone as the marshal was in *High Noon."*

As he got older, Cooper tended more and more to be concerned about the West and its portrayal and tended to be disturbed by lack of historical authenticity in Western films. Since his own career as a Western star had helped to reinforce the myth of the American fictional West rather than a re-creation of historical data, it is ironic that Cooper should turn to that position.

High Noon is indeed not a tale about the true West, but like so many Westerns a presentation of contemporary ideas in the most durable popular genre, the Western. In a sense, the myths of the West—and Cooper as an actor is one of them—are as culturally important as what actually transpired on the frontier a century ago. Will Kane tells us more about how we view our history and myths than any real data we might find about Wild Bill Hickok, Billy the Kid or Buffalo Bill. Cooper's career as a Western figure lasted thirty-five years, as long in fact as the time between the end of the Civil War and the start of the twentieth century, as long as the historical time of the real West.

FIFTEEN

PLAYING WITH
A LEGEND

Late in 1951, Cooper had agreed to join Carl Foreman as a partner in Carl Foreman Productions, but in the fall Cooper pulled out. The idea was that the Foreman company would finance and release three films through Robert L. Lippert. Stockholders in the Foreman company were to be Foreman, his attorney Sidney Cohn, Cooper, his attorney I. H. Prinzmetal and publicist Henry C. Rogers.

Then Foreman appeared before the House Un-American Activities Committee and was labeled an unfriendly witness when he refused to answer questions about former affiliation with the Communist Party. Though Foreman had clearly expressed his contempt for the committee and his belief that their actions were improper, and he had exercised his quite legal right to refuse to speak, he was immediately attacked by Hollywood gossip columnists Hedda Hopper and Louella Parsons.

Reached in Idaho where he was fishing and hunting, Cooper confirmed that he had decided not to join the Foreman company and added, "I was convinced of Foreman's loyalty, Americanism and ability as a picture maker. My opinion of Foreman has not changed." An official announcement issued for Cooper said that Cooper "has received notice of considerable reaction and thinks it better for all concerned that he not purchase this stock."

In an interview for this book, Foreman recalled his association with Cooper: "I think that within his limitations, and I don't use that word pejoratively, he was an excellent actor, with complete control and awareness of what he was doing. He was, in fact, a most intelligent man. So far as I could see, and I was very close to his relationship with the director, they had no problems, and he was completely responsive to Fred Zinnemann.

"In later years I made a practice of sending him my scripts in order to give him first refusal on them, such as *The Bridge on the River Kwai*, *The Key* and *The Guns of Navarone*. Unfortunately, by that time the illness which ultimately killed him had begun to take its toll and he was no longer capable of taking on such physically demanding roles."

Concerning their possibility of a business venture together, Foreman says, "There was such a possibility, but this was prevented by the pressure of the Hollywood blacklist. Cooper came under severe attack from John Wayne and Ward Bond, as well as others in the so-called Motion Picture Alliance for the Preservation of American Ideals, as well as Warner Brothers and various right-wing publications, and I released him from his commitment in order to avoid damage to his career. That was at the same time that I was blacklisted by my own company, the Stanley Kramer Company."

Though Cooper's withdrawal had obviously been a blow to his plans, Foreman at the time stated, "Gary Cooper is the finest kind of an American and one of the most decent men I have ever met. I regret to lose him as a business associate and I hope to keep him always as a friend." Shortly after this announcement, the blacklisted Foreman left for England.

When he returned from hunting, Coop found that Warner Brothers had him scheduled for another film with little financial backing and only a slight improvement in the name power of the supporting cast. The impact of *High Noon* had not set in for the studio, which had obviously planned the new film before *High Noon*'s success.

Springfield Rifle was, not surprisingly, a Western. The director was Andre De Toth, who had begun his career in Hungary with five films directed in Hungarian in 1939. In the United

States he did several films but became known as a director of Westerns with *Ramrod, Man in the Saddle* and *Carson City.* When he came to *Springfield Rifle,* he was definitely not considered a top-name director. In fact, he would never in his career quite make the big-budget category, though he would direct such films as *House of Wax, The Indian Fighter, Monkey on My Back, Hidden Fear* and *Play Dirty.*

Cooper's co-star in the film was Phyllis Thaxter. Support came from David Brian, Paul Kelly, Lon Chaney (who had appeared in *High Noon*) and some young potential stars including Martin Milner, Fess Parker and Alan Hale, Jr.

Cooper, looking far more healthy than he did in *High Noon,* plays Major Alex Kearney, a Union officer who sets up a spy operation to find out why a Northern cavalry post can't supply the horses needed for the Civil War. Kearney goes undercover to get the villains, but he can't tell his wife and son, who don't know whether to regard his behavior as treachery, cowardice or madness.

With the popularity of *High Noon* just making its mark, Warner Brothers decided to get top composer Max Steiner to do the score. The film received moderately good reviews, and Cooper was given equally moderate praise for handling himself well. In one of the many ironies of filmmaking, an examination of *Springfield Rifle* shows that Cooper's improved health indeed reflects on his performance. He is more comfortable with his body and hand movements, is capable of prolonged dialogue and projects the comfortable relationship between actor and persona that had won him his popularity. In short, Cooper's performance as an actor is probably better in *Springfield Rifle* than it was in *High Noon,* in which he had been effectively used instead of affectively acting.

For his next film, Cooper went to an independent producer, which purchased a major novel and gave him a rising director and a chance to spend a number of months in Samoa. *Return to Paradise* was based on the book by James A. Michener. The film was produced by Theron Warth, Robert Wise and Mark

Robson, who also directed. Robson, a Canadian, had begun as a director for producer Val Lewton at RKO. His first film, *The Seventh Victim,* and two Boris Karloff features, *Bedlam* and *Isle of the Dead,* had led to directing honors for *Champion* and *Home of the Brave.* He would later direct such films as *Trial, The Harder They Fall, The Prize* and *Von Ryan's Express.*

The film was shot on the remote Samoan island of Upolo, 5,000 miles from Hollywood, but it was not the primitive paradise that had been suggested. The population had a higher literacy rate than that of the United States, and the natives were fully and Westernly clothed. Cooper became a scuba fan, spending hours spearfishing when he could get away from filming. The easygoing Cooper reported that he had been dubbed "Talofa" by the Samoans working on the film. To him it sounded like "tall loafer," which suited him. In fact, *talofa* was a Samoan greeting and not a nickname at all.

Later, recalling the island, Coop said, "We shot our picture in the ugliest village on the island. The rest of the villages were too beautiful. The public just wouldn't have believed, otherwise, that we weren't shooting on a half-million-dollar set designed by Cedric Gibbons."

"The natives got bored quickly," he said. "That was our biggest production problem. We used too many natives in the picture, but getting them to take their work seriously was difficult."

Director Robson recalled the production as a lot of fun but also full of headaches. "You must remember that there's little time sense in that section of Samoa, and the people just won't be hurried. The heat and humidity of the country make working very difficult. You have to drive yourself to it." Once, when he needed 500 people for a nine o'clock call the next morning, Robson said he went to the local chief and explained his problem. The chief promised to have the people ready for work. When they didn't show up, Robson went back to the chief, who explained that the people had gone to a celebration on the other side of the island instead of working.

Robson also had difficulty with the natives who had speaking roles. Well versed in still photography, they thought they should remain perfectly still when the camera was rolling. "Keeping them acting naturally was a continuous battle," Robson recalled. He felt that the production was almost jinxed. For one key scene, he had trained Roberta Haynes, who played opposite Cooper, to do an intricate native dance called the Siva. A ship strike kept the camera equipment from being delivered, and the dance had to wait two months. When cinematographer Winton Hoch finally arrived, he had with him only enough film for a day of shooting. Robson used the film to shoot Samoa from the air. Meanwhile he kept rehearsing the natives, and Cooper fished and drank a native root drink called *kava*. Then, when the boat with sufficient film actually arrived, Robson rushed to get aboard and took a fifteen-foot fall, almost breaking his neck.

In the film, which is set in 1929, Cooper plays Mr. Morgan, a wandering American of little means who arrives on a small Polynesian island to discover that it is ruled by Pastor Corbett (Barry Jones), who controls the natives in a kind of religious moral tyranny. Morgan opposes Corbett and his "wardens," marries a native (Haynes) and urges the natives to revolt against Corbett's repression. When Corbett reforms, Morgan leaves the island. Years later he returns and is united with his native daughter Turia (Moira MacDonald).

Wearing old clothes, a battered hat and T-shirt throughout the film, Cooper looks comfortable. Coop's portrayal as a hedonist was not looked on with favor by reviewers. His portrayal of Morgan, however, makes an interesting contrast to his portrayal of Roark in *The Fountainhead*. Both men believe in placing oneself first, but for Morgan the goal is enjoyment of life, an enjoyment he thinks others should share. Morgan's loose-jointed movements, lack of concern over dress and posture and soft speech are in sharp contrast to Roark, who sees himself as having a mission. Roark stands tall, wears almost uniformlike suits, speaks sharply and directly and is disinterested in others. Morgan, throughout the film, looks directly at other characters, shows interest in understanding and sharing. Roark looks through other characters and often turns away from them in private triumph. For Roark, life is a game to win. For Morgan, life is a game to enjoy. Cooper's range was such that he could be both Roark and Morgan.

When 1953 began, Coop was fifty-one years old and clearly on top again. *High Noon* had established a new Cooper image. He had gone from young hero in the 1930s to mature protagonist in the 1940s and was now the determined aging and often disillusioned man of the 1950s. His next film was *Blowing Wild,* a tale of bandits and wildcat oil-drilling in Mexico in 1929. To support Cooper, Warner Brothers teamed him for the third time with Barbara Stanwyck, with additional support from Ruth Roman, Anthony Quinn and Ward Bond. Dimitri Tiomkin, who had done the music for *High Noon,* did the score for *Blowing Wild* and wrote a song specially for the film, as he had done for *High Noon. High Noon* had broken ground in having someone—Tex Ritter—actually sing "Do Not Forsake Me, Oh My Darlin'" on the sound track. It was the first time in a major Hollywood picture that this had been done. It soon became commonplace and in fact almost obligatory, particularly in Westerns. Frankie Laine sang the Tiomkin–Paul Francis Webster song "Blowing Wild—the Ballad of Black Gold" for the new Cooper Western. He also sang the title song for the Burt Lancaster/Kirk Douglas film *Gunfight at the O.K. Corral.* So associated was Laine with this genre that Mel Brooks made a joke of his relationship to such tracks by having Laine sing the title song to *Blazing Saddles.*

Director of *Blowing Wild* was Hugo Fregonese, an Argentinian who moved from directing in his native country in the 1940s to directing Westerns in the United States in the 1950s. His credits had included *Saddle Tramp, Apache Drums, Untamed Frontier* and the uncharacteristic *My Six Convicts.*

Blowing Wild is a somber near-Western shot entirely in Mexico for Warner Brothers release. Barbara Stanwyck plays

Marina, the wife of Ward Conway (Quinn), but she is in love with Jeff Dawson (Cooper) and eventually murders her husband to be with the man she loves. Horrified when he discovers what she has done, Dawson is about to kill her, but is interrupted by a bandit raid that results in Marina being blown up in a dynamite explosion. During this final explosion, Cooper was injured when fragments of a dynamited bridge struck him, resulting in contusions and severe bruises.

The reviewers were not particularly kind to Cooper and found some difficulty in accepting this move to bitterness and tragedy.

After the film was finished and he had recovered, Cooper agreed to join the American Federation of Labor's Irving Brown in Europe for some anticommunist propaganda work. Cooper was a longtime member of the AFL's Screen Actors' Guild. The AFL wanted to take advantage of recent riots and anticommunist protests in Eastern Europe and thought the well-known and conservative Cooper might help. He agreed, and in June he went with Brown to West Berlin to meet with fifty-five of Berlin's labor and literary leaders.

According to columnist Victor Riesel, "Earlier he [Cooper] spoke to 500 officials of the postal, telegraph and telephone workers. He impressed them with America's freedom. He told them how he had helped to organize a union of actors. Then he said he had just looked into East Berlin."

According to Riesel, Cooper had compared the Soviet police of East Berlin with the Nazi storm troopers. His speech apparently so impressed the conservative Germans that *Welt Arbeit,* a conservative newspaper, ran Cooper's picture talking to German workers on its front page. Brown also walked with Cooper through what Riesel called "the Red Belt of Paris" where, with Brown translating, Cooper talked to procommunist workers.

While in Paris, Cooper underwent additional hernia surgery at the hands of a New Orleans surgeon, Dr. Alton Ochsner, who flew to Europe to do the work. When he returned to Hollywood from Paris, Cooper did not move back into a hotel but into the family home. It was reported that he would stay there with Rocky and Maria until he had to leave for Mexico, where he would be shooting his next film, *Garden of Evil.*

Meanwhile he had purchased the film rights to A. B. Guthrie's *The Way West* for $65,000. He would sell the rights a short time later at a profit. He also sold the rights to *The Girl on the Via Flaminia* for $50,000, a clear profit.

Rocky Cooper commented to reporters, "We don't like announcements. What we have decided to do in our own minds is our personal business. . . . Gary is staying at home. You can put any interpretations on it that you like." She also said that the family would have Christmas together at their home after *Garden of Evil* was finished.

In *Garden of Evil,* his first Cinemascope picture, Coop was reunited with Henry Hathaway. Co-starring in the Western were Richard Widmark and Susan Hayward, who had appeared with Coop in *Beau Geste.* In addition to the highly respected director and co-stars, Twentieth Century Fox provided a supporting cast which included Cameron Mitchell, Rita Moreno and Hugh Marlowe.

The tale involves a trio of nineteenth-century soldiers of fortune played by Coop (Hooker), Widmark (Fiske) and Mitchell (Daly), who are approached by Leah Fuller (Susan Hayward) to escort her through Indian territory to rescue her husband (Marlowe), who is trapped in a cave-in. They agree, when gold is offered as a reward. Emotions, greed and jealousy mar the trip. When they get to the Indian land called the Garden of Evil, they rescue the husband and start back. Indians attack, killing all but Hooker, Fiske and Leah. Hooker and Fiske, who is a gambler, draw cards to see who will stay to hold off the Indians and who will take the woman to safety. Fiske loses, and Hooker takes off with the woman, who tells him that the gambler cheated in the draw. Returning to help him, he finds Fiske dying amidst the bodies of the Indians.

Hathaway would become increasingly interested in tales of small groups of men and women who have to take an isolated, dangerous journey and find their true emotions in the process. Self-seeking gamblers turn hero, and smug heroes begin to question themselves. Hathaway would repeat the theme in such films as *Legend of the Lost, From Hell to Texas, Nevada Smith, Five Card Stud* and *Shootout.* In *Garden of Evil,* it is the disillusioned Cooper character who finds that he is a hero or must be one and the Widmark character who dies with newfound dignity.

During the course of shooting, in December, 1953, a story came out of Uruapan, where the film was being shot, that a screen fight had gotten out of control and Cooper, Widmark and Mitchell had started a real brawl, resulting in assorted cuts and bruises. According to the report, Cooper wound up with a sprained wrist, a black eye and a cut lip. "I didn't mean to clobber anybody," Cooper reportedly said. "I was just trying to make the branningan look good."

Since all reports on Cooper had been affirmative and it was difficult to find anyone who had an unkind word about him, the possibility of a real enemy was something to pursue in exploring his life and character. In fact, the rumor has persisted since the making of *Garden of Evil* that Widmark and Cooper disliked each other.

In an interview for this book, Widmark said quite the contrary: "I met Gary Cooper in the fall of 1953 in the office of Henry Hathaway at Twentieth Century Fox with Susan Hayward. We were preparing to make a picture, *Garden of Evil,* in Mexico. My first reaction was instant liking. I had admired him very much in movies. Meeting him in person was even better. Usually I have been disappointed in meeting public figures, especially actors. But not this time. That initial liking developed into a strong friendship during the three-month moviemaking period and continued after our work together.

"Our working relationship couldn't have been better. He was a true professional. Earthy, no phony star attitude—always prepared—knew exactly what he was going to do—always on time—a perfect work mate. Some of the current crop of so-called movie stars please take note. He was helpful in that he was a total professional. He was very gregarious. Loved to socialize and unlike his movie image, was very articulate. He was a paradox in that he was a very sophisticated man—loved good living, fine cars, pretty ladies—loved to laugh and have a good time—and yet he was a true man of the outdoors. We used to walk in the Mexican mountains between shots, and he knew every animal track, every leaf—everything having to do with nature.

"Since I like the outdoors myself, we became very close on the location. We were together all day long and most evenings had dinner together or with a group of compatible souls. He had a new Mercedes delivered to him in Mexico City, and he and I drove to a location some 200 miles distant. What I am telling you should negate any news reports that we didn't get along. We were buddies. He was like a brother. And a hell of a lot of fun to be with. I miss him."

As far as Widmark could tell, Cooper was in perfect health, though Coop did tell him that, when he had been in Mexico the year before, he had had a tapeworm from eating raw steak.

Widmark, who is a forceful and forthright assessor of filmacting, replied in answer to a question about Cooper's ability as an actor, "In my opinion he was one of the *best* movie actors. He was able to project a good part of what he was as a man—strong, yet sensitive and sympathetic—and humorous. He had a great sense of humor. And physically of course he had it all—tall, handsome, a good voice. He was underrated in my opinion, for like all good actors he made his work look effortless—as if he were doing nothing—you saw no wheels turning—what every artist in any field tries to achieve. True, his range was limited, which made him the great movie star that he was, for in most cases, a movie star with a long career plays versions of one character that has been established in the minds of the public. That's what Coop did. And he was unsurpassed as that movie personage. Technically, he knew every facet of moviemaking. Knew how to make his points in the simplest and truest way. His concentration was remarkable, and he really *talked* to you in a scene. In fact I was taken aback in the first scene we did together, for it can be so rare for an actor to work with someone who is really *talking* to you. It's what separates the men from the boys—and it's difficult to do. And above all he really *listened*.

"His relaxation was also remarkable," Widmark went on. "I remember one scene we did was the classic 'two guys going to sleep on the ground with their heads in the saddle.' Coop had the opening line. Hathaway called action. I waited. No line. Then I heard Coop snoring. I poked him and whispered, 'Hey Coop, we're rolling.' He awoke with a start. 'Oh—oh yeah—' and started. He was a rare one. For me, he had no weaknesses as an actor. He was the perfect actor."

Cooper did return to Hollywood that Christmas to be with his family, but it was clear that there was as yet no reconciliation. Early in 1954, he went to Mexico for the third time in two years.

This time it was to make *Vera Cruz,* a Hecht-Lancaster production with Burt Lancaster, Denise Darcel, Cesar Romero and a supporting cast that included Ernest Borgnine, Charles Bronson and Jack Elam. Coop was a hot property and had been pursued by a number of producers before he agreed to do *Vera Cruz.* Lancaster and Harold Hecht had done their best to prepare a script that would give Cooper what they thought would interest him, but months passed from the time the script had initially been delivered to Cooper, and Hecht, with millions tied up in the project, began to worry. "We had almost written the script with a tape measure to be sure Cooper had enough strong scenes," Hecht said later. "When he maintained a foreboding silence, we were certain he had something up his sly sleeve. Clearly his lawyers had advised him to appear vague and undecided."

Hecht had the script rewritten to favor Cooper even more heavily. Still there was no word from him. A meeting was finally arranged with the actor at Romanoff's Restaurant. Hecht thought Coop looked particularly unhappy. Hecht asked if he had read the new script. "Yup," replied Cooper. "I liked the first one better." He said he would like to do the film, but he wanted a bit longer to think about it. He waited until forty-eight hours before actual shooting was to start.

Directing the film was Robert Aldrich. His first directing effort had been *The Big Leaguer* with Edward G. Robinson in 1951, followed by *World for Ransom* with Dan Duryea; in 1954 he had directed Lancaster in *Apache. Vera Cruz* was his fourth film as a director. He would go on to direct such films as *Attack, Whatever Happened to Baby Jane?, The Flight of the Phoenix, The Dirty Dozen, Emperor of the North, Hustle* and *The Longest Yard.*

Aldrich was, and continues to be, interested in love-hate relationships, situations in which two individuals are bound together in mutual fascination though it is inevitable that they clash. One of the two is often vibrant, comical, treacherous, childish, appealing and possibly insane—in this case Lancaster's Joe Erin. The other is a tough, determined, conservative individual rooted in the past, in this case Cooper's Ben Trane. It was exactly this kind of relationship that had existed between the Cooper and Brennan characters in *The Westerner.*

By 1954, Cooper's Western persona was so well known that it required little explanation, and the Cooper character did not have to deal in words to keep his semi-mad friend at bay. The very introduction of Cooper at the start of the movie is a reference to the image he had taken by the early 1950s. A narrator informs us that men were streaming into Mexico after the 1866 Revolution, that they usually came in groups, but "some came alone." As these words are heard, we see Cooper riding in the vast wilderness. He is the epitome of the man alone. We later find that Ben Trane is a Southerner who has lost all he had in the Civil War. The gold he hopes to get will help him restore his pride. Trane joins forces with Joe Erin and his gang. Erin is a killer for hire who agrees to fight for the forces of Emperor

Maximilian against the rebels. The Erin gang is given the assignment of escorting Countess Marie Duvarre (Denise Darcel) to Vera Cruz. In fact she is being used as a decoy to transport a gold shipment for the emperor. Trane and Erin plan to steal the gold, but the emperor's guards flee with it. After what he has seen of the brutality of the emperor and his forces, Trane is convinced that the gold should be turned over to the rebels in spite of his own need for it. Erin pretends to go along, but when the gang actually recovers the gold, Erin shoots one of his own loyal men, and Trane reluctantly shoots Erin.

Lancaster's Erin is a comic display. He shows his teeth in a grin parodying his patented smile. He eats food like a savage and displays a wild, grubby charm that draws attention. Cooper's primary acting task as Trane is to show his growing fondness for Erin, to build to the point where it is evident that he is in anguish over the fact that he must kill the man.

Though the film is surely a violent comedy of the kind Aldrich has specialized in right up to *The Choirboys,* it is also evident that Cooper's Trane is a potentially tragic figure whose very presence keeps the comedy from becoming a gross, bloody joke.

For the film, the often-ailing fifty-two-year-old Cooper had to undergo considerable action. The most dangerous stunt, however, was reserved for Coop's longtime friend and double Slim Talbot. In the single most spectacular trick in the film, Trane is forced to jump a broad chasm on his horse. Talbot doubled for Coop and came close to not making the leap, which turned out to be a bit longer and more difficult than planned.

Cooper's bad luck held true to form. During filming of an attack he led, the actor was wounded. An extra's Winchester was fired accidentally, and the wadding from the blank shell struck Cooper at short range, piercing his shirt and burning his skin. He was treated on the El Molino de las Flores location and rushed to a hospital in Mexico City, where the pieces of wadding were removed by a surgeon. The wound kept him from working for two days.

While *Vera Cruz* was being shot, Russian film director Gregori Alexandrov, who had co-directed and co-written *October, The General Line* and *Que Viva Mexico* with the famous Russian filmmaker Sergei Eisenstein and had gone on to become one of Russia's top directors, was attending the Cannes Film Festival. At Cannes, Alexandrov said that he would like Cooper to appear in his next film as a "very pleasant American." He assured reporters that the American character would be a sympathetic one.

Informed in Mexico City of the tentative offer, Cooper was at first angry. "With ruthless government censorship and oppression in Russia, the idea of a foreigner appearing in a Soviet film is senseless and to no purpose," he said. He softened a bit, however, and told a reporter that he might consider acting in a Russian film if it "brought some true knowledge of the outside world to the Russian people and contributed to better understanding and enlightenment among the different countries."

He added: "The whole thing is a wild dream and impossible with the government that now exists in Russia. And I certainly would not want to be associated with anything that would be used for Communist propaganda."

A month later, while *Vera Cruz* was still being shot, another report came out of Mexico City saying Cooper was about to divorce his wife and marry San Antonio model Lorraine Chanel. When confronted with the report, Cooper told the International News Service that he and his wife would be back together. "Miss Chanel and I are friends, very good friends," he said. "But that's all there is to it."

Interviewed while still in his Western costume after a day's work, Coop added, "Lorraine is a fine girl and I don't like to see her hurt by the gossip mongers. . . . Yes, I take Lorraine out, among others."

When he returned from Mexico, Cooper did move back in with his family, and it was made clear that a reconciliation had definitely taken place. With Maria seventeen and about to graduate from Marymount, Coop made it clear that he was home to stay and ready to be a family man.

"Rocky has done a magnificent job with our daughter," he said at the time. "I think Maria is the finest young girl I've ever known. She is religious; she is wise beyond her years; she loves to ski, ride horseback, and she participates in all the sports I enjoy."

In preparation for his return, the Cooper main bedroom had been redesigned. An unusually high washbasin had been installed in the bathroom so he wouldn't have to bend and strain his back. A supposedly restful window had also been designed so that at the push of a button, artificial rain would pour down outside.

The year 1955 was the first in which Cooper made a television appearance. He and Dick Powell were co-guests on the "Steve Allen Show," at that time a sit-down talk-format show.

By June of 1955, Cooper had over eighty screen credits to his name. His films had grossed an estimated $250,000,000, and he had earned almost $6,000,000. Cooper did his best to stand back briefly and enjoy the fruits of his labor. He spent as much time as possible driving one of his Mercedes Benzes at eighty or ninety miles an hour on country roads, went hunting with his friends and spent time scuba diving and playing tennis. He also found time to spend with his mother and was frequently seen with her at Romanoff's throughout 1956. His hearing problem was growing more acute, but so were his other ailments. His ulcer forced him to cut down on smoking and drinking, but he had trouble curtailing his enormous appetite.

For his next film, Cooper decided to stay indoors and go back to the film genre he had once been afraid of, biography. The project was *The Court-Martial of Billy Mitchell.* The impressive cast included Charles Bickford, Ralph Bellamy, Rod Steiger, Elizabeth Montgomery, Fred Clark, James Daly and Peter Graves.

Otto Preminger, who had begun his career in Germany, was

named as director of the *Billy Mitchell* film. By 1956 his direct-
ing credits included *Laura, Fallen Angel, Forever Amber,
Whirlpool, The Moon Is Blue, River of No Return* and *Carmen
Jones.* "We were lucky to get Otto Preminger as director,"
Cooper said shortly before the film was released. "He has imagi-
nation and is sound and thorough."

Preminger, who had, and has, a reputation as a difficult man
to please, wrote in his autobiography, "Cooper was a great film
star. Nobody will dispute that. But during our work together
I discovered that he was also an actor. In fact, the actor Cooper
created a film star. The slow, hesitant speech and movement,
the downward look, the so-called shit-kicking were invented by
him in order to face the camera with a semblance of the complete reality that the medium demands. In life he was different,
a charming, witty, intelligent and entertaining companion appreciated by men and adored by women."

In the film, Cooper plays Brigadier General Billy Mitchell,
who tries to convince the military of the importance of air
power following World War I. Because of his persistence,
Mitchell is reduced to colonel and sent to a post in Texas.
Mitchell, who displayed much of the same determination of Dr.
Wassell, begins to write letters to point out what he believes in.
Following a number of air disasters, Mitchell charges the War
and Navy departments with "incompetence and criminal negli-
gence." He is arrested, and his court-martial is conducted in
secret in a warehouse to keep down the publicity, but word
leaks out. People including a congressman come to Mitchell's
support, but the prosecutor, Major Allan Guillion (Rod Steiger),
makes Mitchell, who is tired and ill from malaria, look foolish
and gives the impression that Mitchell is simply seeking publicity. Found guilty, Mitchell is suspended for five years.

Before the film was released, Cooper described the climactic
scene. "Rod Steiger, who plays a lawyer brought in by the
prosecution, in one scene takes Mitchell and twists him on the
witness stand, which really happened. Mitchell gets up and
tries to explain in a rather inarticulate way, and this prosecut-

ing lawyer tears him to shreds. Hope they leave that scene in."

The scene was left in, inviting another reexamination of Cooper's screen persona. The actor, who in so many films had stood up after an hour or so of shy quietness and delivered an articulate blast at his enemies, here crumbled to ineptitude in his crucial scene. The great American hero in the 1950s was reduced to shaky confusion. Corruption and self-interest triumphed, and the aging Cooper again played a bitter figure who had to face disappointment and even defeat.

Though the real Mitchell apparently had a fanatic drive perhaps approaching madness, Cooper's screen Mitchell is a man who seems to know what the world has in store for him, a man who has tried a thousand times and is wearily continuing though he knows he is doomed.

Critics and audiences did not respond to this bleak biographical presentation. *Time* wrote, "Gary Cooper plays the flamboyant Billy for a sort of militant old maid, and his historic cry for justice for the air services sometimes seems almost as exciting as an old maid's protest that the neighbor's cat has swallowed her beloved canary."

Shortly after release of the film, Cooper appeared on the Ed Sullivan television show and did a live reenactment of part of the courtroom scene of *The Court-Martial of Billy Mitchell.* He appeared quite ill at ease in this dramatic television debut.

Cooper's next project had been waiting for him for a decade. In 1946 screenwriter Michael Wilson had adapted the novel *The Friendly Persuasion* by Jessamyn West. Paramount bought the script from Liberty Films, and William Wyler saw it. As far as Wyler was concerned, the film needed Cooper as Jess Birdwell, the Quaker whose family's religious commitment to peace is put in jeopardy by the coming of the Civil War.

Cooper, however, was tied up with other contracts, and Wyler put the project aside. In 1956, Wyler decided to get Cooper and produce the film himself. Allied Artists agreed to release it. There was only one problem. The studio refused to let Wilson's name appear in the credits, and so in fact it is one of the few films ever made that has no screenwriting credit at all. The reason for the studio's decision was the recent ruling that allowed a studio to deny credit to someone who had refused to answer charges of Communist affiliations, and in 1951, Wilson had used the Fifth Amendment before the House Un-American Activities Committee. Ironically, the screenplay for *Friendly Persuasion* was nominated for an Academy Award for best adaptation.

In addition to Cooper, the Birdwell family consisted of Dorothy McGuire as the wife and Anthony Perkins, Richard Eyer and Phyllis Love as the children. In the film, the coming of war makes Josh (Perkins) wonder about his courage. When an attack on his southern Indiana town by raiders from the South is announced, Josh goes to fight. His father Jess does not agree with him but decides that he hasn't the right to force him to choose pacifism, that every man must decide for himself.

In the battle, Josh is wounded and Jess's best friend is killed. In a fit of rage, Jess trails the killer but finds he cannot commit murder. He lets the man go and goes home with his son, who now is confident that the road of peace is the road he wishes to follow.

Wyler's reasons for wanting Cooper in the role of Jess are fairly clear. Jess must display a great deal of anguish and soul-searching, but because of his convictions they must remain internal. Coop's face and body have to demonstrate his feeling of helplessness. A turn of the palms outward, very naturally, is a Cooper indication of such helplessness. At the same time, as a Quaker leader, Jess must be open and direct, with no sign of deviousness. Instead of his usual man of action, a man who settles things with his gun and fists when he is pushed to the wall, Cooper is here a man who rejects everything his earlier characters had stood for.

When asked about his role in the film, Cooper replied that he played a "kind of backsliding Quaker. The story it is based on was written by a cousin of Vice-President Nixon. The yarn actually was about their great-great-grandparents." Cooper failed to mention the irony of a pacifist screenplay written by a blacklisted writer about the ancestors of Richard Nixon, one of the House Un-American Activities Committee's strongest supporters.

Though Cooper would receive no recognition for his performance beyond some affirmative reviews, Perkins would be nominated for an Academy Award, Dorothy McGuire would be voted the best actress of the year by the National Board of Review, and Wyler would get another best direction nomination for an Oscar.

Friendly Persuasion did lead to Cooper's only venture as a professional singer. In August, 1956, he recorded "Marry Me, Marry Me" from the film, which led him to quip, "I hope all of this won't ruin my career."

Cooper's mind, however, was already on other matters. Allied Artists and United Artists had announced joint distribution of what was to be Cooper's next film, *Ariane.* The announcement stated that the fifty-five-year-old actor would co-star with Audrey Hepburn and Maurice Chevalier in the film, which would be produced and directed by Billy Wilder. *Ariane,* with its name changed to *Love in the Afternoon,* went into production in August, 1956.

SIXTEEN

INTO THE SUNSET

Billy Wilder, who had co-scripted Ball of Fire, *chose Cooper* for the lead in *Love in the Afternoon.* Wilder's directing credits were impressive; they included *Double Indemnity, Lost Weekend, Sunset Boulevard, Ace in the Hole, Stalag-17, Sabrina, The Seven-Year Itch* and *The Spirit of St. Louis.* His choice of the fifty-five-year-old Cooper to play opposite Audrey Hepburn in a romantic comedy was strange on the surface but in keeping with the offbeat casting he enjoyed exploring. In many ways, the Cooper character was an aged version of the one he had played in *Bluebeard's Eighth Wife.* As some of the directors of Westerns, like Aldrich, chose to use the rapidly aging Cooper as a commentary on his earlier Western characters, Wilder chose to use Cooper in a kind of commentary on the Lubitsch versions of the man.

In *Love in the Afternoon,* Audrey Hepburn plays Ariane, the daughter of a private detective, played by Maurice Chevalier. She reads a report by her father about an American playboy, Frank Flannagan, and becomes fascinated. After warning Flannagan that the husband of one of his conquests is trying to kill him, Ariane agrees to meet the American. Charmed by his urbanity, Ariane continues to see him. In an attempt to match his reputation, she confesses to many affairs. To check her stories, Flannagan hires Chevalier to investigate her. The detective discovers it is his own daughter and tells the American, who agrees to leave Paris. Ariane follows him, declares her love, and the two leave together.

At the time of the film, *Life* magazine featured a one-page spread on Cooper and Cary Grant, who was making *An Affair to Remember.* The headline read: "Gary, Cary Remain Frisky Past Fifty." Cooper was shown in a Turkish bath scene looking a bit emaciated and every bit his age. The *New York Herald Tribune* was affirmative about Cooper's performance but not terribly enthusiastic. Writing in that paper, William K. Zinsser said, "Cooper, under Audrey Hepburn's influence, swiftly declines from the suave libertine to the perplexed schoolboy, and there is a quiet humor in the quizzical look that crosses his face as he ponders the strange forces that are assailing him."

A further irony in the life of Cooper, who was a walking testimonial to accident and disease, was that, after the film was finished, President Eisenhower appointed him a member of the Citizens' Advisory Committee on the Physical Fitness of American Youth, along with Bing Crosby and Esther Williams.

Cooper also found time to make an appearance on September 21, 1958, on the "Jack Benny Show." In the episode, in which Benny tries to get a part in Cooper's next picture, Coop sings "Bird Dog." The appearance was clearly a favor to Benny, who also got other reticent stars to make television appearances on his show: Helen Hayes, Humphrey Bogart, James Stewart, Barbara Stanwyck, Claudette Colbert, Fred MacMurray, Kirk Douglas, Irene Dunne, Bing Crosby, Marilyn Monroe and Gregory Peck. Part of the Cooper appearance was later incorporated into the 1969 Jack Benny twentieth-anniversary special.

In his next film, *Ten North Frederick,* Cooper was again cast as a past-middle-aged man in love with a young woman (Suzy Parker). Part of this casting in both the Wilder film and *Ten North Frederick* obviously came from Cooper's off-screen publicity, but in fact, the portrayals in the two films are quite different. In *Love in the Afternoon,* Coop plays a playboy, confident, sure of himself, irresponsible. In *Ten North Frederick,* he is a tired man whose shoulders droop, whose eyes never quite open all the way, whose suits are a bit rumpled or loose-fitting.

In the film, based on a novel by John O'Hara, Coop plays Joe

Chapin, a businessman whose wife (Geraldine Fitzgerald) wants to push him high in politics, to the presidency if possible. In both *The Cowboy and the Lady* and *Meet John Doe,* Coop had played the natural man who shoots down the hollow dream of another man who wants to be president. In *Ten North Frederick,* he is a somewhat henpecked, meek man. Politicians double-cross him, and his wife taunts him. He goes to retrieve his daughter, who has run away, and falls in love with her roommate. Joe finally becomes ill and dies, though he is reconciled with his daughter before the last moment. The film can also be viewed as a bizarre commentary on Cooper's earlier *Good Sam,* in which all the goodness of the character is finally rewarded. In *Ten North Frederick,* we discover the reverse. Good Joe is stepped on by everyone.

This was a sober role for Cooper, in keeping with O'Hara, but out of keeping with Cooper. Not only is he a pathetic character, he actually dies nonheroically. It was a part that required little physical activity, but it was also a part that greatly changes his image as it turns into tragedy. It is not surprising that the role had first been offered to Spencer Tracy, who turned it down.

The film was directed by Philip Dunne, who also wrote the script from the O'Hara novel. O'Hara, who had appeared in a small role in *The General Died at Dawn,* liked the film version of *Ten North Frederick.*

"I was deeply moved," O'Hara wrote in a letter, "and I was pleased with the production." About Cooper, O'Hara wrote, "it is the greatest performance Gary has ever given." The critics, however, did not concur, though Paul V. Beckley in the *New York Herald Tribune* found Cooper's portrait of an Eastern gentleman "quite effective."

As he had throughout his career when the box office dropped and the reviews were unsupportive, Coop headed for a Western. His next film was *Man of the West,* directed by Anthony Mann. According to critic Andrew Sarris in his book *The American Cinema,* Mann "directed action movies with a kind of tough-guy authority that never found favor among the more cultivated critics of the medium." *Man of the West* was no exception.

In the film, Cooper was supported by Julie London, Lee J. Cobb, Arthur O'Connell, Jack Lord, John Dehner and Royal Dano. Cooper was again in opposition to a wild gang leader, Dock Tobin (Lee J. Cobb). As in earlier films—*The Westerner, Vera Cruz*—Cooper's love/hate relationship with the friend/enemy is at the heart of the story. In *Man of the West* Coop plays Link Jones, a man who has long since left the gang of Dock Tobin and gone straight. Following the robbery of a train on which he is a passenger, Jones determines to get back the money stolen from him. He goes after the robbers but finds himself saddled with two of the passengers, played by Julie London and Arthur O'Connell. When they fall into the hands of the Tobin gang, Jones pretends that he has come to rejoin the gang. The gang members don't believe him, but Tobin, who is half-mad, can't quite make up his mind.

Finally there is a shoot-out, and Jones kills all of the gang members before his final confrontation with Tobin, who has raped Billie Ellis (Julie London). "You've outlived your kind, and you've outlived your time," Jones shouts at Tobin, in an ironic commentary, perhaps, on the kind of heroic Western hero Coop himself was still playing in *Man of the West.*

The irony of that statement is not lost in the presentation of Cooper's character, seen riding alone again when the title of the film first appears. In the original theatrical version in CinemaScope, the Man of the West (Cooper) is alone against a vast background.

The film opens by establishing Jones's character. He aids a man having a problem with a ladder. A short time later, Cooper gets his only real comic moment. When he boards a train to Fort Worth and the train takes off, Jones becomes frightened and reaches over to grasp the man in front of him. It is Jones's first train ride, and the fear in his wide-eyed look makes him appear vulnerable. On the train both the London and O'Connell characters try to engage Jones in conversation, but the

Man of the West remains characteristically silent to the point where the woman asks him, "Do you talk?"

Once back with the gang, Jones must play a role. He must convince the gang that he is one of them, while making it clear to the audience and Billie that he is not. In fact, the character lies constantly to keep himself and those for whom he is responsible alive, and the ability to lie convincingly is essential. In a sense, the story is similar to *The Westerner,* where the Cooper character's life depended on his lying convincingly, to Walter Brennan's Roy Bean.

In a later scene, the taciturn Jones loses control, reverts to what he once was. Following a fight with Coaley (Lord), who has been taunting him, Cooper takes Coaley's clothes off and stands over the man with his teeth tight in rage, his hands around his neck, as he hisses, "How does it feel?" The father figure from *Friendly Persuasion* is surely back to the Western image of the man who believes in kill or be killed. At the same time, Cooper's Jones is responsive and sensitive. When Billie tells him she loves him, Jones is moved, but he does not return her feeling. He explains that he has a wife and family and simply wants to get back to them. When Billie is turned away, Jones reaches out to touch her, to console her and then withdraws his touch before completing it, knowing he cannot give her comfort by his touch. Later when he reluctantly shoots Claude (Dehner), Jones, himself wounded, goes to him and again hesitantly reaches out to touch and comfort a person whose emotions he understands. At the end of the film, when Jones is forced to kill Tobin, Cooper shows the man's tension not by words but by a slight clenching of his right fist and an even more slight tightening of his lips. For what he is about to do, he is sorry, but he knows he will do it. What complicates the conclusion even more is the fact that he wants to kill Dock Tobin and must if he is to be free of his past.

Director Anthony Mann, normally a person of few words, said of Cooper, "Those blue, blue eyes are the greatest that have ever looked at another human being. They tell fantastic things.

You can read his every thought, his deepest emotion in those eyes. Then, of course, there's the size of him, the length of him —epic for western roles. No one can walk down a street in a Stetson hat like Cooper."

Following release of the film, Cooper commented on why he had not made a Western for five years before accepting *Man of the West.* "Most Westerns are just easterns with men wearing big hats. They're cops-'n-robbers stories. I turn down 99 out of every 100 offered me . . ."

Between pictures, Coop, his wife and daughter, now twenty and studying art, took lessons in skin-diving in their pool. His hip injury by now was so painful that he could no longer ski or play tennis. The Coopers had become interested in skin-diving a few months earlier when they had taken a short vacation in France and had made a few dives off Cape Antibes and brought up a few pieces of amphora from sunken Greek galleons. Back in California, the Coopers began to dive off Santa Catalina Island.

Before his next film, again with a Western setting, Cooper disappeared for a number of weeks, part of which he spent in Sun Valley hunting with Ernest Hemingway. When asked about Hemingway on his return, Coop responded, "He writes in the morning and goes out shooting rabbits or birds in the afternoon." When asked about rumors that he had spent part of the missing weeks getting a face lift, Cooper denied it, saying to columnist Earl Wilson that he had had surgery but not a face lift. "I got this great plastic surgeon to take a cyst out of my jaw. Then he fixed up the other side. I had it banged in a fight. Sure, they called it a face lift in the papers. Once they say it, what the hell you going to do?" Cooper added that his weight was a steady 185, a result of a controlled diet brought on by his recurring ulcer.

The revitalized Coop immediately went into production of *The Hanging Tree,* based on a short novel by Dorothy M. Johnson that had won the Western Writers of America Golden Spur Award. The director was Delmer Daves, who had experience as an actor, writer, producer and director. As director, he had specialized in Westerns such as *Broken Arrow, Jubal, The Last Wagon, 3:10 to Yuma* and *Cowboy*. The supporting cast included Maria Schell, Karl Malden, George C. Scott and Ben Piazza. Coop's old friend and double Slim Talbot had a small role as a stagecoach driver.

Principal exterior shooting was done about forty miles from Yakima, Washington, where an entire mining camp was constructed. Many of the decisions for construction and shooting were made by Cooper since the film was a Baroda Production, a company Cooper had set up primarily to allow him to control his roles. Baroda was the name of the street on which Cooper lived. All of the remaining features he was to star in would be Baroda productions released through various companies.

In the film, Joe Frail (Cooper) is a doctor with a troubled past who goes to a small mining town in the Montana territory to gamble, fight and do a minimum of healing. Frail befriends a young man (Piazza) and a Swiss girl, Elizabeth (Schell). He finances a small mine for the young man, the girl and Frenchy Plante (Malden). The mine proves to be rich, and Frenchy proves to be attracted to Elizabeth. When Frenchy is attacking Elizabeth, Doc Frail shoots him. The miners take Doc to be hanged, but Elizabeth saves him by giving them her mine.

Karl Malden, in an interview for this book, remembered Cooper with affection and gratitude. "When I first met him," Malden said, "I was in awe of him. I had never been on a horse and was a little cocky about the whole thing. When it came time to get on the horse, the animal balked and Cooper came over to me and told me quietly, 'Don't ever trust a horse.' It wasn't said with any overbearing air, just a friendly way, a very friendly way.

"During the shooting of the film, Cooper used to get in his car and just drive for hours and I'd often go with him, but he was not in good health and you could see it though he didn't complain. He couldn't, for example, sit up on the horse. He had to lean strongly to his left." In fact, for years, Cooper had been gradually moving further and further to his left when on horseback. The movement, as noted earlier, had begun as early as *The Virginian,* but by *The Hanging Tree* it was pronounced. Cooper had incorporated a physical problem into a character mannerism. Two hands on the horn of his saddle, Cooper would list to the left as if resting and move to a position in which he could pay rapt attention to the other characters in the scene.

Malden got the opportunity to do more than observe Cooper as an actor. As it turned out, Malden wound up directing a good chunk of the film. "The director, Delmer Daves, got sick and had to be hospitalized," Malden recalled. "The producers [Martin Jurow and Richard Shepherd] and Cooper, who was backing the film, got together and decided to ask me to direct. There was quite a bit left to do. I told them I wasn't prepared, but Cooper encouraged me. I had directed some theater and a movie, *Time Limit,* but I hadn't thought about directing this picture. Cooper said, 'You can do it,' and he promised his support. This was on a weekend. On that Sunday, Maria Schell and Cooper met with me to rehearse a scene, and we shot it the next day.

"I found that Cooper couldn't communicate with me in words when I told him how I thought a scene should be done. He said, 'Show me,' and I did, acting out the scene with Maria, improvising. Then he took over and did exactly what I wanted him to do, not at all rigid as people have said. If there was a problem, it was with the directors who used him. Look, for example, at the scene in *The Hanging Tree* where he is fixing the medicine and Maria comes in." Malden's point about this scene, which he directed, is similar to the point made two decades earlier about Cooper's naturalness as a doctor handling medicines. Malden ultimately directed many of the interior scenes and the scene in which his character is killed by Cooper's.

"Cooper knew himself and he knew the lens of the camera," Malden continued. "A musician has his instrument, a painter his canvas, a sculptor his medium. An actor has himself, his abilities, his limitations. Cooper knew what to avoid and what to do. He always relaxed in front of the camera and concentrated on the role. He knew what would appear on the screen and he played for it. People have often mistaken his ability to relax on the set for indifference, but he was very interested in the making of the film, the acting process.

"I'm indebted to Cooper not only for giving me the chance to direct and having confidence in me, but for insisting that I be given billing with him and Maria Schell above the title. That was his idea.

"I regret that I didn't get to know him until late in his life. I did meet him socially after the film and felt he was my friend. When you were his friend, you were a friend for life. There was never any discussion of my doing another film with him, but I would have done it gladly if he had wanted me."

The reviews were solidly affirmative, and *Variety* went so far as to say that "Cooper has one of his best roles. His mystery and tight-lipped refusal to discuss [his past] perfectly suit his laconic style." However, on his trip to promote the film, Cooper got more questions about his health and face lift than about *The Hanging Tree*.

In 1959, Coop also did a guest spot in *Alias Jesse James,* a comedy Western produced by and starring his friend Bob Hope. He appeared as himself, wearing Western attire, a tin star and six-guns. Considering his aversion to Westerns on television, it is ironic that Cooper should be a guest in the film along with a string of television Western stars playing their television roles—Hugh O'Brian as Wyatt Earp, Ward Bond as Major Seth Adams from "Wagon Train," James Arness as Matt Dillon, Fess Parker as Davy Crockett, Gail Davis as Annie Oakley, James Garner as Bret Maverick, Jay Silverheels as Tonto, and Roy Rogers, Gene Autry and Cooper as themselves.

Between films, the fifty-eight-year-old Cooper converted to Catholicism. His growing interest in Catholicism was reported to have gone as far back as 1953 when he and his wife had been given an audience by Pope Pius XII. Cooper's wife had been born a Catholic and his daughter also had been a Catholic from birth. The conversion was announced to the world by Radio

Vatican. Cooper's wife announced, "It took him a long time to make up his mind, but he has finally seen the light." Cooper himself sent word through a spokesman that he did not wish to "make a big thing" of his conversion. There was no word from Cooper's mother, an Episcopalian, about how she took the move. Cooper's illness apparently played a role in his decision, but he did not speak on the subject at the time.

Also between movies, Cooper agreed to visit Russia on a goodwill tour with Edward G. Robinson, producer Harold Hecht and opera singer Mattiwilda Dobbs. However, there was no opportunity for much interchange. According to the Associated Press, a series of Soviet attacks on foreign movies led to a cool reception for the group.

Back home, Cooper considered and rejected the chance to co-star with Deborah Kerr in Fred Zinnemann's *The Sundowners,* partly because it was to be shot in Australia, which was, he thought, too far from home and partly because his physician apparently advised against it. Robert Mitchum got the role.

Coop's next film, *They Came to Cordura,* was to be his last with a Western setting. The film was directed and co-written by Robert Rossen, who had worked years as a screenwriter before getting his first directing opportunity. His writing credits included *Marked Woman, The Roaring Twenties, The Sea Wolf* and *A Walk in the Sun.* His first directing/writing assignment had been *Body and Soul,* and he went on to do *All the King's Men,* and, the year following *They Came to Cordura,* he wrote and directed *The Hustler.*

In *They Came to Cordura,* based on a novel by Glendon Swarthout, Cooper again became a character who seemed a commentary on his past heroism. He plays Major Thomas Thorn, who has been disgraced for showing cowardice in battle. Assigned as awards officer in the 1916 Mexican expedition against Pancho Villa, he selects five men as candidates for the Congressional Medal of Honor. Because the men are wanted quickly for World War I propaganda purposes, Thorn has to lead them through the rocky desert country to Cordura. They pick up Adelaide Geary (Rita Hayworth), who has been accused of helping Villa. Along the way, each of the five would-be heroes—Van Heflin, Tab Hunter, Richard Conte, Michael Callan and Dick York—proves to be lacking in some basic humanity. They almost fall into categories of sin, one man being venal, another ambitious, a third slothful, etc. Only the supposedly cowardly Thorn proves to be totally dedicated, honest and selfless. In his dedication to getting the men through to Cordura, he almost destroys himself. Eventually, the men recognize Thorn's self-sacrifice and help him.

Although Cooper's Thorn talks of having been a coward, we never see him display any cowardice, and the act of which he is accused and accuses himself is not seen. In the film he is presented only as the resolute, loyal soldier forced into a position of leadership he does not want but must accept.

The film, shot primarily in and near St. George, Utah, was a physically demanding one for Cooper. It is filled with fights, desert treks, physical feats. At the end, Cooper has to pull a small four-wheel railroad rig carrying several of the exhausted heroes. He does this in full military uniform in the Utah sun. He looks physically beaten at the end of the film and apparently was close to it.

Cooper thought he worked particularly well with Hayworth. In interviews following the film, it was clear that he was bothered by criticism of his having played opposite a younger Audrey Hepburn in *Love in the Afternoon.* "Rita and I hit it off fine in *Cordura,*" he said. "She does a bang-up job in the picture. I think if I play opposite girls that look over twenty-five I'm all right. It's a funny thing, though. When you play in a Western, nobody is bothered by how old the girl is. Of course when you hit my age you have to have an adult love story."

When the film was released, the reviews were negative, and the movie did not do well financially. Robert Rossen placed blame for the criticism on the producer, William Goetz and the Baroda Company, which essentially meant Gary Cooper. Rossen said that the film had not been edited according to his script and ideas. To rectify this, he purchased the rights to the film and said he would reedit it and rerelease it. The next year he began working on *The Hustler.* Then, after making *Lilith,* Rossen died in 1966 before he could complete his reediting of *Cordura.*

Cooper next went back into his sea costume for *The Wreck of the Mary Deare.* The film was based on a best-selling novel by Hammond Innes. Innes owned a ten-ton ocean racer that he sailed several thousand miles a year. One night in 1953, off Cherbourg, Innes had come upon a steamer apparently drifting in the mist with only one light visible. The eerie sight of an apparently abandoned ship stirred Innes. Before he had a chance to signal the apparently drifting craft, the steamer started its engines, turned on its lights and moved away. "This experience gradually crystallized in my mind until I saw that steamer as the *Mary Deare,* ploughing along the coast of France, almost running a smaller boat down, not stopping because she'd been abandoned in panic with her engines still running," Innes wrote in a *New York Times* piece.

The first quarter of the film is essentially a two-man show with the fifty-eight-year-old Cooper as Gideon Patch and thirty-five-year-old Charlton Heston as John Sands on the abandoned *Mary Deare.* In a London court of inquiry, Patch avoids answering questions about what happened to the captain and crew of the *Mary Deare.* When everything looks bleakest for him, Sands joins Patch in a diving exploration of the now sunken *Mary Deare* to find evidence to clear Patch. Proof is found, and Patch not only cleared but proven to have been a loyal officer.

Interviewed for this book, Charlton Heston gave his recollections of Cooper and the film. "I had met Coop the first year I was in Hollywood, 1950," Heston recalled. "Then, the next year, while I was doing *The Greatest Show on Earth,* my wife Lydia and I went to a party at Tyrone Power's house, and I met him again. Lydia was his dinner partner, and on the way home she said, 'You know, Gary Cooper was nicer to me than anyone I've met in Hollywood so far,' which I think is an apt summation of the prevailing opinion of Cooper. He was a consummate gentleman, totally professional, and a terribly nice man.

"Then several years later I did *Ben Hur,* which included another commitment to Metro, though I was totally free-lance by then. I was somewhat apprehensive about what Metro might offer, but when they said they wanted me to do *Wreck of the Mary Deare* with Gary Cooper, I leaped at it.

"I very much wanted to do *Macbeth* at a festival at the same time we were shooting *Mary Deare,* and I asked my agent to work it out somehow and see if I could get time off. There were a lot of scenes in the film that didn't involve me, and I thought it might be done. Anyway, they finally allowed me to take four weeks off in the middle of the shooting schedule and do *Macbeth,* which was an enormous concession which couldn't be granted me without Cooper's approval. Not only was Cooper the star of the picture, it was also being produced for MGM by Julian Blaustein and Cooper's Baroda Company. Coop said, 'Good luck with the show,' and after I did it and came back, he said, 'How did it go?' There was no hint that he was doing me a favor.

"The picture was rather difficult physically, as you know, particularly the diving. It was not at all easy for me. I had to learn to dive to do it. Cooper already knew how to dive, and as I know now, it's not easy when you're past forty. He kept himself in fine shape, did all the dives he was supposed to. He worked all day and it was terribly exhausting. He'd come out debilitated from the big water-filled tank at Metro where he had the full-scale mock-up of a section of the freighter. In every shot we had to get wet and dirty and remain under an awful physical pressure.

"We used to go out to dinner together several times a week when we were in London for shooting. He really palled around with me. We went to restaurants and the theater. I don't make friends easily, and I don't have a great many friends that I value, and while it would be presumptuous to say I became his close friend, it was very certain that we were friends, and it was a friendship that I was very proud of."

Heston said that, when he was a boy, Cooper had been his favorite actor, and, when they worked on *Mary Deare,* he paid attention to the way Cooper worked. "He had enormous presence both on the set, in person, and of course on the screen. It's fashionable even now to dismiss Cooper as an actor. I think this is a serious error. He could do a great deal with very little. He never did much with the reading of a line. He seemed to seek out some interesting physical accent for a scene. There was great integrity in what he did and weight in his person. When an actor looks at dailies, he almost inevitably looks at his own image. The only time I ever found myself forgetting to look at myself was when Cooper was in the scene. He projected the kind of man Americans would like to be, probably more than any actor that's ever lived."

After the film was finished, Heston and Cooper went diving together at Catalina. Heston invited Cooper over to see the new house he was building high on a hill in Beverly Hills. "I remember," said Heston, "the house was unfinished, and I had started to put in my workout equipment, and, callowly unaware of his physical problems, I was showing him some of the equipment and said he should look into it. He said yes he would do it, handled it so nicely. I showed him a collection of Hemingway first editions I have, my only complete first editions, because I knew of his friendship with Hemingway. He said, 'You don't have them autographed, do you?' I said I had never met Hemingway and I understood he was not an easy person to approach. 'You shoot birds, don't you?' Cooper said. I said I'd done it but was not very good. And he said, 'Every fall I go up at the opening of the bird season with Hemingway. This time you'll come along and bring those books with you.' That fall I went to do *El Cid,* and they had gone before I got back. That was the last time I saw him."

The Wreck of the Mary Deare returned to several of the classic Cooper character traits and situations. Once again,

Cooper's character is forced to a public trial where he stands mute. This time, however, in contrast to *The Court-Martial of Billy Mitchell,* Cooper's character returns to those portrayed in the earlier films, particularly *Souls at Sea,* and emerges from the trial in triumph.

In the film, directed by Michael Anderson and written by novelist Eric Ambler, Cooper got his final good reviews. John L. Scott in the *Los Angeles Times* wrote, "Cooper emerges with the stronger role, but both he and Heston have been well chosen." Others, including Howard Thomson in *The New York Times,* noted that Cooper looked a bit old and weary from his supposed exploits in the film, but praised the film and Cooper's performance.

Shortly after release, on April 13, 1960, Cooper was admitted to Massachusetts General Hospital in Boston, supposedly for a prostate gland condition. The next day he underwent surgery. Ten days later he was released. A little over a month later, on May 30, Cooper was admitted to Cedars of Lebanon Hospital for "minor corrective surgery." The surgery involved removal of part of his bowel. On June 9, he was released and the surgery he had undergone was not labeled "major." His physicians knew he had cancer and were doing their best to treat it, although Cooper was apparently not told of his real condition.

In August, Cooper was apparently recovered and explained, "I was living with uremic poison for a couple of years. I knew about it but you just keep putting those things off. Then I made arrangements to make a couple of pictures in Europe. I didn't want to have any trouble while in a strange country, so I had the prostate operation." As for the intestinal surgery, Cooper said, "I had an obstruction that was about to strangle my intestines. It's a good thing I got it taken care of."

Cooper said he had plans to make three films, which would take him into 1962. First he would go to London to make *Last Train to Babylon,* based on a novel by Max Ehrlich. This would be followed by the film version of the novel *View From the*

Fortieth Floor, and he would then do a Western which had not yet been given a title. As it turned out, Cooper would do only the first project, which would be retitled *The Naked Edge,* and be produced by his Baroda Company and Marlon Brando's Pennebaker Productions.

On January 9, 1961, the Friars' Club honored Cooper with a $200-a-plate charity dinner. A total of 849 club members and friends paid the price to honor and rib Cooper. Principal speakers for the event were Georgie Jessel, who was master of ceremonies, Audrey Hepburn, Dimitri Tiomkin, Governor "Pat" Brown, Carl Sandburg, Jack Warner, Samuel Goldwyn, Dean Martin, Jack Benny, Henry Ford II and Tony Curtis. Bob Hope, who had been scheduled to appear, was forced to cancel because of illness.

Cooper was visibly nervous throughout the event and admitted afterward, "I was just plain scared to death."

Among the comments:

Jack Warner—"I've always had great faith in Gary. What the hell else could you have at $20,000 a week?"

Carl Sandburg—Cooper is "an institution while he's alive. He represents something of the clean spirit—the man unafraid in danger—the lack of the phony in man."

Sam Goldwyn—"He doesn't say much, but what he says makes a helluva lot of sense."

Milton Berle—"Cooper is Randolph Scott with novocaine lips. He's the Grandpa Moses of the prairie. For thirty years he's lived a clean, respectable life—unfortunately, not his."

After three standing ovations, Cooper rose with tears in his eyes.

"I've never seen so much fuss by so many over so little," he said. "Seeing all these friends in this way makes me know my life has not been wasted."

The day after the Friars' Club testimonial, Cooper went to Sun Valley to hunt. Supposedly, during his outing with Hemingway, he and the author also discussed the possibility of his appearing in the forthcoming film *Adventures of a Young Man,* based on a number of Hemingway stories. Hemingway was very anxious to get the film under way. According to A. E. Hotchner, he needed the $125,000 Twentieth Century Fox had offered him, though he thought it was less than the stories were worth. Hemingway was not thinking seriously of his friend Cooper in *Adventures of a Young Man,* but he did have him in mind for a film version of *Across the River and Into the Trees.* Cooper was very interested, and plans were made to pursue the project late in 1961 or 1962.

In the winter, Cooper was interviewed by *Newsweek* and spoke on what was becoming his favorite public subject, television Westerns. "Look," he said, "did you ever see anything so idiotic as some of these TV cowboys? Hell, they grab the saddle with the wrong hand when they mount. And they can't ride anyway. And look at how they carry their guns, down around their knees somewhere so they can make a production job out of drawing."

More poignantly, Cooper spoke for the first time about quitting his profession. "People hang on after they should quit," he said. "The urge to act stays with you. Sometimes in the middle of a scene I find myself saying a piece of dialogue from fifteen years ago. Situations tend to repeat themselves, and there's a limit to the things you can do with one face and one carcass."

Cooper had already begun the making of *The Naked Edge* when he talked to *Newsweek.* The film was shot entirely in London with Michael Anderson again directing with Deborah Kerr, Eric Portman, Diane Cilento, Hermione Gingold, Peter Cushing and Michael Wilding. The producers were Walter Seltzer and George Glass.

Interviewed for this book, Seltzer recalled, "I met Cooper casually a number of times before we worked together on *The Naked Edge.* Michael Anderson and I sent the script to him in the West Indies, where Cooper was at the time. It was a very different role for him, as he recognized, and that was one of the reasons he wanted to do it. He also said he wanted to work in

Europe, and this film was shot entirely in England. Although he was certainly gravely ill during the making of the picture, he never let it show, and he never let it slow down the film. There were very few retakes, and the film certainly was on time.

"I remember we ended just before Christmas, and I arranged for a portrait to be done of him. I met him at the studio and he told me, 'I really like working in London. The pace is slow and it has a good feeling to it.'

"I do remember two incidents about him worth recalling," Seltzer continued. "One evening Coop and I were invited to a dinner of the Variety Clubs of England with Prince Philip as main speaker. It was tie and tails, and Cooper looked magnificent, very comfortable. He certainly stole the show, and I commented to him on the ride back, 'How did the great American cowboy manage to look so at home in an international gathering of high society?' 'Well," said Coop, 'a few years back I made the rounds of Europe with the Countess diFrasso and got to like it.' "

"One ironic thing did happen while we were shooting the picture," Seltzer added. "Cooper was very nearly killed. We were on location at the Tower of London and had portable dressing rooms for him and Deborah Kerr. Two minutes after Cooper left his dressing room for a shot, his dressing room exploded, destroyed completely, probably a faulty heater."

The role was certainly different for Cooper. He played an American businessman, George Radcliffe, whose wife (Kerr) suspects him of being a murderer. "Problem is to play it on the innocent side," Cooper said about his role during shooting, "and still bring out to the audience the circumstances that seem to make me guilty. Well, there's a bigger problem. I don't know whether people will believe that Gary Cooper could commit a crime."

To keep the effects of illness from his performance required both makeup and a wig, but it was still clear that he was not the Gary Cooper of the past. One relatively simple scene with Kerr required twelve takes, mostly because Cooper was having difficulty with his lines. Following the scene, Cooper went to his dressing room upset and blaming the contrivance of the script and story for the problem.

When the film was finally released after his death, the reviews were not favorable. Brendan Gill, writing in *The New Yorker,* stated, "The qualities that made Cooper a great star had little to do with acting, and since he must have been very uncomfortable in this absurd and unpleasant role, he leaves the make-believe largely to Deborah Kerr."

"I met Gary Cooper when I first went to Hollywood in 1946," Deborah Kerr recalled when interviewed for this book. "We met socially, and I became very good friends with him and his beautiful wife Rocky. They invited me many times to their house, and indeed it was at a party at their new and very 'modern' home that I had the honor to be seated next to President Kennedy, who was then Senator Kennedy. His [Kennedy's] extraordinary charm and personality was quite startling! It is an occasion I shall never forget. He had a magnetism and an ability to make one feel one was the only person in the room. But we are talking of Gary Cooper. And actually Coop possessed the very same qualities that I have described about President Kennedy. Coop, though, had a shyness and a quietness that hid his very dry wit. He was truly a 'gentle-man' and I never met anyone who did not have the greatest affection for him.

"We did not work together until his last movie, *The Naked Edge,*" she continued. "He knew he was a very sick man, and we would lunch together almost every day, and he would reminisce and reminisce about his early days in the movies. It was fascinating but, for me, of course rather sad. When he worked, he was always humorous and cooperative, and to match his wonderful inborn timing was a joy as well as a lesson.

"He was," said Kerr, "a complete 'natural' as an actor. Acting and comedy timing came as naturally to him as a fish knows how to swim. He was a lovely man. What more can I say? They don't make 'em like that any more."

When the film was finished, Cooper commented, "Nothing I've done lately, the last eight years or so, has been especially worthwhile. I've been coasting along. Some of the pictures I've made recently I'm genuinely sorry about."

Reflecting on his life for *McCall's* early in 1961, Coop pointed out that his twenty-three-year-old daughter was a "level-headed youngster" who was studying at the Chouinard Art Institute in Los Angeles. He added that on occasion he had asked Maria if she wanted to appear in any of his films, and she had always turned him down.

Although his films were estimated to have made a total of more than $300,000,000 and he had easily made more than ten million, Cooper claimed that "I'm not rich. I don't own oil wells like Bing Crosby and Bob Hope. I couldn't afford to retire and take up painting."

Cooper's next and final public project was in the medium he had disdained, television. Television gave him the opportunity to go out as a Western figure. The show was an NBC "Project 20" one-hour special called "The Real West," based on still photographs taken in the last century, which Cooper hosted and narrated. The show aired on March 29, 1961. Although it was advertised as his first television appearance, it was far from that. In addition to his appearances on the "Jack Benny Show," Coop had done guest spots on the "Ed Sullivan Show," the "Steve Allen Show" and the "Perry Como Show." In addition, he had appeared on Academy Award night television coverage.

Discussing "The Real West," Cooper told a reporter, "Along with fiction I think a certain amount of historical fact should be given now and then so kids and people don't get the idea that all you have to do is kill a lot of people and you're a Westerner."

To another reporter Cooper commented about his image as

a personality and an actor. "People don't recognize me as much as they used to. Only the older people. The kids today have Frankie Avalon and Elvis Presley. They pretty much leave me alone. It's not like it was in the old days. They've taken all the real glamour out of the picture business by exposing the whole thing to the public—all the inside pictures and stories of how it's done and how that pretty star actually loves to cook a small steak with her own hands and be just like the folks next door."

On April 7, 1961, it was announced that several honorary Oscars would be given at the Academy Awards ceremony that year. Cooper was to get one and Stan Laurel another. When the ceremony was held in Santa Monica on April 17, Cooper was too ill to be present. His friend Jimmy Stewart accepted the award for him. It was presented by William Wyler, who said, "Many people, including Gary himself, don't know how good an actor he really is."

Stewart, who knew the nature of Cooper's illness, was near tears when he accepted the award, and he addressed his remarks to Coop and his family. "I am very honored to accept this award tonight for Gary Cooper," Stewart said. "I am sorry he's not here to accept it, but I know he's sitting by the television set tonight, and, Coop, I want you to know I'll get it to you right away. With it goes all the friendship and affection and the admiration and the deep respect of all of us. We're very, very proud of you, Coop. All of us are tremendously proud."

On April 19, Cooper's family announced that the actor had cancer and knew it. A week later Cooper's physician confirmed that the actor was suffering from "advanced cancer" and that there had been a worsening of his condition. Cooper was being treated at his Bel Air home, and there were no plans to hospitalize him.

Calls, letters and telegrams began to flood the Cooper home. President Kennedy called and spoke to Cooper for about five minutes. Cooper also reported to a visitor that Hemingway had called him. "Papa phoned . . . told me he was sick, too. I bet him that I will beat him out to the barn." A few friends were allowed to visit, including Stewart and his wife, Sam Goldwyn, producer Jerry Wald and a limited number of others.

On May 6, more than 600 movie personalities crowded into a hall of the Cannes Film Festival Palace in France for the official award presentation on behalf of André Malraux, French Cultural Affairs Minister, making Cooper an officer in the Order of Arts and Letters. The award, a medal, was given to Fred Zinnemann, who said he would take it to Cooper in California.

On May 7, 1961, Gary Cooper became sixty years old. Heavily sedated, he had been receiving the sacraments of the Roman Catholic Church every few days. Six days later, he was dead.

At the funeral on May 16, the pallbearers were James Stewart, Jack Benny, Henry Hathaway and producers William Goetz, Jerry Wald and Charles Feldman. Honorary pallbearers included John Wayne, Henry Ford II, Bing Crosby, Burt Lancaster, Dick Powell, Kirk Douglas, Danny Kaye, Tony Curtis, Peter Lawford and Ernest Hemingway. Hemingway was reportedly too ill to attend. Less than two months later the sixty-two-year-old writer took his own life.

Condolences were cabled to the Cooper family from all over the world, including from Pope John XXIII. Attending the funeral were Cooper's brother Arthur and his eighty-six-year-old mother Alice. Mrs. Cooper informed the press that those desiring to send contributions instead of flowers should direct their contributions to the Sloan-Kettering Institute for Cancer Research in New York City. Burial was in the Holy Cross Cemetery in Los Angeles.

The world's newspapers responded to Cooper's death in various ways:

Italy's *Corriere della Sera*—"With him there is ended a certain America . . . that of the frontier and of innocence which had or was believed to have an exact sense of the dividing line between good and evil."

Sweden's *Svenska Dagladet*—"He had the soul of a boy, a pure, simple, nice, warm boy's soul . . . he was the incarnation of the honorable American."

Germany's *Die Welt*—"He had been a key figure of our days. . . . He was the symbol of trust, confidence and protection. . . . He is dead now. What a miracle that he existed."

The *New York Times*—"A new generation of moviegoers and television viewers may want a different sort of hero—perhaps a man more baffled by life. But it is sad to see Gary Cooper go."

To honor Cooper's memory, the American Institute of Fine Arts created a scholarship in his name to enable one deserving artist each year to study art in Hollywood. Announcement of the scholarship was made by Mary Pickford, honorary president of the institute. Initial contributions were made by Pickford and Bing Crosby Enterprises. To further honor Cooper's memory, the jury at the Cannes Film Festival instituted a new yearly Gary Cooper Award for outstanding human values. The first award was given to the film *A Raisin in the Sun.* Sidney Poitier accepted the award on behalf of the producer.

The month following the funeral, it was disclosed that Cooper had left half of his estate, estimated at more than one million dollars, to his widow. An additional $5,000 each was left to Cooper's brother Arthur, a nephew, Howard Cooper, a niece, Mrs. Georgia C. Burton, and $1,000 to Our Lady of Gethsemane Abbey in Kentucky and $10,000 to the Motion Picture Relief Fund, Inc. The remainder went into a trust for Maria Cooper and to Cooper's mother.

The crew who had worked with Cooper on "The Real West" went to work to create a tribute to the actor, "The Tall American." Don Hyatt, who produced both television shows, stated: "He had courage right out of *High Noon* . . . we didn't know why, but he was in great pain when he worked with us and he remained respectful, kind and considerate to everyone. So that's what we're trying to show—that Gary Cooper was as real as what people thought he was on the screen."

In the course of the television show, "The Tall American," Walter Brennan, who did the narration, said, "He could be at ease with a prince, because he was a kind of royalty himself— the greatest of his line, and maybe the last."

"The Tall American" aired on NBC in March of 1963 and was

praised by critics. Wrote Cecil Smith in the *Los Angeles Times,* " 'The Tall American' offered this man in his warmth, his simplicity, his towering dignity."

Following the funeral and aftermath, Cooper's widow and daughter moved to New York. But first they made some presentations. "Gary's own saddle, hat, chaps and holster were really the world's," Rocky Cooper said, "and I turned them over to the Museum of the West in Oklahoma. Many of the saddles, guns and Stetson hats that Gary kept from his movies we gave to the Museum of Memorabilia in Hollywood."

SEVENTEEN

THE MEANING OF
A CAREER

In spite of his Oscars and his praise, Gary Cooper apparently lived with the belief that he was not an accomplished actor. Part of this stemmed from the high esteem placed on stage experience, experience that Cooper never had. Part of it obviously came from his own genuinely humble attitude toward himself and his accomplishments. That he was truly a humble man can be seen in the support he received from those with whom he worked and lived. To find someone who has an unkind word to say about Cooper is a near impossibility.

Usually, when one is doing research for a book on a person in the public spotlight, incidents arise, remarks are dropped, people have a sore they wish bared or someone makes a revelation they then ask not to be used. Nothing like that arose in the research and interviewing for this book. The few things people did ask to be withheld, and that have been withheld, related not to Cooper's personality but to details of his health or business agreements.

If Cooper was criticized for anything, it was for his sexual behavior and political choices. That he liked women was clearly evident throughout his life. That he was highly conservative politically is also evident. That he was vain about his appearance is to a degree also clear, but it was a vanity born out of professional pride and the realization that his career was based upon how he looked.

One can conjecture about Cooper's personality and how it came to be. In spite of his claims of independence as a boy, his parents kept a relatively firm grip on him, protected him from trouble and supported him right up to the point where he began to make a living as a film actor. In practice, he had no idea of what it meant to be poor or worried about money. Cooper was never totally comfortable with the recognition that he had never suffered deprivation of even a minimal kind. Consequently, when asked about his life, he tended to create a fiction that would support his persona. He presented to others the cowboy from Montana, the man of few words who respected and was ill at ease with women. He was the man who had known trouble and survived. He was the common man.

In fact, he was a quite uncommon man. As a young man, his intellectual pursuits and interests were nonexistent. By the time he reached his forties, however, he had developed into a respected businessman, an intelligent conversationalist and a determined individualist. By 1940, the comment recurs over and over from people who worked with Cooper: "He was so different off-camera than on."

He was not a dynamic man. He was, in many ways, a man alone who could retreat into himself, which he frequently did. The ease with which he fell asleep in public is a sign of such ability to retreat from the world. The desire to participate in solitary sports and activities—skiing, hunting, diving, riding and driving—are indicative of the private man. In this he was strange, an actor who felt uneasy with the public, a man who did not enjoy the reaction of his fans.

The impulse always exists to reduce a public personality to a list of characteristics, a catalogue of traits and beliefs. Most people, like Gary Cooper, are a complex amalgam of emotions and reactions. They do not always understand themselves, and from the outside we have even more trouble trying to understand them. The danger lies in attempting to oversimplify their natures, their being, their thoughts and abilities. Even when, as with Cooper, they impel you in the direction of the myth they wish to stand for, it is a disservice to accept that myth. If a person is not ultimately reducible to a few pages or sentences, ideas or feelings, then so be it—sympathize to the degree we wish, and appreciate to the degree we are able.

In looking back over Gary Cooper's career and what we have explored of it, there are some patterns that might help relate the life of the man to his screen image.

One can see Cooper's career as falling into six periods:

1. 1926–1930: THE NAIVE YOUNG HERO. In this four-year period, Cooper made twenty-three films, an average of five a year from *The Winning of Barbara Worth* to *The Spoilers*. More than half were Westerns or military pictures, films in which Cooper appeared as the tentative, shy young man, loose and limber of body, sure of the moral position he shared with the world. In this pre-Depression era, Cooper represented the young American who believed in the triumph of simple virtues and the commitment to them. In his life, Cooper was, in fact, developing more and more confidence, was at the peak of his physical appearance and health, was in fact by the conclusion of this period not a tentative, shy man at all.

2. 1930–1936: CYNICISM AND DISILLUSION. In this six-year period, Cooper made nineteen films, an average of a little over three a year, from *Morocco* to *Desire*. Only one of these films was a Western. The Western image of affirmation submerged with the Depression. Instead Cooper emerged as a tense and cautious figure, one who distrusted others, one loath to commit himself to others though he could be touched.

3. 1936–1941: ALTRUISM AND DEDICATION. In this four-year period, Cooper made fourteen films, from *Mr. Deeds Goes to Town* to *Sergeant York*. Cooper's character was now a determined man, a man who saw hope in the future and was willing to sacrifice himself for the future of mankind. Many of these movies were set in the past.

4. 1942–1947: INTELLECT AND PURPOSE. In this five-year period, Cooper made eight films, from *Ball of Fire* through *Unconquered*. In these war years and aftermath of the war period, Cooper was a man out of his environment, a man who could handle the riddle of an unfamiliar world and triumph by his native wit and determination even when others distrusted

him. The only exceptions to this pattern in this period are the two films Cooper himself produced, *Casanova Brown* and *Along Came Jones,* both of which present an earlier Cooper image, an attempt to create a variation on what he had done before. It seems that the public image of Cooper changed slowly while he himself wanted to try broader variations on his image. It was surely a source of unhappiness to Cooper that whenever he attempted to vary too much from his public image in a particular period, the public failed to respond.

5. 1948–1956: THE MAN ALONE. In this eight-year period, Cooper made sixteen films, from *The Fountainhead* to *The Court-Martial of Billy Mitchell.* It is significant that half of the films he made in this period are Westerns, often harking back to the period of his tentative shyness. Only now, Cooper was the rapidly aging man who stood resolutely against the world. That *The Virginian* should be the culmination of his earlier Western period and *High Noon* the peak for his second Western period is not a coincidence. Cooper and others saw the similarity of the two films. Their differences are equally striking. Will Kane in *High Noon* seeks help from his society. The Virginian wanted to be on his own. Will Kane learns the bitter lesson of having to be alone. The Virginian never has to face this issue. Throughout this period, the Cooper character is faced with defeat and indecision, a character alone by choice, as in *The Fountainhead,* or because his society rejects him, as in *The Court-Martial of Billy Mitchell.* It is the confounding Cold War period, in which the Cooper character's old values are rejected.

6. 1956–1961: QUESTIONING THE PAST. In this five-year period, Cooper made eight films, from *Love in the Afternoon* through *The Naked Edge.* The period is ushered in by a transition film, *Friendly Persuasion,* a film in which Cooper's character discarded his guns and rejected the violence that the characters in the other periods had accepted with little question. This questioning of the past continues to the end of Cooper's life. It is significant that this is the period in which Cooper had the most control of his parts, was producing his own films, but

felt he had let his public down. Cooper was now trying to extend his range as an actor and was willing to do this by questioning his image in the past. His role as the lover in *Love in the Afternoon* is an ironic comment on his past comedy images. In his Westerns of this period, he is a self-sufficient but highly reluctant, somber man. His final films are constantly questioning his past. In *They Came to Cordura,* the very essence of filmic courage that Cooper represented was questioned and in his final film, *The Naked Edge,* the possibility of Cooper's even being a vicious murderer was proposed. It is true in all these cases that the Cooper character was ultimately heroic, but the films played with the image, toyed with possibilities and the public image Cooper represented. Certainly his work is not less good in this period though he did suffer physically. What was reacted to by critics and public was what Cooper now represented, the weary questioner of the American mythic past.

It is perhaps appropriate that Cooper's two Oscars for acting should be for two separate periods, one in which he was an optimistic hero of the past and the other in which he was a pessimistic retainer of the past. In fact more than sixty of Cooper's films were set in the past. It may well have been what he represented in our history and culture as well as his performances in these films for which he was honored.

As one critic said, Gary Cooper's face was the map of America. In it, we read our past. We liked it or did not like it, but we could not turn away from the compelling man who represented it.

SELECTED BIBLIOGRAPHY

Books

Bancroft, F. M. *A Short History of Dunstable School 1888–1963,* Dunstable, G. W. Parsons, 1963, p. 8.

Behlmer, Rudy, ed. *Memo From: David O. Selznick,* New York: Avon, 1972, pp. 179, 180, 183, 194, 198–201.

Brownlow, Kevin. *The Parade's Gone By,* Berkeley: University of California Press, 1968, pp. 114–117, 187.

Capra, Frank. *The Name Above the Title: An Autobiography,* New York: Macmillan, 1971, pp. 182–183, 187, 221.

Carpozi, George. *The Gary Cooper Story,* New York: Arlington House, 1970.

Corey, Jeff. "Gary Cooper: Natural Talent." In *Close-up,* edited by Danny Peary, New York: Workman Publishing Co., 1978.

Davies, Marion. *The Times We Had,* New York: Bobbs-Merrill, Inc., 1975, pp. 182, 183.

Dickens, Homer. *The Films of Gary Cooper,* Secaucus, N.J.: Citadel Press, 1971.

Dmytryk, Edward. *It's a Hell of a Life But Not a Bad Living,* New York: New York Times Book Company, 1978, pp. 96, 97.

Durgnat, Raymond. "Six Films of Josef von Sternberg." In *Movies and Methods,* edited by Bill Nichols, Berkeley: University of California Press, 1976, p. 265.

Easton, Carol. *The Search for Sam Goldwyn,* New York: William Morrow, 1976, pp. 73–74.

Escoubé, Lucienne. *Gary Cooper: Le Cavalier de L'Ouest,* Paris: Les Editions du Cert, 1965.

Farrell, Barry. *Pat and Roald,* New York: Random House, 1969, pp. 64, 65.

Fein, Irving. *Jack Benny: An Intimate Biography,* New York: G. P. Putnam's Sons, 1976, pp. 181, 481, 483.

Graham, Sheilah. *Confessions of a Hollywood Columnist,* New York: William Morrow, 1969, pp. 286–292.

Greene, Graham. "The Real Glory." In *Graham Greene on Film,* edited by John Russell Taylor, New York: Simon & Schuster, 1972, p. 262.

Griffith, Richard. *Samuel Goldwyn: The Producer and His Films,* New York: Simon & Schuster, 1956, pp. 18–19.

Guiles, Fred Lawrence. *Marion Davies,* New York: McGraw-Hill, 1972, p. 271.

Higham, Charles, and Greenberg, Joel. *The Celluloid Muse,* New York: Signet, 1969, pp. 130–133, 151, 169–171, 180–181.

Hotchner, A. E. *Papa Hemingway,* New York: Random House, 1966, pp. 201, 202, 237, 239, 258, 264, 289, 290.

Johnston, Alva. *The Great Goldwyn,* New York: Random House, 1937, p. 88.

Madsen, Axel. *William Wyler,* New York: Thomas Y. Crowell, 1973, pp. 193–195.

Maltin, Leonard. *Behind the Camera,* New York: Signet, 1971, p. 53.

Maltin, Leonard. *The Real Stars,* New York: Curtis Books, 1970, p. 226.

Martin, Pete. *Hollywood Without Makeup,* New York: Bantam, 1949, p. 138.

McGann, Kevin. "Ayn Rand in the Stockyard of the Spirit." In *The Modern American Novel and the Movies,* edited by Gerald Peary and Roger Shatzkin, New York: Frederick Ungar, 1978, pp. 325–335.

Marx, Arthur. *Goldwyn: A Biography of the Man Behind the Myth,* New York: W. W. Norton, 1976, pp. 278–279.

Moore, Dickie. "Sergeant York." In *Hollywood Kids,* edited by Leonard Maltin, New York: Popular Library, 1978, pp. 75–79.

Morella, Joe, and Epstein, Edward Z. *The IT Girl: The Incredible Story of Clara Bow,* New York: Delacorte, 1976, pp. 88–105.

O'Hara, John. *Selected Letters of John O'Hara,* edited by Matthew J. Bruccoli, New York: Random House, 1978, pp. 270–271, 320.

Preminger, Otto. *Preminger: An Autobiography,* New York: Doubleday, 1977, p. 147.

Quinn, Anthony. *The Original Sin,* Boston: Little, Brown and Company, 1972, pp. 238–247, 258.

Schickel, Richard. *The Men Who Made the Movies,* New York: Atheneum, 1975, pp. 205–206.

Sternberg, Josef von. *Fun in a Chinese Laundry,* New York: Macmillan, 1965, p. 255.

Vidor, King. *On Filmmaking,* New York: David McKay, 1972, pp. 56–57.

Walsh, Raoul. *Each Man in His Time,* New York: Farrar, Straus and Giroux, 1974, pp. 356–357.

Walton, Donald. *A Rockwell Portrait,* New York: Sheed Andrews and McMeel, 1978.

Warshow, Robert. "The Westerner." In *Film: Anthology,* edited by Daniel Talbot, New York: Simon & Schuster, 1959, pp. 171–173, 204.

Yablonsky, Lewis. *George Raft,* New York: McGraw-Hill, 1974, pp. 62, 116.

Articles

American Film Institute Center for Advanced Film Study. "Dialogue on Film: Carl Foreman." *American Film,* April 1979, pp. 35–46.

Anthony, Paul. "A Lesson for Every Woman." *Photoplay,* October 1961, pp. 59, 60, 89–91.

Archerd, Army. "Gary Cooper to Friars: Who? Me!" *Variety,* January 11, 1961, pp. 1–2.

Arvad, Inga. "Call for Coop." *Photoplay,* December 1945, pp. 54–55, 118–119.

Associated Press. "Gary Cooper Movie Battle Turns Real." December 18, 1953.

Bankhead, Tallulah. "The Man I Can't Forget." *American Weekly,* April 14, 1953, pp. 9–11.

Bosquet, Jean. "JFK's Call Cheers Film Star." *Los Angeles Examiner,* April 23, 1961.

Busby, Marquis. "The New Two-Gun Man." *Photoplay,* April 1930, pp. 50, 121.

Carle, Teet. "Gary Cooper: The Man Who Seemed Eternal." *Hollywood Studio,* May 1972, pp. 6, 7, 25.

Carroll, Harrison. "Gary Cooper and Wife End Separation." *Los Angeles Herald Express,* November 9, 1953.

Chicago Tribune. "People." April 22, 1979, sec. 3, p. 1 on Maria Cooper Janis.

Colliers. "Gary Cooper Spears a Kahala in Samoa." December 20, 1952.

Collins, Imogene. "A New Love for Coop?" *Modern Screen,* August 1951, pp. 31, 66.

Committee on Un-American Activities, House of Representatives, 80th Congress, First Session, Hearings Regarding the Communist Infiltration of the Motion Picture Industry. Thursday, October 23, 1947, pp. 219–224. Testimony of Gary Cooper.

Cooper, Gary. "The Big Boy Tells His Story." *Photoplay,* Part I: April, 1929, pp. 64–65; 133–135; Part II: May, 1929, pp. 70–71, 84–85. (As told to Dorothy Spensley.)

Cooper, Gary. "I Took a Good Look at Myself, and This Is What I Saw." *McCall's,* January 1961, pp. 62, 138–142. (As told to Leonard Slater.)

Cooper, Gary. "The Role I Liked Best." *Saturday Evening Post,* May 6, 1950.

Cooper, Gary. "Well, It Was This Way." *Saturday Evening Post,* Part I: February 18, 1956; Part II, February 25, 1956; Part III: March 3, 1956; Part IV: March 10, 1956; Part V: March 17, 1956; Part VI: March 24, 1956; Part VII: March 31, 1956; Part VIII: April 7, 1956. (As told to George Scullin.)

Cooper, Veronica. "How I Faced Tomorrow." *Good Housekeeping,* September 1963, pp. 81–83, 160–168. (As told to George Christy.)

Crisler, B. R. "Gary Cooper, Cowboy Connoisseur." *New York Times,* September 3, 1939, sec. IV, p. 3:1.

Crowther, Bosley. "Modesty and Mr. Grant." *New York Times,* December 4, 1938, sec. V, p. 9:8. Compares Cooper and Cary Grant.

Crowther, Bosley. "Setting Stars." *New York Times,* May 21, 1961, sec. II, p. 1:8.

Dinter, Charlotte. "Tribute to a Great Guy: Coop." *Photoplay,* July 1961, pp. 47, 83–85.

DuBrow, Rick. "How Ill is Gary Cooper?" *Hollywood Citizen-News,* April 18, 1961.

French, William. "What Hollywood Thinks of Gary Cooper." *Photoplay,* August 1942, pp. 39, 76.

Garber, Arlene. "All About Gary Cooper." *Hollywood Citizen-News,* March 26, 1963, p. B-12.

Gehman, Richard. "Brave Legacy." *Los Angeles Examiner,* "American Weekly," August 13, 1961, pp. 5, 7. Interview with Veronica Cooper.

Goodman, Ezra. "Average Guy: Gary Cooper Reflects on Twenty Years in Film." *New York Times,* December 19, 1948, sec. II, p. 5:8.

Grinnell Scarlet and Black, "Abegglen, Dramatic Club Head Who Barred Cooper, Fan of Star Today." January 4, 1933, p. 1.

Grinnell Scarlet and Black, "Gary Cooper Breaks into Movies After Studying Advertising Here." November 21, 1929, p. 1.

Grinnell Scarlet and Black, "Gary Cooper Comes Back by Airplane to Celebration." October 10, 1929, p. 1.

Grinnell Scarlet and Black, "Gary Cooper is Kept Busy Here," October 23, 1929, p. 1.

Harris, Herbert. "Secrets of Gary Cooper's Boyhood in Britain." *Film Pictorial,* August 15, 1936, pp. 8–9.

Hollywood Citizen-News. "Fine Arts Group Plans Scholarship." May 8, 1961.

Hollywood Citizen-News. "Gary Cooper Hurt in Blast." March 28, 1953.

Hollywood Citizen-News. "Gary Cooper to Undergo Operation." July 25, 1953.

Hollywood Reporter. "Cooper Initials Deal at Warners." October 31, 1947.

Herzog, Dorothy. "This for Art's Sake?" *Motion Picture,* December 1927, pp. 45, 95, 120. On shooting of *Beau Sabreur.*

Hopper, Hedda. "Gary Cooper to Stay Out of Film Deal." *Los Angeles Times,* November 2, 1951,

Hubler, Richard G. "Gary Cooper: Mr. American." *Coronet,* June 1955, pp. 21–28.

Hull, Bob. "Tribute to a Tall American." *Los Angeles Herald-Examiner,* "TV Weekly," March 24, 1963, p. 5.

Hunt, Julie Lang. "Why Gary's Gone Rural Again." *Photoplay,* August 1936, pp. 30–31, 112.

Hyams, Joe. "The Western He Wanted to Do." *New York Herald Tribune,* March 26, 1961.

Jamison, Jack. "Cary versus Gary." *Photoplay,* January 1933, pp. 33, 111.

Johnson, Nunnally. "Along Came Cooper." *Photoplay,* August 1945, pp. 38–39, 96, 99.

Kingsley, Grace. "Favorite Stars." *The New Movie Magazine,* July 1930, p. 37.

Koury, Phil. "Silent Knight." *New York Times,* October 20, 1946, sec. II, p. 5:1.

Leslie, Marion. "I'm Through Being Bossed." *Photoplay,* October 1932, pp. 34, 98.

Life. "Gary, Cary Remain Frisky Past Fifty." August 12, 1957, p. 79.

Life. "Hollywood Mourns a Good Man." May 26, 1961, pp. 26–40.

Life. "Life Goes Hunting at Sun Valley with the Gary Coopers and Ernest Hemingways." November 24, 1941, pp. 116–117.

Life. "Sad News of Cooper." April 28, 1961, p. 74A.

Life. "We Love You, Mr. Cooper." August 25, 1952, p. 22.

Los Angeles Herald-Express. "Gary Cooper Returns Home." December 29, 1943.

Los Angeles Herald-Express. "Gary Cooper: Wife Says He Can Have Divorce if He Wishes." January 30, 1952.

Los Angeles Times. "Cooper Role in Film Lauded by Sgt. York." May 14, 1961, sec. A, p. 3.

Los Angeles Times. "Gary Cooper Forms Baroda Productions." September 22, 1954.

Manners, Dorothy. "Shock at Removal of Cooper's Body." *Los Angeles Herald-Examiner.* May 14, 1974.

Maxwell, Elsa. "American Natural." *Photoplay,* December 1944, pp. 38, 87, 90.

Maxwell, Virginia. "Can a Man Love Two Women?" *Photoplay,* February 1934, pp. 32–33, 119.

McCrea, Joel. "My Friend Coop!" *Photoplay,* October 1939, pp. 19–21, 85–87.

Miron, Charles. "Gary Cooper's Daughter to Enter Convent." *Photoplay,* August 1961, pp. 53, 79.

Morgan, Thomas B. "The American Hero Grows Older." *Esquire,* May 1961, pp. 63–66.

Newsweek. "Communists: Philadelphia Story." August 18, 1947, p. 21.

Newsweek. "Honor and Duty in the Lives of a Bengal Lancer." January 19, 1935, p. 26.

Newsweek. "23 Years After Argonne: Jesse Lasky Brings Life

Story of Sergeant York to Screen." July 14, 1941, pp. 61–62.

Newsweek. "The Urge Stays On." December 12, 1960,

New York Herald Tribune. "Gary Cooper Had a Case of Shyness." August 23, 1942, sec. VI. p. 3.

New York Times. "Academy Award to Joan Fontaine, She Wins for Role in *Suspicion*—Gary Cooper Takes Honors for *Sergeant York.*" February 27, 1942, p. 21:1.

New York Times. "Cooper, Film Star to Wed Debutante." November 29, 1933, p. 23:3.

New York Times. "Cooper Has 60th." May 8, 1961, p. 49:5.

New York Times. "Cooper Hurt Making Film." March 28, 1953, p. 15:6.

New York Times. "Cooper Sues Milk Company." November 15, 1932, p. 19:2.

New York Times. "Cooper Will is Filed." May 21, 1961, p. 86:3.

New York Times. "Daughter to Gary Coopers." September 16, 1937, p. 29:2.

New York Times. "Film Celebrities Robbed." July 31, 1937, p. 30:2.

New York Times. "Film Salaries Cut to Third by Taxes." January 11, 1937, p. 16:2.

New York Times. "France Honors Cooper." May 6, 1961, p. 26:8.

New York Times. "Friars Club Cites Gary Cooper," January 10, 1961, p. 27:1.

New York Times. "Gary Cooper a Convert." April 25, 1959, p. 14:2.

New York Times. "Gary Cooper Backs Dewey," November 2, 1944, p. 12:8.

New York Times. "Gary Cooper Dead of Cancer; Film Star, 60, Won 2 Oscars." May 14, 1961, p. 1:4.

New York Times. "Gary Cooper Enters Hospital." May 31, 1960, p. 27:1.

New York Times. "Gary Cooper Gets the Third Degree." March 3, 1935, sec. VIII, p. 4.

New York Times. "Gary Cooper Has Operation." August 9, 1951, p. 17:4.

New York Times. "Gary Cooper Has Surgery." April 15, 1960, p. 13:4.

New York Times. "Gary Cooper Has Surgery." June 1, 1960, p. 43:2.

New York Times. "Gary Cooper Ill at Home." April 19, 1961, p. 32:1.

New York Times. "Gary Cooper Ill on Coast." January 25, 1945, p. 16:4.

New York Times. "Gary Cooper in Hospital." April 14, 1960, p. 35:2.

New York Times. "Gary Cooper is Displeased." March 28, 1954, p. 22:1. On Russian director.

New York Times. "Gary Cooper Leaves Hospital." June 10, 1960, p. 37:1.

New York Times. "Gary Cooper Quits Hospital." April 26, 1960, p. 40:6.

New York Times. "Gary Cooper Resting After Operation." December 9, 1951, p. 84:6.

New York Times. "Gary Coopers Arrive in Bermuda." March 27, 1936, p. 25:3.

New York Times. "Gary Coopers Separated." May 17, 1951, p. 38:2.

New York Times. "Gary Cooper's $482,819 Tops List of Salaries Given Out by Treasury." August 3, 1941, p. 30:2.

New York Times. "Gary Cooper to Enter Hospital." May 15, 1945, p. 23:4.

New York Times. "Gary Cooper Weds in Quiet Ceremony." December 16, 1933, p. 18:4.

New York Times. "Goldwyn Must Defend Suit." October 19, 1936, p. 23:6.

New York Times. "Goldwyn Plea is Heard." October 13, 1936, p. 48:3.

New York Times. "Highest Salaries Paid in Nation in 1936 are Listed by House Committee." January 9, 1938, p. 44:1.

New York Times. "Lupe Velez Denies She is to Wed." February 21, 1929, p. 14:5.

New York Times. "Many Film Stars at Cooper Rites." May 17, 1961, p. 37:3.

New York Times. "Pallbearers Listed for Cooper Funeral." May 15, 1961, p. 31:4.

New York Times. "Widow Gets Cooper Estate." June 9, 1961, p. 66:7.

New York Times. "Youth Fitness Unit Set." June 1, 1957, p. 19:8.

Nugent, Frank S. "The All-American Man." *New York Times Magazine,* July 5, 1942, p. 18.

Parsons, Louella O. "Gary Cooper in Hospital." *Los Angeles Herald Examiner,* December 20, 1948,

Parsons, Louella O. "The Gary Coopers' New Formula For Happy Marriage." *Los Angeles Herald Examiner,* "Pictorial Living," November 21, 1954, pp. 12–13.

Parsons, Louella O. "Gary Coopers Will Separate." *Los Angeles Herald Examiner,* May 17, 1951, sec. I, p. 3.

Parsons, Louella. "Restless Hearts." *Photoplay,* March 1951, pp. 50, 95–96.

Pryor, Thomas M. "By Way of Report." *New York Times,* August 27, 1944, sec. II, p. 3:1.

Rhea, Marian. "The Laws of Averages." *Photoplay,* March 1941, pp. 33, 71.

Riesel, Victor. "Gary Cooper Talks to Reds." *Hollywood Citizen-News,* October 1, 1953.

St. Johns, Adela Rogers. "Gary the Great." *Photoplay,* April 1938.

St. Nicholas, The Magazine of Youth. "When I Was a Boy: Six Famous Americans Tell You of their Most Vivid Memories and Problems as Boys." November 1935, p. 21.

Samuels, Charles. "Gary Cooper—Mr. Everybody." *Motion Picture,* January 1946, p. 30.

Scott, Vernon. "The Gary Cooper Story." *Hollywood Citizen-News,* Part I: May 15, 1961; Part II: May 16, 1961; Part III: May 17, 1961.

Service, Faith. "Has Gary Changed?" *Movie Classic,* June 1933, p. 34.

Smith, Cecil. "Cooper Profile—One of the Noblest." *Los Angeles Times,* March 28, 1963, part IV, p. 10.

Suckow, Ruth. "Grinnell." *College Humor,* May 1930, pp. 58, 109.

Time. "Coop." March 3, 1941, pp. 78–82. Cover story.

Tower, Samuel A. "Hollywood Communists 'Militant,' but Small in Number, Stars Testify." *New York Times,* October 24, 1947, p. 1:2.

TV Guide. "Strong But Not So Silent." March 25, 1961, pp. 9–11.

Variety. "Gary Cooper Buys Half Interest in Two Lippert Productions." October 17, 1950, p. 4.

Variety. "Pressure Cooper, Other Partners to Quit Foreman." October 3, 1951, p. 1.

Wix, John. "Gary Cooper, Wife Will Reconcile." *Los Angeles Examiner,* April 14, 1954.

Wood, Tom. "Gary Cooper." *Look,* May 16, 1944, pp. 38, 42.

Zeitlin, David I. *Fred Zinnemann.* Directors Guild of America, 1966. A monograph in honor of the director upon winning 1966 DGA Directoral Award.

FILMOGRAPHY:
THE FILMS OF GARY COOPER

Note: Dates indicated are dates of release and do not necessarily reflect the order in which films were made.

Cooper appeared as an extra in about thirty films in 1925 and 1926. Among them were:

Dick Turpin   (1925)
starring Tom Mix.
The Thundering Herd   (1925)
starring Tom Mix with Noah Beery, Raymond Hatton, Lois Wilson and Jack Holt.
Wild Horse Mesa   (1925)
with Jack Holt and Billie Dove.
The Lucky Horseshoe   (Fox, 1925)
with Tom Mix, Billie Dove and Ann Pennington.
The Vanishing American   (1925)
with Richard Dix, Lois Wilson and Noah Beery.
The Eagle   (United Artists, 1925)
with Rudolph Valentino, Vilma Banky and Louise Dresser.
The Enchanted Hill   (1926)
with Florence Vidor, Jack Holt and Noah Beery.
Watch Your Wife   (1926)
with Virginia Valli and Pat O'Malley.

Cooper appeared as a supporting actor in the following short films in 1925–1926:

1926   TRICKS   Davis Distributing Company

Director: Bruce Mitchell
Scenarist: Mary C. Bruning
Cast: Marilyn Mills and J. Frank Glendon

1926   THREE PALS   Davis Distributing Company

Director: Bruce Mitchell
Scenarist: Mary C. Bruning
Cast: Marilyn Mills and J. Frank Glendon

1926   LIGHTNIN' WINS   Independent Pictures

Director: Hans Tiesler
Cast: Lightnin' the Super Dog and Eileen Sedgwick

1926   THE WINNING OF BARBARA WORTH
United Artists

Director: Henry King
Producer: Samuel Goldwyn
Scenarist: Frances Marion
Photographer: George Barnes
Editor: Viola Lawrence
Art Director: Carl Oscar Borg
Associate Photographer: Gregg Toland
Titler: Rupert Hughes
Musical Score: Ted Henkel
Based on the novel by Harold Bell Wright
Cast: Ronald Colman (Willard Holmes), Vilma Banky (Barbara
Worth), Charles Lane (Jefferson Worth), Paul McAllister (The Seer),
E. J. Ratcliffe (James Greenfield), Gary Cooper (Abe Lee), Clyde Cooke
(Tex), Erwin Connelly (Pat), Sam Blum (Blanton).

1927   IT   Paramount

Director: Clarence Badger
Producers: Clarence Badger, Elinor Glyn
Associate Producer: B. P. Schulberg
Scenarists: Hope Loring, Louis D. Lighton
Adaptation: Elinor Glyn
Photographer: H. Kinley Martin
Editor: E. Lloyd Sheldon
Titler: George Marion, Jr.
Cast: Clara Bow (Betty Lou), Antonio Moreno (Cyrus Waltham), Wil-
liam Austin (Monty), Jacqueline Gadson (Adela Van Norman), Julia
Swayne Gordon (Mrs. Van Norman), Priscilla Bonner (Molly), Eleanor
Lawson (First Welfare Worker), Rose Tapley (Second Welfare
Worker), Gary Cooper (Reporter), Elinor Glyn (Herself), Lloyd Corri-
gan (Cabin Boy).

1927   CHILDREN OF DIVORCE   Paramount

Director: Frank Lloyd
Producer: E. Lloyd Sheldon
Scenarists: Hope Loring, Louis D. Lighton
Photographer: Victor Milner
Editor: E. Lloyd Sheldon
Associate Producer: B. P. Schulberg
Based on the novel by Owen McMahon Johnson
Cast: Clara Bow (Kitty Flanders), Esther Ralston (Jean Waddington), Gary Cooper (Ted Larrabee), Einar Hanson (Prince Ludovico de Sfax), Norman Trevor (Duke de Gondreville), Hedda Hopper (Katherine Flanders), Edward Martindel (Tom Larrabee), Julia Swayne Gordon (Princess de Sfax), Tom Ricketts (The Secretary), Albert Gran (Mr. Seymour), Iris Stuart (Mousie), Margaret Campbell (Mother Superior), Percy Williams (Manning), Joyce Marie Coad (Little Kitty), Yvonne Pelletier (Little Jean), Don Marion (Little Ted).

1927   ARIZONA BOUND   Paramount

Director: John Waters
Scenarists: John Stone, Paul Gangelon
Adaptation: Marion Jackson
Photographer: C. Edgar Schoenbaum
Titler: Alfred Hustwick
Based on a story by Richard Allen Gates
Cast: Gary Cooper (The Cowboy), Betty Jewel (The Girl), Jack Dougherty (Buck O'Hara), Christian J. Frank (The Stranger), El Brendel, Charles Crockett, Joe Butterworth, Guy Oliver, Guinn "Big Boy" Williams, Thelma Todd.

1927   WINGS   Paramount

Director: William A. Wellman
Producer: Lucien Hubbard
Scenarists: Hope Loring, Louis D. Lighton
Photographer: Harry Perry
Editor: Lucien Hubbard
Associate Producer: B. P. Schulberg
Titler: Julian Johnson
Editor-in-Chief: E. Lloyd Sheldon
Musical Score: John S. Zamecnik
Based on an original story by John Monk Saunders
Cast: Clara Bow (Mary Preston), Charles "Buddy" Rogers (Jack Powell), Richard Arlen (David Armstrong), Jobyna Ralston (Sylvia Lewis),

Gary Cooper (Cadet White), Arlette Marchal (Celeste), El Brendel
(Herman Schwimpf), "Gunboat" Smith (The Sergeant), Richard
Tucker (Air Commander), Julia Swayne Gordon (Mrs. Armstrong),
Henry B. Walthall (Mr. Armstrong), George Irving (Mr. Powell),
Hedda Hopper (Mrs. Powell), Nigel de Brulier (Peasant), Roscoe Karns
(Lt. Cameron), James Pierce (MP), Carl Von Haartman (German
Officer).

1927   NEVADA   Paramount

Director: John Waters
Scenarists: John Stone, L. G. Rigby
Photographer: C. Edgar Schoenbaum
Titler: Jack Conway
Based on the novel by Zane Grey
Cast: Gary Cooper (Jim Lacy), Thelma Todd (Hettie Ide), William
Powell (Clan Dillion), Philip Strange (Ben Ide), Ernie S. Adams (Cash
Burridge), Christian J. Frank (Sheriff of Winthrop), Ivan Christy (Caw-
thorne), Guy Oliver (Sheriff of Lineville), Evelyn Brent.

1927   THE LAST OUTLAW   Paramount

Director: Arthur Rossen
Scenarists: John Stone, J. Walter Ruben
Adaptation: J. Walter Ruben
Photographer: James Murray
Assistant Director: George Crook
Based on a story by Richard Allen Gates
Cast: Gary Cooper (Sheriff Buddy Hale), Betty Jewel (Janet Lane),
Jack Luden (Ward Lane), Herbert Prior (Bert Wagner), Jim Corey
(Butch), Billy Butts (Chick), and Flash, the Wonder Horse.

1928   BEAU SABREUR   Paramount

Director: John Waters
Scenarist: Tom J. Geraghty
Photographer: C. Edgar Schoenbaum
Production Supervisor: Milton E. Hoffman
Assistant Director: Richard Johnston
Editor-in-Chief: E. Lloyd Sheldon
Editor: Rose Lowenger
Titler: Julian Johnson
Based on the novel *Beau Geste* by Percival Christopher Wren
Cast: Gary Cooper (Major Henri de Beaujolais), Evelyn Brent (Mary

Vanbrugh), Noah Beery (Sheikh El Hamel), William Powell (Becque), Roscoe Karns (Buddy), Mitchell Lewis (Suleiman the Strong), Arnold Kent (Raoul de Redon), Raoul Paoli (Dufour), Joan Standing (Maudie), Frank Reicher (General de Beaujolais), Oscar Smith (Djikki), and Alberto Morin.

1928   LEGION OF THE CONDEMNED   Paramount

Director and Producer: William A. Wellman
Associate Producer: E. Lloyd Sheldon
Scenarists: John Monk Saunders, Jean De Limur
Photographer: Henry Gerrard
Editor: Alyson Shaffer
Titler: George Marion, Jr.
Editor: E. Lloyd Sheldon
Based on an original story by John Monk Saunders
Cast: Fay Wray (Christine Charteris), Gary Cooper (Gale Price), Barry Norton (Byron Dashwood), Lane Chandler (Charles Holabird), Francis McDonald (Gouzalo Vasques), Albert Conti (Von Hohendorff), Charlotte Bird (Tart in Cafe), Voya George (A Gambler), Freeman Wood (A Bored Man), E. H. Calvert (The Commandant), Toto Guette (A Mechanic).

1928   DOOMSDAY   Paramount

Director and Producer: Rowland V. Lee
Scenarist: Donald W. Lee
Adaptation: Doris Anderson
Photographer: Henry Gerrard
Editor: Robert Bassler
Titler: Julian Johnson
Based on the novel by Warwick Deeping
Cast: Florence Vidor (Mary Viner), Gary Cooper (Arnold Furze), Lawrence Grant (Percival Fream), Charles A. Stevenson (Captain Hesketh Viner).

1928   HALF A BRIDE   Paramount

Director: Gregory La Cava
Scenarists: Doris Anderson, Percy Heath
Photographer: Victor Milner
Editor: Verna Willis

Titler: Julian Johnson
Production Supervisor: B. P. Fineman
Based on the story "White Hands" by Arthur Stringer
Cast: Esther Ralston (Patience Winslow), Gary Cooper (Captain Edmunds), William J. Worthington (Mr. Winslow), Freeman Wood (Jed Session), Mary Doran (Betty Brewster), Guy Oliver (Chief Engineer), Ray Gallagher (Second Engineer).

1928   LILAC TIME   A First National Picture

Director and Producer: George Fitzmaurice
Scenarist: Carey Wilson
Adaptation: Willis Goldbeck
Titler: George Marion, Jr.
Musical Score: Nathaniel Shilkret
Editor: Al Hall
Photographer: Sid Hickox
Song: "Jeannine, I Dream of Lilac Time", Music by Nathaniel Shilkret and Lyrics by L. Wolfe Gilbert
Based on the play by Jane Cowl and Jane Murfin and the book by Guy Fowler
Cast: Colleen Moore (Jeannine), Gary Cooper (Captain Philip Blythe), Eugenie Besserer (Widow Berthelot), Kathryn McGuire (Lady Iris), Cleve Moore (Flight Commander), Arthur Lake (The Unlucky One), Jack Stone (The Kid), Dan Dowling, Stuart Knox, Jack Ponder, Harlan Hilton (Aviators), George Cooper (Sergeant Hawkins), Edward Dillon (Corporal "Smitty"), Emile Chautard (The Mayor), Edward Clayton (The Enemy Ace), Paul Hurst (Hospital Orderly), Philo McCullough (German Officer), Nelson McDowell (A French Drummer), and Richard Jarvis.

1928   THE FIRST KISS   Paramount

Director and Producer: Rowland V. Lee
Scenarist: John Farrow
Photographer: Alfred Gilks
Editor: Lee Helen
Titler: Tom Reed
Based on the story "Four Brothers" by Tristram Tupper
Cast: Fay Wray (Anna Lee), Gary Cooper (Mulligan Talbot), Lane Chandler (William Talbot), Leslie Fenton (Carol Talbot), Paul Fix (Ezra Talbot), Malcolm Williams ("Pap"), Monroe Owsley (Other Suitor).

1928   THE SHOPWORN ANGEL   Paramount

Director: Richard Wallace
Producer: Louis D. Lighton
Scenarists: Howard Estabrook, Albert Shelby Le Vino
Photographer: Charles Lang
Editor: Robert Bassler
Titler: Tom Miranda
Song: "A Precious Little Thing Called Love" by Lew Davis and J. Fred
Coots
Based on the story by Dana Burnet
Cast: Nancy Carroll (Daisy Heath), Gary Cooper (William Tyler), Paul
Lukas (Bailey), Emmett King (The Chaplain), Mildred Washington
(Daisy's Maid), and Roscoe Karns.

1929   WOLF SONG   Paramount

Director and Producer: Victor Fleming
Scenarists: John Farrow, Keene Thompson
Photographer: Allen Siegler
Editor: Eda Warren
Associate Producer: B. P. Fineman
Assistant Director: Henry Hathaway
Songs: "Mi Amado" and "Yo Te Amo Means I Love You" by Richard
Whiting (Music) and Alfred Bryan (Lyrics)
Titler: Julian Johnson
Based on the novel by Harvey Fergusson
Cast: Gary Cooper (Sam Lash), Lupe Velez (Lola Salazar), Louis Wol-
heim (Gullion), Constantine Romanoff (Rube Thatcher), Michael Va-
vitch (Don Solomon Salazar), Ann Brody (Duenna), Russell (Russ)
Columbo (Ambrosia Guiterrez), Augustina Lopez (Louisa), George
Rigas (Black Wolf), Leone Lane (Dance Hall Girl).

1929   BETRAYAL   Paramount

Director: Lewis Milestone
Scenarists: Hans Kraly, Leo Birinsky
Photographer: Henry Gerrard
Musical Score: J. S. Zamecnik
Editor: Del Andrews
Associate Producer: David O. Selznick
Titler: Julian Johnson
Based on a story by Victor Schertzinger and Nicholas Soussanin

Cast: Emil Jannings (Poldi Moser), Esther Ralston (Vroni), Gary Cooper (Andre Frey), Jada Welles (Hans), Douglas Haig (Peter), Bodil Rosing (Andre's mother).

1929   THE VIRGINIAN   Paramount

Director: Victor Fleming
Producer: Louis D. Lighton
Scenarist: Howard Estabrook
Photographers: J. Roy Hunt, Edward Cronjager
Editor: William Shea
Sound Recorder: M. M. Paggie
Assistant Director: Henry Hathaway
Titler: Joseph L. Mankiewicz
Based on the novel by Owen Wister and play by Kirk La Shelle
Cast: Gary Cooper (The Virginian), Walter Huston (Trampas), Richard Arlen (Steve), Mary Brian (Molly Wood), Chester Conklin (Uncle Hughey), Eugene Pallette (Honey Wiggin), E. H. Calvert (Judge Henry), Helen Ware ("Ma" Taylor), Victor Potel (Nebraskey), Tex Young (Shorty), Charles Stevens (Pedro), Jack Pennick (Slim), George Chandler (Ranch Hand), Willie Fung (Hong, the cook), George Morrell (Reverend Dr. McBride), Ernie S. Adams (Saloon Singer), Ethan Laidlaw (Posseman), Ed Brady (Greasy), Bob Kortman (Henchman), James Mason (Jim), Fred Burns (Ranch Hand), Nena Quartero (Girl in Bar).

1930   ONLY THE BRAVE   Paramount

Director: Frank Tuttle
Scenarist: Edward E. Paramore, Jr.
Adaptation: Agnes Brand Leahy
Photographer: Harry Fischbeck
Editor: Doris Drought
Based on a story by Keene Thompson
Cast: Gary Cooper (Captain James Braydon), Mary Brian (Barbara Calhoun), Phillips Holmes (Captain Robert Darrington), James Neill (Vance Calhoun), Morgan Farley (Tom Wendell), Guy Oliver (General U. S. Grant), John H. Elliot (General Robert E. Lee), E. H. Calvert (The Colonel), Virginia Bruce (Elizabeth), Elda Voelkel (Lucy Cameron), William Le Maire (The Sentry), Freeman S. Wood (Elizabeth's Lover), Lalo Encinas (General Grant's Secretary), Clinton Rosemond (Butler), William Bakewell (Young Lieutenant).

1930   PARAMOUNT ON PARADE   Paramount

Directors: Dorothy Arzner, Otto Brower, Edmund Goulding, Victor
Heerman, Edwin H. Knopf, Rowland V. Lee, Ernst Lubitsch, Lothar
Mendez, Victor Schertzinger, Edward Sutherland, Frank Tuttle
Producer: Albert A. Kaufman
Production Supervisor: Elsie Janis
Photographers: Harry Fischbeck, Victor Milner
Production Designer: John Wenger
Editor: Merrill White
Cast: Richard Arlen, Jean Arthur, William Austin, George Bancroft,
Clara Bow, Evelyn Brent, Mary Brian, Clive Brook, Virginia Bruce,
Nancy Carroll, Ruth Chatterton, Maurice Chevalier, Gary Cooper,
Leon Errol, Stuart Erwin, Kay Francis, Skeets Gallagher, Harry
Green, Mitzi Green, James Hall, Phillips Holmes, Helen Kane, Dennis
King, Abe Lyman and His Band, Fredric March, Nino Martini, David
Newell, Jack Oakie, Warner Oland, Zelma O'Neal, Eugene Pallette,
Joan Peers, William Powell, Charles "Buddy" Rogers, Lillian Roth,
Stanley Smith, Fay Wray and Jackie Searle, Mischa Auer, Cecil Cun-
ningham, Henry Fink, Jack Luden, Jack Pennick, Rolfe Sedan, Robert
Greig, Iris Adrian.

1930   THE TEXAN   Paramount

Director: John Cromwell
Scenarist: Daniel N. Rubin
Adaptation: Oliver H. P. Garrett
Photographer: Victor Milner
Editor: Verna Willis
Assistant Director: Henry Hathaway
Associate Producer: Hector Turnbull
From "A Double-Dyed Deceiver" by O. Henry
Cast: Gary Cooper (Enrique ["Quico"], The Llano Kid), Fay Wray (Con-
suelo), Emma Dunn (Señora Ibarra), Oscar Apfel (Thacker), James
Marcus (John Brown), Donald Reed (Nick Ibarra), Soledad Jiminez
(The Duenna), Veda Buckland (Mary, The Nurse), Cesar Vanoni (Pas-
quale), Edwin J. Brady (Henry), Enrique Acosta (Sixto), Romualdo
Tirado (Cabman), Russell (Russ) Columbo (Singing Cowboy).

1930   SEVEN DAYS' LEAVE   Paramount

Director: Richard Wallace
Producer: Louis D. Lighton
Scenarists: John Farrow, Don Totheroh
Photographer: Charles Lang

Editor: George Nicholls, Jr.
Assistant Director: John Cromwell
Based on the play *The Old Lady Shows Her Medals* by Sir James M. Barrie
Cast: Gary Cooper (Kenneth Dowey), Beryl Mercer (Sarah Ann Dowey), Daisy Belmore (Emma Mickelham), Nora Cecil (Amelia Twymley), Tempe Piggott (Mrs. Haggerty), Arthur Hoyt (Mr. Willings), Arthur Metcalfe (Colonel), Basil Radford (Corporal), Larry Steers (Aide de Camp).

1930   THE MAN FROM WYOMING   Paramount

Director: Rowland V. Lee
Scenarists: John V. A. Weaver, Albert Shelby Le Vino
Photographer: Harry Fischbeck
Editor: Robert Bassler
From a story by Joseph Moncure March and Lew Lipton
Cast: Gary Cooper (Jim Baker), June Collyer (Patricia Hunter), Regis Toomey (Jersey), Morgan Farley (Lieutenant Lee), E. H. Calvert (Major-General Hunter), Mary Foy (Inspector), Emile Chautard (French Mayor), Ed Deering (Sergeant), William B. Davidson (Major), Ben Hall (Orderly).

1930   THE SPOILERS   Paramount

Director: Edward Carewe
Scenarists: Agnes Brand Leahy, Bartlett Cormack
Photographer: Harry Fischbeck
Editor: William Shea
Based on the book by Rex Beach
Cast: Gary Cooper (Glenister), Kay Johnson (Helen Chester), Betty Compson (Cherry Malotte), William "Stage" Boyd (McNamara), Harry Green (Herman), Slim Summerville (Slapjack Slim), James Kirkwood (Dextry), Lloyd Ingraham (Judge Stillman), Oscar Apfel (Voorhees), George Irving (William Wheaton), Knute Ericson (Ship Captain), Merrill McCormick (Miner), Charles K. French (Man in Bar).

1930   MOROCCO   Paramount

Director: Josef von Sternberg
Scenarist: Jules Furthman

Photographer: Lee Garmes
Art Director: Hans Dreier
Editor: Sam Winston
Musical Score: Karl Hajos
Based on the novel *Amy Jolly* by Benno Vigny
Cast: Gary Cooper (Tom Brown), Marlene Dietrich (Amy Jolly), Adolphe Menjou (Kennington), Ullrich Haupt (Adjutant Caesar), Juliette Compton (Anna Dolores), Francis McDonald (Corporal Tatoche), Albert Conti (Colonel Quinnevieres), Eve Southern (Madame Caesar), Michael Visaroff (Barratire), Paul Porcase (Lo Tinto), Theresa Harris (Camp Follower).

1931   FIGHTING CARAVANS   Paramount

Directors: Otto Brower, David Burton
Scenarists: Edward G. Paramore, Jr., Keene Thompson, Agnes Brand Leahy
Photographers: Lee Garmes, Henry Gerrard
Editor: William Shea
Art Director: Robert Odell
Based on the novel by Zane Grey
Cast: Gary Cooper (Clint Belmet), Lilly Damita (Felice), Ernest Torrence (Bill Jackson), Fred Kohler (Lee Murdock), Tully Marshall (Jim Bridger), Eugene Pallette (Seth Higgins), Roy Stewart (Couch), May Boley (Jane), James Farley (Amos), James Marcus (The Blacksmith), Eve Southern (Faith), Donald MacKenzie (Gus), Syd Saylor (Charlie), E. Alyn Warren (Barlow), Frank Campeau (Jeff Moffitt), Charles Winninger (Marshal), Frank Hagney (The Renegade), Jane Darwell (Pioneer Woman), Irving Bacon (Barfly), Harry Semels (Brawler), Iron Eyes Cody (Indian After Firewater).

1931   CITY STREETS   Paramount

Director: Rouben Mamoulian
Producer: E. Lloyd Sheldon
Scenarist: Oliver H. P. Garrett
Adaptation: Max Marcin
Photographer: Lee Garmes
Editor: William Shea
Based on an original screenplay by Dashiell Hammett
Cast: Gary Cooper (The Kid), Sylvia Sidney (Nan), Paul Lukas (Big Boy Maskal), William "Stage" Boyd (McCoy), Guy Kibbee (Pop Cooley), Stanley Fields (Blackie), Wynne Gibson (Agnes), Betty Sinclair (Pansy), Barbara Leonard (Girl), Terry Carroll (Esther March), Edward Le Saint (Shooting Gallery Patron), Robert Homans (Inspector),

Willard Robertson (Detective), Hal Price (Shooting Gallery Onlooker), Ethan Laidlaw (Killer at Prison), George Regas (Machine-gunner), Bob Kortman (Servant), Leo Willis (Henchman), Bill Elliott (Dance Extra), Allan Cavan (Cop), Bert Hanlon (Baldy), Matty Kemp (Man Stabbed With Fork), and Kate Drain Lawson.

1931   I TAKE THIS WOMAN   Paramount

Director: Marion Gering
Scenarist: Vincent Lawrence
Photographer: Victor Milner
Assistant Director: Slavko Vorkapich
Based on the novel *Lost Ecstasy* by Mary Roberts Rinehart
Cast: Gary Cooper (Tom McNair), Carole Lombard (Kay Dowling), Helen Ware (Aunt Bessie), Lester Vail (Herbert Forrest), Charles Trowbridge (Mr. Dowling), Clara Blandick (Sue Barnes), Gerald Fielding (Bill Wentworth), Albert Hart (Jake Mallory), Guy Oliver (Sid), Syd Saylor (Shorty), Mildred Van Dorn (Clara Hammell), Leslie Palmer (Phillips), Ara Haswell (Nora), Frank Darien (The Station Agent), David Landau (The Circus Boss).

1931   HIS WOMAN   Paramount

Director: Edward Sloman
Scenarists: Adelaide Heilbron, Melville Baker
Photographer: William Steiner
Editor: Arthur Ellis
Based on the novel *The Sentimentalist* by Dale Collins
Cast: Gary Cooper (Captain Sam Whalan), Claudette Colbert (Sally Clark), Averill Harris (Mate Gatson), Richard Spiro (Sammy), Douglass Dumbrille (Alisandroe), Raquel Davida (Maria Estella), Hamtree Harrington (Aloysius), Sidney Easton (Mark), Joan Blair (Gertrude), Charlotte Winters (Flo), Herschell Mayall (Mr. Morrisey), Joe Spurin Calleia (The Agent), Lon Haschal (Captain of Schooner), Harry Davenport (Customs Inspector), John T. Doyle (Doctor), Edward Keane (Boatswain), Barton MacLane, Donald McBride, Preston Foster (Crewmen).

1932   MAKE ME A STAR   Paramount

Director: William Beaudine
Adaptation: Sam Wintz, Walter De Leon, Arthur Kober
Photographer: Allen Siegler

Editor: Leroy Stone
Based on the book *Merton of the Movies* by Harry Leon Wilson and the subsequent play by George S. Kaufman and Moss Hart
Cast: Stuart Erwin (Merton Gill), Joan Blondell ("Flips" Montague), Zasu Pitts (Mrs. Scudder), Ben Turpin (Ben), Charles Sellon (Mr. Gashwiler), Florence Roberts (Mrs. Gashwiler), Helen Jerome Eddy (Tessie Kearns), Arthur Hoyt (Hardy Powell), Dink Templeton (Buck Benson), Ruth Donnelly (The Countess), Sam Hardy (Jeff Baird), Oscar Apfel (Henshaw), Frank Mills (Chuck Collins), Polly Walters (Doris Randall).
Guest Stars (As Themselves): Tallulah Bankhead, Clive Brook, Maurice Chevalier, Claudette Colbert, Gary Cooper, Phillips Holmes, Fredric March, Jack Oakie, Charlie Ruggles, Sylvia Sidney.

1932   THE DEVIL AND THE DEEP   Paramount

Director: Marion Gering
Scenarist: Benn Levy
Photographer: Charles Lang
Sound Recorder: J. A. Goodrich
Art Director: Bernard Herzbrun
Editor: Otho Lovering
Based on a story by Harry Hervey
Cast: Tallulah Bankhead (Pauline Sturm), Gary Cooper (Lieutenant Sempter), Charles Laughton (Commander Charles Sturm), Cary Grant (Lieutenant Jaeckel), Paul Porcasi (Hassan), Juliette Compton (Mrs. Planet), Henry Kolker (Hutton), Dorothy Christy (Mrs. Crimp), Arthur Hoyt (Mr. Planet), Gordon Westcott (Lieutenant Toll), Jimmie Dugan (Condover), Kent Taylor (A Friend), Lucien Littlefield (Shopkeeper), Peter Brocco (Wireless Operator), Wilfred Lucas (Court Martial Judge), Dave O'Brien, Harry Guttman, George Magrill (Submarine Crewmen).

1932   IF I HAD A MILLION   Paramount

Directors: Ernst Lubitsch, Norman Taurog, Stephen Roberts, Norman McLeod, James Cruze, William A. Seiter, H. Bruce Humberstone
Scenarists: Claude Binyon, Whitney Bolton, Malcolm Stuart Boylan, John Bright, Sidney Buchanan, Lester Cole, Isabel Dawn, Boyce DeGaw, Walter De Leon, Oliver H. P. Garrett, Harvey Gates, Grover Jones, Ernst Lubitsch, Lawton Mackall, Joseph L. Mankiewicz, William Slavens McNutt, Seton I. Miller, Tiffany Thayer
Producer: Louis D. Lighton
Based on a story by Robert D. Andrews
Cast: Gary Cooper (Gallagher), George Raft (Eddie Jackson), Wynne Gibson (Violet), Charles Laughton (The Clerk), Jack Oakie (Mulligan),

Frances Dee (Mary Wallace), Charles Ruggles (Henry Peabody), Alison Skipworth (Emily), W. C. Fields (Rollo), Mary Boland (Mrs. Peabody), Roscoe Karns (O'Brien), May Robson (Mrs. Walker), Gene Raymond (John Wallace), Lucien Littlefield (Zeb), Richard Bennett (John Glidden), Grant Mitchell (The Prison Priest), Joyce Compton (Marie), Cecil Cunningham (Agnes), Irving Bacon (Chinaware Salesman), Blanche Frederici (Head Nurse, Old Ladies' Home), Gail Patrick (Secretary), Fred Kelsey, Willard Robertson (Doctors), Jack Pennick (Sailor), Berton Churchill (Warden), James Burtis (Jailer).

1932   A FAREWELL TO ARMS   Paramount

Director: Frank Borzage
Scenarists: Benjamin Glazer, Oliver H. P. Garrett
Photographer: Charles Lang
Editor: Otho Lovering
Art Directors: Hans Dreier, Roland Anderson
Assistant Directors: Arthur Jacobson, Lou Borzage
Based on the novel by Ernest Hemingway
Cast: Helen Hayes (Catherine Barkley), Gary Cooper (Lieutenant Frederic Henry), Adolphe Menjou (Major Rinaldi), Mary Philips (Helen Ferguson), Jack La Rue (The Priest), Blanche Frederici (Head Nurse), Henry Armetta (Bonello), George Humbert (Piani), Fred Malatesta (Manera), Mary Forbes (Miss Van Campen), Tom Ricketts (Count Greffi), Robert Couterio (Gordoni), Gilbert Emery (British Major), Peggy Cunningham (Molly), Agustino Borgato (Giulio), Paul Porcasi (Inn Keeper), Alice Adair (Cafe Girl).

1932   THE SLIPPERY PEARLS

A two-reel short made by the Masquers Club. Stars from all the studios appeared. Salaries were donated to Hollywood charities. The cast included Norma Shearer, Edward G. Robinson, Irene Dunne, Buster Keaton, Barbara Stanwyck, Joan Crawford, Gary Cooper, Laurel & Hardy, Loretta Young, Wynne Gibson, Fay Wray, Wallace Beery, and others.

1932   VOICE OF HOLLYWOOD   Tiffany

Short featuring Farina as the studio M.C., John Wayne as the announcer and Thelma Todd as "Miss Information." Guests included George Bancroft, El Brendel, Jackie Cooper, Lupe Velez, and Gary Cooper.

1933   TODAY WE LIVE   Metro-Goldwyn-Mayer

Director and Producer: Howard Hawks
Adaptation: Edith Fitzgerald, Dwight Taylor
Photographer: Oliver T. Marsh
Editor: Edward Curtis
Dialogue: William Faulkner
Art Director: Cedric Gibbons
From the story "Turnabout" by William Faulkner
Cast: Joan Crawford (Diana Boyce-Smith), Gary Cooper (Bogard), Robert Young (Claude), Franchot Tone (Ronnie), Roscoe Karns (McGinnis), Louise Closser Hale (Applegate), Rollo Lloyd (Major), Hilda Vaughn (Eleanor).

1933   ONE SUNDAY AFTERNOON   Paramount

Director: Stephen Roberts
Producer: Louis D. Lighton
Scenarists: William Slavens McNutt, Grover Jones
Photographer: Victor Milner
Editor: Ellsworth Hoagland
Art Directors: Hans Dreier, W. B. Ihnen
Based on the stage play by James Hagan
Cast: Gary Cooper (Biff Grimes), Fay Wray (Virginia Brush), Neil Hamilton (Hugo Barnstead), Frances Fuller (Amy Lind), Roscoe Karns (Snappy Downs), Jane Darwell (Mrs. Lind), Clara Blandick (Mrs. Brush), Sam Hardy (Dr. Startzman), Harry Schultz (Schneider), James Burtis (Dink Hoops), A. S. Byron (Foreman), Jack Clifford (Watchman).

1933   DESIGN FOR LIVING   Paramount

Director: Ernst Lubitsch
Producer: Ernst Lubitsch
Scenarist: Ben Hecht
Photographer: Victor Milner
Editor: Francis Marsh
Art Director: Hans Dreier
Based on the play by Noel Coward
Cast: Fredric March (Tom Chambers), Gary Cooper (George Curtis), Miriam Hopkins (Gilda Farrell), Edward Everett Horton (Max Plunkett), Franklin Pangborn (Mr. Douglas), Isabel Jewell (Lisping Stenographer), Harry Dunkinson (Mr. Egelbauer), Helena Phillips (Mrs. Egelbauer), James Donlin (Fat Man), Vernon Steele (First Manager), Thomas Braidon (Second Manager), Jane Darwell (Housekeeper),

Armand Kaliz (Mr. Burton), Adrienne D'Ambricourt (Propriet-
ress of Café), Wyndham Standing (Max's Butler), Nora Cecil
(Tom's Secretary), Grace Hayle (Woman on Staircase), Olaf Hytten
(Englishman at Train), Mary Gordon (Theatre Chambermaid),
Lionel Belmore, Charles K. French (Theatre Patrons), Rolfe Sedan
(Bed Salesman).

1933   ALICE IN WONDERLAND   Paramount

Director: Norman McLeod
Producer: Louis D. Lighton
Scenarists: Joseph L. Mankiewicz, William Cameron Menzies
Photographers: Henry Sharp, Bert Glennon
Editor: Ellsworth Hoagland
Musical Score: Dimitri Tiomkin
From *Alice's Adventures in Wonderland* and *Alice Through the Look-
ing-Glass* by Lewis Carroll
Cast: Charlotte Henry (Alice) and (in alphabetical order) Richard
Arlen (The Cheshire Cat), Roscoe Ates (The Fish), William Austin (The
Gryphon), Billy Barty (The White Pawn and The Baby), Billy Bevan
(The Two of Spades), Colin Campbell (Garden Frog) Harvey Clark
(Father William), Gary Cooper (The White Knight), Jack Duffy (Leg
of Mutton), Harry Ekezian (First Executioner), Leon Errol (Uncle
Gilbert), Louise Fazenda (The White Queen), W. C. Fields (Humpty
Dumpty), Alec B. Francis (The King of Hearts), Skeets Gallagher (The
White Rabbit), Meyer Grace (Third Executioner), Cary Grant (The
Mock Turtle), Ethel Griffies (Governess), Lillian Harmer (The Cook),
Raymond Hatton (The Mouse), Sterling Holloway (The Frog), Edward
Everett Horton (The Mad Hatter), Roscoe Karns (Tweedledee), Colin
Kenny (The Clock), Baby Le Roy (Joker), Lucien Littlefield (Father
William's Son), Mae Marsh (The Sheep), Charles McNaughton (Five
of Spades), Polly Moran (The Dodo Bird), Jack Oakie (Tweedledum),
Patsy O'Byrne (The Aunt), Edna May Oliver (The Red Queen), George
Ovey (Plum Pudding), May Robson (The Queen of Hearts), Charlie
Ruggles (The March Hare), Jackie Searl (Dormouse), Alison Skip-
worth (The Duchess), Ned Sparks (The Caterpillar), Will Stanton
(Seven of Spades), Ford Sterling (The White King), Joe Torillo (Second
Executioner), Jacqueline Wells (Alice's Sister).

1933   OPERATOR 13   Metro-Goldwyn-Mayer

Director: Richard Boleslavsky
Producer: Lucien Hubbard
Scenarists: Harry Thew, Zelda Sears, Eva Green
Photographer: George Folsey

Art Director: Cedric Gibbons
Editor: Frank Sullivan
Musical Score: Dr. William Axton
Cast: Marion Davies (Gail Loveless), Gary Cooper (Captain Jack Gailliard), Jean Parker (Eleanor), Katharine Alexander (Pauline), Ted Healy (Doctor Hitchcock), Russell Hardie (Littledale), Henry Wadsworth (John Pelham), Douglass Dumbrille (General Stuart), Willard Robertson (Captain Channing), Fuzzy Knight (Sweeney), Sidney Toler (Major Allen), Robert McWade (Colonel Sharpe), Marjorie Gateson (Mrs. Shackleford), Wade Boteler (Gaston), Walter Long (Operator 55), Hattie McDaniel (Cook), Francis McDonald (Denton), William H. Griffith (Mac), James Marcus (Staff Colonel), The Four Mills Brothers, Sam McDaniel (Old Bob), Buddy Roosevelt (Civilian), Frank McGlynn, Jr., Wheeler Oakman (Scouts) Don Douglas (Confederate Officer), Si Jenks (White Trash), Reginald Barlow (Colonel Storm), Ernie Alexander, Richard Powell (Confederate Sentries), Belle Daube (Mrs. Dandridge), Wilfred Lucas (Judge), Bob Stevenson (Guard), Martin Turner (Wickman), Frank Burt (Confederate Lieutenant), Wallie Howe (Clergyman), William Henry (Young Lieutenant), Richard Tucker (Execution Officer), Arthur Grant (Chaplain), Sherry Tansey (Officer), Lia Lance (Witch Woman), Charles Lloyd (Union Private), DeWitt C. Jennings (Artillery Man), Sam Ash (Lieutenant), Ernie Adams (Orderly), Clarence Hummel Wilson (Claybourne), Franklin Parker (John Hay), Claudia Coleman (Nurse), Sterling Holloway (Wounded Soldier), Sherry Hall (Army Officer), Douglas Fowley (Union Officer), Frank Marlowe (Confederate Officer), Fred Warren (Grant), John Elliott (Lee), Frank Leighton (Union Major), James C. Morton (Secret Service Man), Hattie Hill, John Kirkley (Slaves), John Larkin, Poppy Wilde (Party Guests).

1934   NOW AND FOREVER   Paramount

Director: Henry Hathaway
Producer: Louis D. Lighton
Scenarists: Vincent Lawrence, Sylvia Thalberg
Photographer: Harry Fischbeck
Editor: Ellsworth Hoagland
Art Directors: Hans Dreier, Robert Usher
Based on an original story, "Honor Bright," by Jack Kirkland and Melville Baker
Cast: Gary Cooper (Jerry Day), Carole Lombard (Toni Carstairs), Shirley Temple (Penelope Day), Sir Guy Standing (Felix Evans), Charlotte Granville (Mrs. J. H. P. Crane), Gilbert Emery (James Higginson), Henry Kolker (Mr. Clark), Tetsu Komai (Mr. Ling), Jameson Thomas

(Chris Carstairs), Harry Stubbs (Mr. O'Neill), Egon Bercher (Doctor), Andre Charon (Inspector), Agostino Borgato (Fisherman), Richard Loo (Hotel Clerk), Look Chan (Assistant Manager), Akim Tamiroff (French Jeweller), Buster Phelps (Boy With Skates), Rolfe Sedan (Hotel Manager), Ynez Seabury (Girl), Sam Harris (Man at Pool), Grace Hale (Lady in Store), Ronnie Cosby (little boy).

1935   THE LIVES OF A BENGAL LANCER   Paramount

Director: Henry Hathaway
Producer: Louis D. Lighton
Scenarists: Waldemar Young, John L. Balderston, Achmed Abdullah
Adaptation: Grover Jones, William Slavens McNutt
Photographer: Charles Lang
Art Directors: Hans Dreier, Roland Anderson
Editor: Ellsworth Hoagland
Musical Score: Milan Roder
Based on the novel by Major Francis Yeats-Brown
Cast: Gary Cooper (Lieutenant McGregor), Franchot Tone (Lieutenant Fortesque), Richard Cromwell (Lieutenant Stone), Sir Guy Standing (Colonel Stone), C. Aubrey Smith (Major Hamilton), Monte Blue (Hamzulia Khan), Kathleen Burke (Tania Volkanskaya), Colin Tapley (Lieutenant Barrett), Douglass Dumbrille (Mohammed Khan), Akim Tamiroff (Emir), Jameson Thomas (Hendrickson), Noble Johnson (Ram Singh), Lumsden Hare (Major General Woodley), J. Carrol Nash (Grand Vizier), Rollo Lloyd (The Ghazi [Prisoner]), Charles Stevens (McGregor's Servant), Boswhan Singh (Nuim Shah), Abdul Hassan (Ali Hamdi), Mischa Auer (Afridi), Clive Morgan (Lieutenant Norton), Eddie Das (Servant), Leonid Kinskey (Snake Charmer), Hussain Hasri (Muezzin), James Warwick (Lieutenant Gilhooley), George Regas (Kushal Khan), Major Sam Harris, Carli Taylor (British Officers), Ram Singh, Jamiel Hasson, James Bell, General Ikonnikoff, F. A. Armenta (Indian Officers), Claude King (Experienced Clerk), Reginald Sheffield (Novice), Ray Cooper (Assistant to Grand Vizier), Myra Kinch (Solo Dancer), Lya Lys (Girl on Train).

1935   THE WEDDING NIGHT   A Samuel Goldwyn
Picture Released Through United Artists

Director: King Vidor
Producer: Samuel Goldwyn
Scenarist: Edith Fitzgerald
Photographer: Gregg Toland

Art Director: Richard Day
Musical Director: Alfred Newman
Editor: Stuart Heisler
Based on an original story by Edwin Knopf
Cast: Gary Cooper (Tony Barrett), Anna Sten (Manya), Ralph Bellamy (Fredrik), Helen Vinson (Dora Barrett), Siegfried Rumann (Nowak), Esther Dale (Kaise), Leonid Snegoff (Sobieski), Eleanor Wesselhoeft (Mrs. Sobieski), Milla Davenport (Grandmother), Agnes Anderson (Helena), Hilda Vaughn (Hezzie), Walter Brennan (Jenkins), Douglas Wood (Heywood), George Meeker (Gilly), Hedi Shope (Anna), Otto Yamaoka (Taka), Violet Axzelle (Frederica), Ed Ebele (Uncle), Robert Louis Stevenson II, Auguste Tollaire, Dave Wengren, George Magrill, Bernard Siegel, Harry Semels (Men at Wedding), Robert Bolder (Doctor), Alphonse Mantell (Waiter), Miami Alvarez (Guest at Party), Constance Howard, Jay Eaton, Jay Belasco (Guests at Party), Richard Powell (Truck Driver).

1935   PETER IBBETSON   Paramount

Director: Henry Hathaway
Producer: Louis D. Lighton
Scenarists: Vincent Lawrence, Waldemar Young
Adaptation: Constance Collier
Additional Scenes: John Meehan, Edwin Justus Mayer
Photographer: Charles Lang
Musical Score: Ernst Toch
Editor: Stuart Heisler
Art Directors: Hans Dreier, Robert Usher
Musical Director: Nat W. Finston
Based on the novel by George du Maurier and play by John Nathaniel Raphael
Cast: Gary Cooper (Peter Ibbetson), Ann Harding (Mary, Duchess of Towers), John Halliday (Duke of Towers), Ida Lupino (Agnes), Douglass Dumbrille (Colonel Forsythe), Virginia Weidler (Mimsey), Dickie Moore (Gogo), Doris Lloyd (Mrs. Dorian), Elsa Buchanan (Madame Pasquier), Christian Rub (Major Duquesnoit), Donald Meek (Mr. Slade), Gilbert Emery (Wilkins), Marguerite Namara (Madame Ginghi), Elsa Prescott (Katherine), Marcelle Corday (Maid), Adrienne D'Ambricourt (Nun), Theresa Maxwell Conover (Sister of Mercy), Colin Tapley (First Clerk), Clive Morgan (Second Clerk), Ambrose Barker (Third Clerk), Thomas Monk (Fourth Clerk), Blanche Craig (The Countess).

1935   STAR NIGHT AT THE COCONUT GROVE

Hollywood notables arrive at the night spot. Stars included Mary Pickford, Bing Crosby, Gary Cooper, Jack Oakie, John Mack Brown and Leo Carrillo.

1936   DESIRE   Paramount

Director: Frank Borzage
Producer: Ernst Lubitsch
Scenarists: Edwin Justus Mayer, Waldemar Young, Samuel Hoffen-
stein
Photographer: Charles Lang
Art Directors: Hans Dreier, Robert Usher
Musical Score: Frederick Hollander
Editor: William Shea
From a play by Hans Szekely and R. A. Stemmle
Cast: Marlene Dietrich (Madeleine de Beaupre), Gary Cooper (Tom Bradley), John Halliday (Carlos Margoli), William Frawley (Mr. Gibson), Ernest Cossart (Aristide Duval), Akim Tamiroff (Police Official), Alan Mowbray (Dr. Edouard Pauquet), Zeffie Tilbury (Aunt Olga), Harry Depp (Clerk), Marc Lawrence (Valet), Henry Antrim (Chauffeur), Armand Kaliz (Jewelry Clerk), Gaston Glass (Jewelry Clerk), Albert Pollet (French Policeman), George Davis (Garage Man), Constant Franke (Border Official), Robert O'Connor (Customs Official), Stanley Andrews (Customs Inspector), Rafael Blanco (Haywagon Driver), Alden Chase (Hotel Clerk), Tony Merlo (Waiter), Anna Delinsky (Servant), Alice Feliz (Pepi), Enrique Acosta (Pedro), George Mac Quarrie (Clerk With Gun), Isabel La Mal (Nurse), Oliver Eckhardt (Husband), Blanche Craig (Wife), Rollo Lloyd (Mayor's Office Clerk), Alfonso Pedrosa (Oxcart Driver).

1936   MR. DEEDS GOES TO TOWN   Columbia

Director and Producer: Frank Capra
Scenarist: Robert Riskin
Photographer: Joseph Walker
Editor: Gene Havlick
Musical Director: Howard Jackson
Art Director: Stephen Goosson
Based on the story "Opera Hat" by Clarence Budington Kelland
Cast: Gary Cooper (Longfellow Deeds), Jean Arthur (Babe Bennett), George Bancroft (MacWade), Lionel Stander (Cornelius Cobb), Doug-

lass Dumbrille (Cedar), Raymond Walburn (Walter), Margaret Mat-
zenauer (Madame Pomponi), H. B. Warner (Judge Walker), Warren
Hymer (Bodyguard), Muriel Evans (Theresa), Ruth Donnelly (Mabel
Dawson), Spencer Charters (Mal), Emma Dunn (Mrs. Meredith), Wyr-
ley Birch (Psychiatrist), Arthur Hoyt (Budington), Stanley Andrews
(James Cedar), Pierre Watkin (Arthur Cedar), John Wray (Farmer),
Christian Rub (Swenson), Jameson Thomas (Mr. Semple), Margaret
Seddon (Jane Faulkner), Margaret McWade (Amy Faulkner), Russell
Hicks (Dr. Malcolm), Gustav Von Seyffertitz (Dr. Frazier), Edward Le
Saint (Dr. Fosdick), Charles (Levison) Lane (Hallor), Irving Bacon
(Frank), George Cooper (Bob), Gene Morgan (Waiter), Walter Catlett
(Morrow), Edward Gargan (Second Bodyguard), Paul Hurst (First Dep-
uty), Paul Porcasi (Italian), Franklin Pangborn (Tailor), George F.
("Gabby") Hayes (Farmers' Spokesman), Mary Lou Dix (Shop Girl),
George Meeker (Brookfield), Barnett Parker (Butler), Patricia
Monroe, Lillian Ross (Hat Check Girls), Peggy Page (Cigarette Girl),
Janet Eastman (Shop Girl), Bud Flannigan (Dennis O'Keefe) (Re-
porter), Dale Van Sickel (Lawyer), and Cecil Cunningham, Bess Flow-
ers, Ann Doran, Billy Bevan, Beatrice Curtis, Beatrice Blinn, Pauline
Wagner, Frank Hammond, Charles Sullivan, Flo Wix, Hal Budlong,
Ethel Palmer, Juanita Crosland, Vacey O'Davoren.

1936   HOLLYWOOD BOULEVARD   Paramount

Director: Robert Florey
Producer: A. M. Botsford
Scenarist: Marguerite Roberts
Photographer: George Clemens
Cameraman: Karl Struss
Musical Score: Gregory Stone
Editor: Harvey Johnston
Cast: John Halliday (John Blakeford), Marsha Hunt (Patricia Blake-
ford), Robert Cummings (Jay Wallace), C. Henry Gordon (Jordan
Winslow), Frieda Inescort (Alice Winslow), Esther Ralston (Flora),
Esther Dale (Martha), Betty Compson (Betty), Albert Conti (Sanford),
Richard Powell (Moran), Rita La Roy (Nella), Oscar Apfel (Dr. Inslow),
Purnell Pratt (Mr. Steinman), Irving Bacon (Gus the Bartender), Lois
Kent (Little Girl), Gregory Gay (Russian Writer), Eleanore Whitney
(Herself), Tom Kennedy (Bouncer), Gertrude Simpson (Gossipy
Woman), and Hyman Fink, Thomas Jackson, Ed Cecil, Phil Tead,
Eddie Dunn, Monty Vandegrift, Frances Morris, Ruth Clifford, Joanne
Dudley.
And the following stars from the silent screen: Francis X. Bushman
(Director, Desert Scene), Maurice Costello (Director), Mae Marsh (Car-
lotta Blakeford), Charles Ray (Assistant Director), Herbert Rawlinson

(Manager, Grauman's Chinese Theatre), Jane Novak (Mrs. Steinman), Kathryn "Kitty" McHugh (Secretary), Bryant Washburn (Robert Martin), William Desmond (Guest), Jack Mulhall (Man at Bar), Roy D'Arcy (The Sheik), Creighton Hale (Man at Bar), Mabel Forrest (Mother), Bert Roach (Scenario Writer), Harry Myers, Jack Mower, Frank Mayo, Pat O'Malley (Themselves) and Gary Cooper (Guest at Bar).

1936   THE GENERAL DIED AT DAWN   Paramount

Director: Lewis Milestone
Producer: William Le Baron
Scenarist: Clifford Odets
Photographer: Victor Milner
Musical Score: Werner Janssen
Art Directors: Hans Dreier, Ernst Fegto
Editor: Eda Warren
Based on a novel by Charles G. Booth
Cast: Gary Cooper (O'Hara), Madeleine Carroll (Judy Perrie), Akim Tamiroff (General Yang), Dudley Digges (Mr. Wu), Porter Hall (Peter Perrie), William Frawley (Brighton), J. M. Kerrigan (Leach), Philip Ahn (Oxford), Lee Tung Foo (Mr. Chen), Leonid Kinsky (Stewart), Val Duran (Wong), Willie Fung (Bartender), Hans Fuerberg (Yang's Military Advisor), Sarah Edwards, Paul Harvey (American Couple), Spencer Chan (Killer), Harold Tong, Charles Leong, Thomas Chan, Harry Yip, Swan Yee, Kam Tong (House Boys), Frank Young (Clerk), Walter Wong (Bartender), Carol De Castro (Clerk), Barnett Parker (Englishman), Hans Von Morhart (Mandarin), Dudley Lee, Walter Lem, Thomas Lee, George Wong Wah (Waiters on Train), Tom Ung (Steward on Train), Taft Jung, Sam Laborador, Richard Young, Jung Kai, Harry Leong, Chan Suey, Paul Tom, Loo Loy, Quon Gong, Wong Fong, Leo Abbey, Bob Jowe (Guards), George Chan (Porter), and Clifford Odets, John O'Hara, Sidney Skolsky and Lewis Milestone (Reporters).

1936   THE PLAINSMAN   Paramount

Director and Producer: Cecil B. De Mille
Scenarists: Waldermar Young, Harold Lamb, Lynn Riggs
Adaptation: Jeanie MacPherson
Photographers: Victor Milner, George Robinson
Musical Score: George Antheil
Editor: Anne Bauchens
Associate Producer: William H. Pine
Art Directors: Hans Dreier, Roland Anderson
Musical Director: Boris Morros

Second Unit Director: Arthur Rossen
Set Decorator: A. E. Freudeman
Based on data from the stories *Wild Bill Hickok* by Frank J. Wistach
and *The Prince of Pistoleers* by Courtney Ryley Cooper and Grover
Jones.
Cast: Gary Cooper (Wild Bill Hickok), Jean Arthur (Calamity Jane),
James Ellison (Buffalo Bill Cody), Charles Bickford (John Latimer),
Porter Hall (Jack McCall), Helen Burgess (Louisa Cody), John Miljan
(General George Armstrong Custer), Victor Varconi (Painted Horse),
Paul Harvey (Chief Yellow Hand), Frank McGlynn, Sr. (Abraham
Lincoln), Granville Bates (Van Ellyn), Purnell Pratt (Captain Wood),
Pat Moriarty (Sgt. McGinnis), Charles Judels (Tony the Barber), An-
thony Quinn (A Cheyenne Warrior), George MacQuarrie (General
Merritt), George "Gabby" Hayes (Breezy), Fuzzy Knight (Dave),
George Ernest (An Urchin), Fred Kohler (Jack), Frank Albertson (A
Young Soldier), Harry Woods (Quartermaster Sergeant), Francis Mc-
Donald (Gambler on Boat), Francis Ford (Veteran), Irving Bacon (Sol-
dier), Edgar Dearing (Custer's Messenger), Edwin Maxwell (Stanton),
John Hyams (Schuyler Colfax), Bruce Warren (Captain of the *Lizzie
Gill*), Mark Strong (Wells Fargo Agent), Charlie Stevens (Injun
Charlie), Arthur Aylesworth, Douglas Wood, George Cleveland (Van
Ellyn's Associates), Lona Andre (Southern Belle), Leila McIntyre
(Mary Todd Lincoln), Harry Stubbs (John F. Usher), Davison Clark
(James Speed), C. W. Herzinger (William H. Seward), William Humph-
ries (Hugh McCulloch), Sidney Jarvis (Gideon Welles), Wadsworth
Harris (William Dennison), and Stanhope Wheatcroft, Noble Johnson,
Ted Oliver, James Mason, Bud Osborne, Franklyn Farnum, Lane
Chandler, Hank Bell, Louise Stuart, Gail Sheridan, Bud Flannigan
(Dennis O'Keefe), Blackjack Ward, Jane Keckley, Cora Shumway, Tex
Driscoll, Wilbur Mack, Francis Sayles.

1936   LA FIESTA DE SANTA BARBARA

Metro-Goldwyn-Mayer

Technicolor, short with Gary Cooper, Buster Keaton, Ida Lupino, Binnie Barnes, Robert Taylor, Toby Wing, Edmund Lowe, Warner Baxter,
and Harpo Marx, among others.

1937   SOULS AT SEA

Paramount

Director: Henry Hathaway
Scenarists: Grover Jones, Dale Van Every
Photographer: Charles Lang, Jr.
Editor: Ellsworth Hoagland
Art Directors: Hans Dreier, Roland Anderson

Musical Score: W. Franke Harling, Milan Roder, Bernhard (Bernard) Kaun, John Leipold
Musical Director: Borris Morros
Based on a story by Ted Lesser
Cast: Gary Cooper ("Nuggin" Taylor), George Raft (Powdah), Frances Dee (Margaret Tarryton), Harry Carey (Captain of *William Brown*), Olympe Bradna (Babsie), Robert Cummings (George Martin), Porter Hall (Court Prosecutor), George Zucco (Barton Woodley), Virginia Weidler (Tina), Joseph Schildkraut (Gaston de Bastonet), Gilbert Emery (Captain Martisel), Lucien Littlefield (Toymaker—Tina's Father), Paul Fix (Violinist), Tully Marshall (Pecora), Monte Blue (Mate of *William Brown*), Stanley Fields (Capt. Paul M. Granley), Fay Holden (Mrs. Martin), Clyde Cook (Hendry), Rollo Lloyd (Parchy), Wilson Benge (Doctor), Rolfe Sedan, Eugene Borden (Friends of de Bastonet), Lee Shumway (Mate), Ethel Clayton (Passenger), Harvey Clark (Court Clerk), Forbes Murray (Associate Justice), Davison Clark (Bailiff), William Stack (Judge), Charles Middleton (Foreman of Jury), Olaf Hytten (Proprietor), Forrester Harvey (Proprietor of Pub), Jane Weir (Barmaid), Lina Basquette (Brunette in Saloon), Pauline Haddon (Blonde), Lowell Drew (Jury Foreman), Paul Stanton (Defense Attorney), Leslie Francis (Woodley's Secretary), Robert Barrat (The Reverend), Constantine Romanoff (Drinker in Pub), Henry Wilcoxin (Lieutenant Tarryton).

1937   LEST WE FORGET   Metro-Goldwyn-Mayer

Short-subject message in behalf of the Will Rogers Memorial Hospital at Saranac Lake, New York. Gary Cooper and Harry Carey spoke informally about Will Rogers.

1938   THE ADVENTURES OF MARCO POLO
A Samuel Goldwyn Production
Released Through United Artists

Director: Archie Mayo
Producer: Samuel Goldwyn
Scenarist: Robert E. Sherwood
Photographer: Rudolph Mate
Musical Score: Hugo Friedhofer
Musical Director: Alfred Newman
Art Director: Richard Day
Set Decorator: Julia Heron
Editor: Fred Allen
Based on a story by N. A. Pogson
Cast: Gary Cooper (Marco Polo), Sigrid Gurie (Princess Kukachin),

Basil Rathbone (Ahmed), Ernest Truex (Binguccio), Alan Hale (Kaidu), George Barbier (Kublai Khan), Binnie Barnes (Nazama), Lana Turner (Nazama's maid), Stanley Fields (Bayan), Harold Huber (Toctai), H. B. Warner (Chen Tsu), Eugene Hoo (Chen Tsu's Son), Helen Quan (Chen Tsu's Daughter), Soo Yong (Chen Tsu's Wife), Mrs. Ng (Chen Tsu's Mother), Lotus Liu (Visahka), Ferdinand Gottschalk (Persian Ambassador), Henry Kolker (Nicolo Polo), Hale Hamilton (Maffeo Polo), Robert Greig (Chamberlain), Reginald Barlow (Giuseppe), Ward Bond (Mongol Guard), James Leong (Tartar Warrior), Dick Alexander (Ahmed's Aide), Jason Robards (Messenger), Gloria Youngblood, Diana Moncardo, Dora Young, Mia Schioka (Court Girls).

1938   BLUEBEARD'S EIGHTH WIFE   Paramount

Director: Ernst Lubitsch
Producer: Ernst Lubitsch
Scenarists: Charles Brackett, Billy Wilder
Adaptation: Charlton Andrews
Photographer: Leo Tover
Editor: William Shea
Art Directors: Hans Dreier, Robert Usher
Musical Score: Frederick Hollander, Werner R. Heymann
Based on a play by Alfred Savoir
Cast: Claudette Colbert (Nicole de Loiselle), Gary Cooper (Michael Brandon), Edward Everett Horton (The Marquis de Loiselle), David Niven (Albert de Regnier), Elizabeth Patterson (Aunt Hedwige), Herman Bing (Monsieur Pepinard), Warren Hymer (Kid Mulligan), Franklin Pangborn, Armand Cortes (Assistant Hotel Managers), Rolfe Sedan (Floorwalker), Lawrence Grant (Professor Urganzeff), Lionel Pape (Monsieur Potin), Tyler Brooke (Clerk), Tom Ricketts (Uncle Andre), Barlow Borland (Uncle Fernandel), Charles Halton (Monsieur de la Coste—President), Pauline Garon (Customer), Ray De Ravenne (Package Clerk), Sheila Darcy (Maid), Blanche Franke (Cashier), Joseph Romantini (Headwaiter), Alphonse Martell (Hotel Employee), Harold Minjir (Photographer), Gino Corrado (Waiter Who Carries Marquis), Terry Ray (later Ellen Drew) (Secretary), Leon Ames (Ex-Chauffeur), Olaf Hytten (Valet), Grace Goodall (Nurse).

1938   THE COWBOY AND THE LADY
A Samuel Goldwyn Picture
Released Through United Artists

Director: H. C. Potter
Producer: Samuel Goldwyn
Scenarists: S. N. Behrman, Sonya Levien

Photographer: Gregg Toland
Art Director: Richard Day
Musical Score: Alfred Newman
Editor: Sherman Todd
From an original story by Leo McCarey and Frank R. Adams.
Cast: Gary Cooper (Stretch), Merle Oberon (Mary Smith), Patsy Kelly (Katie Callahan), Walter Brennan (Sugar), Fuzzy Knight (Buzz), Mabel Todd (Elly), Henry Kolker (Mr. Smith), Harry Davenport (Uncle Hannibal Smith), Emma Dunn (Ma Hawkins), Walter Walker (Ames), Berton Churchill (Henderson), Charles Richman (Dillon), Fredrik Vogeding (Captain), Arthur Hoyt (Valet), Mabel Colcord (Old Woman), Billy Wayne, Ernie Adams, Russ Powell, Jack Baxley, Johnny Judd (Rodeo Riders).

1939   BEAU GESTE   Paramount

Director and Producer: William A. Wellman
Scenarist: Robert Carson
Photographers: Theodor Sparkuhl, Archie Stout
Editor: Thomas Scott
Art Directors: Hans Dreier, Robert Odell
Musical Score: Alfred Newman
Based on the novel *Beau Geste* by Percival Christopher Wren
Cast: Gary Cooper (Beau Geste), Ray Milland (John Geste), Robert Preston (Digby Geste), Brian Donlevy (Sergeant Markoff), Susan Hayward (Isobel Rivers), J. Carrol Naish (Rasinoff), Albert Dekker (Schwartz), Broderick Crawford (Buddy McMonigal), James Stephenson (Major Henri de Beaujolais), Heather Thatcher (Lady Patricia Brandon), G. P. Huntley, Jr. (Augustus Brandon), James Burke (Lieutenant Dufour), Henry Brandon (Renouf), Arthur Aylesworth (Renault), Harry Woods (Renoir), Harold Huber (Voisin), Stanley Andrews (Maris), Donald O'Connor (Beau at 12), Billy Cook (John at 10), Martin Spellman (Digby at 12), David Holt (Augustus at 12), Ann Gillis (Isobel at 10), Harvey Stephens (Lieutenant Martin), Barry Macollum (Krenke), Ronnie Rondell (Bugler), Frank Dawson (Burdon, the Butler), George Chandler (Cordier), Duke Green (Glock), Thomas Jackson (Colonel in Recruiting Office), Jerome Storm (Sergeant-Major), Joseph Whitehead (Sergeant), Harry Worth, Nestor Paiva (Corporals), George Regas, Francis McDonald (Arab Scouts), Carl Voss, Joe Bernard, Robert Perry, Larry Lawson, Henry Sylvester, Joseph William Cody (Legionnaires), Joe Colling (Trumpeter O. Leo), Gladys Jeans (Girl in Port Said Cafe), and Bob Kortman, Gino Corrado.

1939   THE REAL GLORY   A Samuel Goldwyn Picture
Released Through United Artists

Director: Henry Hathaway
Producer: Samuel Goldwyn
Scenarists: Jo Swerling, Robert R. Presnell
Photographer: Rudolph Mate
Musical Director: Alfred Newman
Editor: Daniel Mandell
Art Director: James Basevi
Associate Director: Richard Talmadge
Cast: Gary Cooper (Doctor Bill Canavan), Andrea Leeds (Linda Hartley), David Niven (Lieutenant McCool), Reginald Owen (Captain Hartley), Broderick Crawford (Lieutenant Larson), Kay Johnson (Mabel Manning), Charles Waldron (Padre Rafael), Russell Hicks (Captain Manning), Roy Gordon (Colonel Hatch), Benny Inocencio (Miguel), Vladimar Sokoloff (Datu), Rudy Robles (Lieutenant Yabo), Henry Kolker (The General), Tetsu Komai (Alipang), Elvira Rios (Mrs. Yabo), Luke Chan (Top Sergeant), Elmo Lincoln (U.S. Captain), John Villasin (Moro Priest), Charles Stevens (Cholera Victim), Karel Sorrell (Young Native Woman), Soledad Jimenez (Old Native Woman), Lucio Villegas, Nick Shaid (Old Native Men), Kam Tong (Filipino Soldier), Martin Wilkins, Bob Naihe, Satini Puailoa, Kalu Sonkur, Sr., George Kaluna, Caiyu Ambol (Moro Warriors).

1940   THE WESTERNER

A Samuel Goldwyn Picture
Released Through United Artists

Director: William Wyler
Producer: Samuel Goldwyn
Scenarists: Jo Swerling, Niven Busch
Photographer: Gregg Toland
Art Director: James Basevi
Musical Score: Dimitri Tiomkin
Editor: Daniel Mandell
Based on an original story by Stuart N. Lake
Cast: Gary Cooper (Cole Hardin), Walter Brennan (Judge Roy Bean), Doris Davenport (Jane-Ellen Mathews), Fred Stone (Caliphet Mathews), Paul Hurst (Chickenfoot), Chill Wills (Southeast), Charles Halton (Mort Borrow), Forrest Tucker (Wade Harper), Tom Tyler (King Evans), Arthur Aylesworth (Mr. Dixon), Lupita Tovar (Teresita), Julian Rivero (Juan Gomez), Lillian Bond (Lillie Langtry), Dana An-

drews (Bart Cobble), Roger Gray (Eph Stringer), Jack Pennick (Bantry), Trevor Bardette (Shad Wilkins), Bill Steele (Tex Cole), Blackjack Ward (Buck Harrigan), James "Jim" Corey (Lee Webb), Buck Moulton (Charles Evans), Ted Wells (Joe Lawrence), Joe De La Cruz (Mex), Frank Cordell (Man), Philip Connor (Johnyancy), Capt. C. E. Anderson (Hezekiah Willever), Arthur "Art" Mix (Seth Tucker), William Gillis (Leon Beauregard), Buck Connor (Abraham Wilson), Dan Borzage (Joe Yates), Speed Hanson (Walt McGary), Gertrude Bennett (Abigail), Miriam Sherwin (Martha), Annabelle Rousseau (Elizabeth), Helen Foster (Janice), Connie Leon (Langtry's Maid), Charles Coleman (Langtry's Manager), Lew Kelly (Ticket Man), Heinie Conklin (Man at Window), Lucien Littlefield (A Stranger), Corbet Morris (Orchestra Leader), Stanley Andrews (Sheriff), Phil Tead (Prisoner), Henry Roquemore (Stage Manager), Bill Bauman (Man Getting Haircut), Hank Bell (Deputy).

1940   NORTHWEST MOUNTED POLICE   Paramount

Director and Producer: Cecil B. De Mille
Scenarists: Alan Le May, Jesse Lasky, Jr., C. Gardner Sullivan
Photographers: Victor Milner, W. Howard Greene
Editor: Anne Bauchens
Art Directors: Hans Dreier, Roland Anderson
Associate Producer: William H. Pine
Musical Score: Victor Young
Dialogue Supervisor: Edwin Maxwell
Based on "Royal Canadian Mounted Police" by R. C. Fetherstonhaugh
Cast: Gary Cooper (Dusty Rivers), Madeleine Carroll (April Logan), Paulette Goddard (Louvette Corbeau), Preston Foster (Sgt. Jim Brett), Robert Preston (Constable Ronnie Logan), George Bancroft (Jacques Corbeau), Lynne Overman (Tod McDuff), Akim Tamiroff (Dan Duroc), Walter Hampden (Chief Big Bear), Lon Chaney, Jr. (Shorty), Montague Love (Inspector Cabot), Francis McDonald (Louis Riel), George E. Stone (Johnny Pelang), William Robertson (Superintendent Harrington), Regis Toomey (Const. Jerry Moore), Richard Denning (Const. Thornton), Robert Ryan (Const. Dumont), Douglas Kennedy (Const. Carter), Clara Blandick (Mrs. Burns), Ralph Byrd (Const. Ackroyd), Lane Chandler (Const. Fyffe), Julia Faye (Wapiskan), Jack Pennick (Sgt. Field), Rod Cameron (Corporal Underhill), James Seay (Const. Fenton), Jack Chapin (Bugler), Eric Alden (Const. Kent), Wallace Reid, Jr. (Const. Rankin), Bud Geary (Const. Herrick), Evan Thomas (Capt. Gower), Davidson Clark (Surgeon Roberts), Chief Thundercloud (Wandering Spirit), Harry Burns (The Crow), Lou Merril (Lesure), Ynez Seabury (Mrs. Shorty), Phillip Terry (Const. Judson), Soledad

Jiminez (Grandmother), Kermit Maynard (Const. Porter), Anthony Caruso, Paul Sutton (Indians).

1940   MEET JOHN DOE   Warner Brothers

Director: Frank Capra
Producer: Frank Capra
Scenarist: Robert Riskin
Photographer: George Barnes
Musical Score: Dimitri Tiomkin
Editor: Daniel Mandell
Art Director: Stephen Goosson
From an original story by Richard Connell and Robert Presnell
Cast: Gary Cooper (John Doe—Long John Willoughby), Barbara Stanwyck (Ann Mitchell), Edward Arnold (D. B. Norton), Walter Brennan (Colonel), James Gleason (Henry Connell), Spring Byington (Mrs. Mitchell), Gene Lockhart (Mayor Lovett), Rod La Rocque (Ted Sheldon), Irving Bacon (Beany), Regis Toomey (Bert Hansen), Warren Hymer (Angelface), Aldrich Bowker (Pop Dwyer), Ann Doran (Mrs. Hansen), Sterling Holloway (Dan), Mrs. Gardner Crane (Mrs. Brewster), J. Farrell MacDonald (Sourpuss Smithers), Pat Flaherty (Mike), Carlotta Jelm, Tina Thayer (Ann's Sisters), Bennie Bartlett (Red the Office Boy), Sarah Edwards (Mrs. Hawkins), Stanley Andrews (Weston), Andrew Tombes (Spencer), Pierre Watkin (Hammett), Garry Owen (Sign Painter), Charlie Wilson (Charlie Dawson), Gene Morgan (Mug), Cyril Thornton (Butler), Edward Earle (Radio M.C.), Mike Frankovich (Radio Announcer), Harry Holman (Mayor Hawkins), Bess Flowers (Newspaper Secretary), Emma Tansey (Mrs. Delancy), Mitchell Lewis (Bennett), Billy Curtis, Johnny Fern (Midgets), Vernon Dent (Man), Suzanne Carnahan (later Susan Peters), Maris Wrixon (Autograph Hounds), Vaughn Glaser (Governor), Selmer Jackson, Knox Manning, John B. Hughes (Radio Announcers at Convention), The Hall Johnson Choir.

1941   SERGEANT YORK   Warner Brothers

Director: Howard Hawks
Producers: Jesse Lasky, Hal B. Wallis
Scenarists: Abem Finkel, Harry Chandlee, Howard Koch, John Huston
Photographer: Sol Polito
Battle Sequences: Arthur Edeson
Editor: William Holmes
Art Director: John Hughes
Musical Score: Max Steiner

Based on the diary of Sergeant York as edited by Tom Skeyhill
Cast: Gary Cooper (Alvin C. York), Walter Brennan (Pastor Rosier
Pile), Joan Leslie (Gracie Williams), George Tobias (Michael T.
"Pusher" Ross), Stanley Ridges (Major Buxton), Margaret Wycherly
(Mother York), Ward Bond (Ike Botkin), Noah Beery, Jr. (Buck Lip-
scomb), June Lockhart (Rose York), Dickie Moore (George York), Clem
Bevans (Zeke), Howard DaSilva (Lem), Charles Trowbridge (Cordell
Hull), Harvey Stephens (Captain Danforth), David Bruce (Bert
Thomas), Charles (Carl) Esmond (The German Major), Joseph Sawyer
(Sergeant Early), Pat Flaherty (Sergeant Harry Parsons), Robert Por-
terfield (Zeb Andrews), Erville Alderson (Nate Tomkins), Joseph Ge-
rard (General Pershing), Frank Wilcox (Sergeant), Donald Douglas
(Captain Tillman), Lane Chandler (Corporal Savage), Frank Marlowe
(Beardsley), Jack Pennick (Corporal Cutting), James Anderson (Eb),
Guy Wilkerson (Tom), Tully Marshall (Uncle Lige), Lee "Lasses"
White (Luke, the Target Keeper), Jane Isbell (Gracie's Sister), Frank
Orth (Drummer), Arthur Aylesworth (Bartender), Rita La Roy, Lucia
Carroll, Kay Sutton (Girls in Saloon), Elisha Cook, Jr. (Piano Player),
William Haade (Card Player), Jody Gilbert (Fat Woman), Victor Kil-
ian (Andrews), Frank Faylen, Murray Alper (Butt Boys), Gaylord
(Steve) Pendleton, Charles Drake (Scorers), Theodore Von Eltz (Prison
Camp Commander), Roland Drew (Officer), Russell Hicks (General),
Jean Del Val (Marshal Foch), Selmer Jackson (General Duncan),
Creighton Hale (AP Man), George Irving (Harrison), Ed Keane (Oscar
of the Waldorf), Byron Barr [Gig Young] (Soldier), and Si Jenks, Ray
Teal, Kit Guard, Dick Simmons.

1941   BALL OF FIRE   A Samuel Goldwyn Production
Released by RKO-Radio Pictures, Inc.

Director: Howard Hawks
Producer: Samuel Goldwyn
Scenarists: Charles Brackett, Billy Wilder
Photographer: Gregg Toland
Editor: Daniel Mandell
Musical Score: Alfred Newman
Art Director: Perry Ferguson
Based on "From A to Z," an original story, by Thomas Monroe and
Billy Wilder
Cast: Gary Cooper (Prof. Bertram Potts), Barbara Stanwyck (Sugar-
puss O'Shea), Oscar Homolka (Prof. Gurkakoff), Henry Travers (Prof.
Jerome), S. Z. Sakall (Prof. Magenbruch), Tully Marshall (Prof. Robin-
son), Leonid Kinsky (Prof. Quintana), Richard Haydn (Prof. Oddly),
Aubrey Mather (Prof. Peagram), Allen Jenkins (Garbage Man), Dana
Andrews (Joe Lilac), Dan Duryea (Duke Pastrami), Ralph Peters

(Asthma Anderson), Kathleen Howard (Miss Bragg), Mary Field (Miss
Totten), Charles Lane (Larson), Charles Arnt (McNeary), Elisha Cook
Jr. (Cook), Alan Rhein ("Horseface"), Eddie Foster (Pinstripe), Aldrich
Bowker (Justice of the Peace), Addison Richards (District Attorney),
Pat West (Bum), Kenneth Howell (College Boy), Tommy Ryan (News
boy), Tim Ryan (Motor Cop), Will Lee ("Benny, the Creep"), Gene
Krupa and His Orchestra, Otto Hoffmann (Stage Door Man), Ed
Mundy (Spieler), Geraldine Fissette (Hula Dancer), June Horne,
Ethelreda Leopold (Nursemaids in Park), Walter Shumway, George
Barton (Garbagemen), Merrilee Lannon, Doria Caron (Girls in Sub
way), Helen Seamon, Catherine Henderson (College Girls), Jack Perry
(Fighting Bum), Lorraine Miller (Girl in Cafe), Mildred Morris (Chorus
Girl), Francis Sayles (Taxi Driver), Gerald Pierce (Delivery Boy), Che
De Vito (Toll Keeper), Pat Flaherty, George Sherwood (Deputies), Den
Lawrence (Irish Gardener), Eddy Chandler, Lee Phelps, Ken Christy,
Dick Rush, Oscar Chalkee Williams (Cops), Johnnie Morris (Justice of
Peace Clerk), Edward Clark (Proprietor of Motor Court).

1942   THE PRIDE OF THE YANKEES

A Samuel Goldwyn Picture
Released by RKO-Radio Pictures, Inc

Director: Sam Wood
Producer: Samuel Goldwyn
Scenarists: Jo Swerling, Herman J. Mankiewicz
Photographer: Rudolph Mate
Production Designer: William Cameron Menzies
Musical Score: Leigh Harline
Art Director: Perry Ferguson
Editor: Daniel Mandell
Produced with the assistance of Mrs. Lou Gehrig, by arrangement
with Christy Walsh. From an original story by Paul Gallico.
Cast: Gary Cooper (Lou Gehrig), Teresa Wright (Eleanor Gehrig), Wal
ter Brennan (Sam Blake), Dan Duryea (Hank Hanneman), Babe Ruth
(Himself), Elsa Janssen (Mom Gehrig), Ludwig Stossel (Pop Gehrig),
Virginia Gilmore (Myra), Bill Dickey (Himself), Ernie Adams (Miller
Huggins), Pierre Watkin (Mr. Twitchell), Harry Harvey (Joe
McCarthy), Robert W. Meusel, Mark Koenig, Bill Stern (Themselves),
Addison Richards (Coach), Hardie Albright (Van Tuyl), Edward Field
ing (Clinic Doctor), George Lessey (Mayor of New Rochelle), Vaughan
Glaser (Doctor in Gehrig Home), Douglas Croft (Lou Gehrig as a boy),
Veloz & Yolanda, Ray Noble and his Orchestra, Frank Faylen (3rd
Base Coach), Lane Chandler (Player in Locker Room), Edgar Barrier
(Hospital Doctor), Gene Collins (Billy, age 8), David Holt (Billy, age 17),
George Offerman, Jr. (Freshman), David Manley (Mayor La Guardia)

Anita Bolster (Sasha's Mother), Jimmy Valentine (Sasha), Spencer Charters (Mr. Larsen), Sarah Padden (Mrs. Roberts), Bernard Zanville (later Dane Clark), Tom Neal (Fraternity Boys), Lorna Dunn (Nurse in Clinic), Emory Parnell (Cop), Dorothy Vaughan (Landlady), Patsy O'Byrne (Scrub Woman), Matt McHugh (Strength Machine Operator), William Chaney (Newsboy), Pat Flaherty (Baseball Player), Mary Gordon (Maid), Francis Sayles (Cab Driver).

1943   FOR WHOM THE BELL TOLLS   Paramount

Director and Producer: Sam Wood
Scenarist: Dudley Nichols
Executive Producer: Buddy De Sylva
Photographer: Ray Rennahan
Musical Score: Victor Young
Art Directors: Hans Dreier, Haldane Douglas
Editors: Sherman Todd, John Link
Production Designer: William Cameron Menzies
From the novel by Ernest Hemingway
Cast: Gary Cooper (Robert Jordan), Ingrid Bergman (Maria), Akim Tamiroff (Pablo), Arturo de Cordova (Agustin), Vladimir Sokoloff (Anselmo), Mikhail Rasumny (Rafael), Fortunio Bonanova (Fernando), Eric Feldary (Andres), Victor Varconi (Primitivo), Katina Paxinou (Pilar), Joseph Calleia (El Sordo), Lilo Yarson (Joaquin), Alexander Granach (Paco), Adia Kuznetzoff (Gustavo), Leonid Snegoff (Ignacio), Leo Bulgakov (Gen. Golz), Duncan Renaldo (Lt. Berrendo), George Coulouris (Andre Massart), Frank Puglia (Capt. Gomez), Pedro De Cordoba (Col. Miranda), Michael Visaroff (Staff Officer), Konstantin Shayne (Karkov), Martin Garralaga (Capt. Mora), Jean Del Val (Sniper), Feodor Chaliapin (Kashkin), Pedro De Cordoba (Frederico Gonzales), Mayo Newhall (Ricardo), Michael Dalmatoff (Benito Garcia, Mayor), Antonio Vidal (Guillermo), Robert Tafur (Faustino Rivero), Armand Roland (Julian), Trini Varela (Spanish Singer), Dick Botiller (Sgt. Elias' Man), Franco Corsaro, Frank Lackteen (Elias' Men), George Sorel (Bored Sentry), John Bleifer (Peasant—Flails Gonzalez), Harry Cording (Man—Flails the Mayor), William Edmunds, Albert Morin, Pedro Regas (Soldiers), Soledad Jiminez (Guillermo's Wife), Luis Rojas (Drunkard), Manuel Paris (Officer of Civil Guards), Jose Tortosa, Ernesto Morelli, Manuel Lopez (Civil Guards), Yakima Canutt (Young Cavalry Man), Tito Renaldo (1st Sentry), Maxine Ardell, Marjorie Deanne, Yvonne De Carlo, Alice Kirby, Marcella Phillips, Lynda Grey, Christopher King, Louise La Planche (Girls in Cafe).

1944   **MEMO FOR JOE**   Produced by RKO Pathe
for National War Fund

Directed by Richard O. Fleischer. Cooper is seen entertaining troops
in the Pacific on his USO tour.

1944   **THE STORY OF DR. WASSELL**   Paramount

Director and Producer: Cecil B. De Mille
Scenarists: Alan Le May, Charles Bennett
Photographer: Victor Milner
Editor: Anne Bauchens
Second Unit Director: Arthur Rossen
Musical Score: Victor Young
Technical Consultant: Commander Corydon M. Wassell
Based on the story by Commander Corydon M. Wassell and the origi-
nal story by James Hilton
Cast: Gary Cooper (Dr. Corydon M. Wassell), Laraine Day (Madeleine
Day), Signe Hasso (Bettina), Carol Thurston (Tremartini), Dennis O'-
Keefe (Benjamin "Hoppy" Hopkins), Carl Esmond (Lt. Dirk Van Daal),
Stanley Ridges (Cdr. William B. Goggins), Renny McEvoy (Joe Lein-
werber), Elliott Reid (William Anderson), Melvin Francis (Himself),
Joel Allen (Robert Kraus), Paul Kelly (Murdock), Oliver Thorndike
(Alabam), James Milligan (Robert Elroy Whaley), Mike Kilian
(Thomas Borghetti), Philip Ahn (Ping), Doodles Weaver (Harold
Hunter), Barbara Britton (Ruth), Richard Loo (Dr. Wei), Davidson
Clark (Dr. Holmes), Si Jenks (The Arkansas Mailman), Morton Lowry
(Lt. Bainbridge), Richard Nugent (Capt. Carruthers), Lester Matthews
(Dr. Wayne), Victor Varconi (Capt. Ryk), George Macready (A Dutch
Officer), Ludwig Donath (Dr. Vranken), Frank Puglia (Java Temple
Guide), Irving Bacon (Missionary), Ottola Nesmith (His Wife), Jody
Gilbert (Head Nurse), Anthony Caruso (Male Nurse), Louis Jean
Heydt (Ensign), Minor Watson (Rear Admiral), Ann Doran (Praying
Woman), Julia Faye (Anne, a Nurse), Ron Randell, Sarah Edwards,
Jack Norton (Passengers), Carlyle Blackwell (An American Marine),
and Douglas Fowley, Miles Mander, Hugh Beaumont, Charles Trow-
bridge, Fred Kohler, Jr., Ivan Triesault, Philip Van Zandt, Yvonne De
Carlo.

1944   **CASANOVA BROWN**
An International Pictures, Inc. Production
Released by RKO-Radio Pictures, Inc.

Director: Sam Wood
Producer and Scenarist: Nunnally Johnson

Photographer: John Seitz
Editor: Thomas Neff
Musical Score: Arthur Lange
Art Director: Perry Ferguson
Based on the short story "The Little Accident" by Floyd Dell and Thomas Mitchell
Cast: Gary Cooper (Casanova Brown), Teresa Wright (Isabel Drury), Frank Morgan (Mr. Ferris), Anita Louise (Madge Ferris), Patricia Collinge (Mrs. Drury), Edmond Breon (Mr. Drury), Jill Esmond (Dr. Zernerke), Emory Parnell (Frank), Isabel Elsom (Mrs. Ferris), Mary Treen (Monica), Halliwell Hobbes (Butler), Larry Joe Olsen (Junior), Byron Foulger (Fletcher), Sarah Padden (Landlady), Eloise Hardt (Doris Ferris), Grady Sutton (Tod), Frederick Burton (Rev. Dean), Robert Dudley (Marriage Clerk), Isabel La Mal (Clerk's Wife), Florence Lake (Nurse Phillips), Ann Evers (Nurse Petherbridge), Frances Morris (Nurse Gillespie), Nell Craig (4th Nurse), Lane Chandler (Orderly), Kay Deslys (Fat Woman Patient), Ottola Nesmith (Patient's Nurse), Lorna Dunn, Kelly Flint, Julia Faye (X-Ray Nurses), Dorothy Tree (Nurse Clark), Isabel Withers (Nurse, helps Casanova), Irving Bacon (Hotel Manager), James Burke (O'Leary), Francis Sayles (Elevator Operator), Phil Tead (License Clerk), Snub Pollard (Father at Baby Window), Grace Cunard, Vera Kornman, Anna Luther, Marian Gray, Sada Simmons (Women at Baby Window), Lelah Tyler (Switchboard Operator), Cecil Stewart (Organist), Helen St. Rayner (Soloist), Stewart Garner (Usher), Mary Young (Mrs. Dean), John Brown (Fire Chief), and Jack Gargan (Intern).

1945   ALONG CAME JONES   A Cinema
Artists Corp. Picture An International Pictures, Inc.
Production Released by RKO-Radio Pictures, Inc.

Director: Stuart Heisler
Producer: Gary Cooper
Scenarist: Nunnally Johnson
Photographer: Milton Krasner
Musical Score: Arthur Lange, Hugo Friedhofer, Charles Maxwell
Editor: Thomas Neff
Editorial Supervision: Paul Weatherwax
Production Designer: Wiard B. Ihnen
From an original novel by Alan LeMay.
Cast: Gary Cooper (Melody Jones), Loretta Young (Cherry de Longpre), William Demarest (George Fury), Dan Duryea (Monte Jarrad), Frank Sully (Cherry's Brother), Russell Simpson (Pop de Longpre), Arthur Loft (Sheriff), Willard Robertson (Luke Packard), Don Costello (Gledhill), Ray Teal (Kriendler), Walter Sande (Ira Waggoner), Lane Chandler (Boone), Frank Cordell (Guard on Coach), Lou Davis, Ed

Randolph, Tommy Coates (Passengers on Coach), Tony Roux (Old Mexican), Erville Alderson (Bartender), Paul Sutton (Man at Bar), Herbert Heywood, Frank Hagney, Ralph Littlefield, Ernie Adams (Townsmen), Lane Watson (Town Character), Paul E. Burns (Small Man), Chris Pin Martin (Store Proprietor), Jack Baxley (Rancher on Street), Doug Morrow (Rifleman), Ralph Dunn (Cotton), Geoffrey Ingham, John Merton, Tom Herbert (Card Players), Charles Morton (Fat Card Player), Lee Phelps (Deputy), Billy Engle (Wagon Driver), Bob Kortman, Frank McCarroll, Hank Bell, Chalky Williams (Posse).

1945   SARATOGA TRUNK   Warner Brothers

Director: Sam Wood
Producer: Hal B. Wallis
Scenarist: Casey Robinson
Photographer: Ernest Haller
Musical Score: Max Steiner
Editor: Ralph Dawson
Art Director: Carl Jules Weyl
From the novel by Edna Ferber
Gary Cooper (Col. Clint Maroon), Ingrid Bergman (Clio Dulaine), Flora Robson (Angelique Buiton), Jerry Austin (Cupidon), John Warburton (Bartholomew Van Steed), Florence Bates (Mrs. Coventry Bellop), Curt Bois (Augustin Haussy), John Abbott (Roscoe Bean), Ethel Griffies (Mme. Clarissa Van Steed), Marla Shelton (Mrs. Porcelain), Helen Freeman (Mrs. Nicholas Dulaine), Sophie Huxley (Charlotte Dulaine), Fred Essler (Monsieur Begue), Louis Payne (Raymond Soule), Sarah Edwards (Miss Diggs), Adrienne D'Ambricourt (Grandmother Dulaine), Jacqueline De Wit (Guilia Forosini), Minor Watson (J. P. Reynolds), J. Lewis Johnson, Libby Taylor, Lillian Yarbo (Servants), Geneva Williams (Blackberry Woman), Ruby Dandridge (Turbaned Vendor), Paul Bryant, Shelby Bacon (Urchins), Peter Cusanelli (Coffee Proprietor), Bertha Woolford (Flower Woman), George Reed (Carriage Driver), Amelia Liggett (Mme. Begue), George Beranger (Leon, the Headwaiter), John Sylvester (Young Man Escort), George Humbert (Jambalaya Proprietor), Edmund Breon (McIntyre), William B. Davidson (Mr. Stone), Edward Fielding (Mr. Bowers), Thurston Hall (Mr. Pound), Alice Fleming (Woman on Piazza), Ralph Dunn (Engineer), Lane Chandler (Al), Glenn Strange (Cowboy), Chester Clute (Hotel Clerk), Theodore Von Eltz (Hotel Manager), Monte Blue (Fireman on Train), Franklyn Farnum (Gambler), Bob Reeves (Soule Bodyguard), Al Ferguson, Hank Bell (Cowhands), Dick Elliott (Politician).

1946   **CLOAK AND DAGGER**
A United States Picture Production
Released by Warner Brothers

Director: Fritz Lang
Producer: Milton Sperling
Scenarists: Albert Maltz, Ring Lardner, Jr.
Photographer: Sol Polito
Musical Score: Max Steiner
Editor: Christian Nyby
Art Director: Max Parker
From an original story by Boris Ingster and John Larkin
Suggested by the book by Corey Ford and Alastair MacBain.
Cast: Gary Cooper (Prof. Alvah Jesper), Lilli Palmer (Gina), Robert
Alda (Pinkie), Vladimir Sokoloff (Polda), J. Edward Bromberg (Trenk),
Marjorie Hoshelle (Ann Dawson), Ludwig Stossel (The German), He-
lene Thimig (Katerin Lodor), Dan Seymour (Marsoli), Marc Lawrence
(Luigi), James Flavin (Col. Walsh), Pat O'Moore (The Englishman),
Charles Marsh (Erich), Don Turner (Lingg), Clifton Young (American
Commander), Ross Ford (Paratrooper), Robert Coote (Cronin), Hans
Schumm, Peter Michael (German Agents), Yola D'Avril, Claire Du
Brey, Lottie Stein (Nurses), Lynne Lyons (Woman in Bank, Dougle),
Rory Mallinson (Paul), Ed Parker, Gil Oerkins (Gestapo), Bruce Lester
(British Officer), Leon Lenoir (Italian Soldier), Otto Reichow, Arno
Frey (German Soldiers), Maria Monteil, Lillian Nicholson (Nuns),
Bobby Santon (Italian Boy), Elvira Curci (Woman in Street), Hella
Crossley (Rachele), Douglas Walton (British Pilot), Vernon Downing
(British Sergeant), Holmes Herbert (British Officer), Frank Wilcox
(American Officer), Michael Burke (OSS Agent).

1947   **UNCONQUERED**   Paramount

Director and Producer: Cecil B. De Mille
Scenarists: Charles Bennett, Frederic M. Frank, Jesse Lasky, Jr.
Photographer: Ray Rennahan
Editor: Anne Bauchens
Art Directors: Hans Dreier, Walter Tyler
Second Unit Director: Arthur Rosson
Musical Score: Victor Young
Based on a novel by Neil H. Swanson.
Cast: Gary Cooper (Captain Christopher Holden), Paulette Goddard
(Abigail Martha Hale), Howard DaSilva (Martin Garth), Boris Karloff
(Guyasuta, Chief of the Senecas), Cecil Kellaway (Jeremy Love), Ward
Bond (John Fraser), Katherine De Mille (Hannah), Henry Wilcoxon
(Capt. Steele), Sir C. Aubrey Smith (Lord Chief Justice), Victor Var-
coni (Capt. Simeon Ecuyer), Virginia Grey (Diana), Porter Hall

(Leach), Mike Mazurki (Dave Bone), Robert Warwick (Pontiac, Chief
of the Ottawas), Richard Gaines (Col. George Washington), Virginia
Campbell (Mrs. Fraser), Gavin Muir (Lt. Fergus McKenzie), Alan
Napier (Sir William Johnson), Nan Sutherland (Mrs. Pruitt), Marc
Lawrence (Sioto), Jane Nigh (Evelyn), Griff Barnett
(Brother Andrews), John Mylong (Col. Henry Bouquet), Lloyd Bridges
(Lt. Hutchins), Oliver Thorndike (Lt. Baillie), Jack Pennick (Jim
Lovat), Paul E. Burns (Dan McCoy), Davidson Clark (Mr. Carroll),
Dorothy Adams (Mrs. Bront), Clarence Muse (Jason), Raymond Hat-
ton (Venango Scout), Julia Faye (The Widow Swivens), Chief Thunder-
cloud (Chief Killbuck), Charles B. Middleton (Mulligan), Tiny Jones
(Bondswoman), Fred Kohler, Jr. (Sergeant), and Iron Eyes Cody, Ray
Teal, Noble Johnson, Byron Foulger, Bob Kortman, Jeff Corey, Lex
Barker, Mike Kilian, Lane Chandler, Jay Silverheels, Isabel Chabing
Cooper.

1947   VARIETY GIRL   Paramount

Director: George Marshall
Producer: Daniel Dare
Scenarists: Edmund Hartmann, Frank Tashlin, Robert Welch, Monte
Brice
Photographers: Lionel Lindon, Stuart Thompson
Editor: LeRoy Stone
Cast: Mary Hatcher (Catherine Brown), Olga San Juan (Amber La
Vonne), DeForest Kelley (Bob Kirby), William Demarest (Barker),
Frank Faylen (Stage Manager), Frank Ferguson (J. R. O'Connell),
Glenn Tryon (Bill Farris), Nella Walker (Mrs. Webster), Torben Meyer
(Headwaiter, Brown Derby), Jack Norton (Busboy), Elaine Riley
(Cashier), Charles Victor (O'Connell's Assistant), Gus Taute (As-
sistant's Assistant), Harry Hayden (Stage Manager, Grauman's Chi-
nese), Janet Thomas, Roberta Jonay (Girls), Wallace Earl (Girl with
Sheep Dog), Dick Keene (Dog Trainer), Ann Doran (Hairdresser),
Jerry James (Assistant Director), Eric Alden (Makeup Man), Frank
Mayo (Director), Russell Hicks, Charles Coleman, Eddie Fetherston
(Men in Steam Bath), Frank Hagney (Attendant).
Guest Stars (As Themselves): Bing Crosby, Gary Cooper, Bob Hope,
Ray Milland, Alan Ladd, Barbara Stanwyck, Paulette Goddard, Doro-
thy Lamour, Sonny Tufts, Joan Caulfield, William Holden, Lizabeth
Scott, Burt Lancaster, Gail Russell, Diana Lynn, Sterling Hayden,
Robert Preston, Veronica Lake, John Lund, William Bendix, Barry
Fitzgerald, Cass Daley, Howard Da Silva, Macdonald Carey, Billy De
Wolfe, Patric Knowles, Mona Freeman, Cecil Kellaway, Virginia
Field, Richard Webb, Arleen Whelan, Johnny Coy, Stanley Clements,
Wanda Hendrix, Mikail Rasumny, George Reeves, Cecil B. De Mille,

Mitchell Leisen, Frank Butler, George Marshall, Pearl Bailey, Spike Jones & His City Slickers, Roger Dann, Jim & Mildred Mulcay, Barney Dean.

1948   GOOD SAM   A Rainbow Productions, Inc. Picture Released by RKO-Radio Pictures, Inc.

Director and Producer: Leo McCarey
Scenarist: Ken Englund
Photographer: George Barnes
Editor: James McKay
Musical Score: Robert Emmett Dolan
Art Director: John B. Goodman
Based on a story by Leo McCarey and John Klorer
Cast: Gary Cooper (Sam Clayton), Ann Sheridan (Lu Clayton), Ray Collins (Reverend Daniels), Edmund Lowe (H. C. Borden), Joan Lorring (Shirley Mae), Clinton Sundberg (Nelson), Minerva Urecal (Mrs. Nelson), Louise Beavers (Chloe), Dick Ross (Claude), Lora Lee Michel (Lulu), Bobby Dolan, Jr. (Butch), Matt Moore (Mr. Butler), Netta Packer (Mrs. Butler), Ruth Roman (Ruthie), Carol Stevens (Mrs. Adams), Todd Karns (Joe Adams), Irving Bacon (Tramp), William Frawley (Tom), Harry Hayden (Banker), Irmgard Dawson, Jane Allan (Girls), Tom Dugan (Santa Claus), Sarah Edwards (Mrs. Gilmore), Ruth Sanderson (Sam's Secretary), Marta Mitrovich (Mysterious Woman), Mimi Doyle (Red Cross Nurse), Franklin Parker (Photographer), Ida Moore (Old Lady), Florence Auer (Woman on Bus), Dick Wessell (Bus Driver), Sedal Bennett (Woman Chasing Bus), Jack Gargan, Bess Flowers (Parents), Almira Sessions (Landlady), Garry Owens (Taxi Driver), Stanley McKay (Young Minister), Bert Roach (Whispering Usher), Bob Tidwell (Telegraph Boy), Ann Lawrence (Salvation Army Girl), Joe Hinds, Francis Stevens (Salvation Army Workers), Joseph Crehan (Casey), William Haade (Taxi Driver).

1948   THE FOUNTAINHEAD   Warner Brothers

Director: King Vidor
Producer: Henry Blanke
Scenarist: Ayn Rand
Photographer: Robert Burks
Editor: David Weisbart
Art Director: Edward Carrere
Musical Score: Max Steiner
From the novel *The Fountainhead* by Ayn Rand
Cast: Gary Cooper (Howard Roark), Patricia Neal (Dominique Francon), Raymond Massey (Gail Wynand), Kent Smith (Peter Keating),

Robert Douglas (Ellsworth Toohey), Henry Hull (Henry Cameron), Ray Collins (Enright), Moroni Olsen (Chairman), Jerome Cowan (Alvah Scarret), Paul Harvey (A Businessman), Harry Woods (The Superintendent), Paul Stanton (The Dean), Bob Alden (Newsboy), Tristram Coffin (Secretary), Roy Gordon (Vice-President), Isabel Withers (Secretary), Almira Sessions (Housekeeper), Tito Vuolo, William Haade (Workers), Gail Bonney (Woman), Thurston Hall (Businessman), Dorothy Christy (Society Woman), Harlan Warde (Young Man), Jonathan Hale (Guy Franchon), Frank Wilcox (Gordon Prescott), Douglas Kennedy (Reporter), Pierre Watkin, Selmer Jackson (Officials), John Doucette (Gus Webb), John Alvin (Young Intellectual), Geraldine Wall (Woman), Fred Kelsey (Old Watchman), Paul Newland, George Sherwood (Policemen), Lois Austin (Woman Guest), Josephine Whittell (Hostess), Lester Dorr (Man), Bill Dagwell (Shipping Clerk), Charles Trowbridge, Russell Hicks, Raymond Largay, Charles Evans (Directors), Morris Ankrum (Prosecutor), Griff Barnett (Judge), G. Pat Collins (Foreman), Ann Doran, Ruthelma Stevens (Secretaries), Creighton Hale (Clerk), Philo McCullough (Bailiff).

1949   IT'S A GREAT FEELING   Warner Brothers

Director: David Butler
Producer: Alex Gottlieb
Scenarists: Jack Rose, Mel Shavelson
Photographer: Wilfrid M. Cline
Art Director: Stanley Fleischer
Editor: Irene Moore
Musical Director: Ray Heindorf
From a story by I. A. L. Diamond
Cast: Dennis Morgan (Himself), Doris Day (Judy Adams), Jack Carson (Himself), Bill Goodwin (Arthur Trent), Irving Bacon (Information Clerk), Claire Carleton (Grace), Harlan Warde (Publicity Man), Jacqueline De Wit (Trent's Secretary), The Mazzone-Abbott Dancers, Wilfred Lucas (Mr. Adams), Pat Flaherty (Gate Guard), Wendy Lee (Manicurist), Nita Talbot, Eve Whitney, Carol Brewster, Sue Casey, Joan Vohs (Models), Lois Austin (Saleslady), Tom Dugan (Wrestling Fan in Bar), James Holden (Soda Jerk), Jean Andren (Headwaitress), Dudley Dickerson (Porter), Sandra Gould (Train Passenger, Upper Berth), Shirley Ballard (Beautiful Girl on Bike), and Errol Flynn (The Groom, Jeffrey Bushfinkle).
Guest Stars (As Themselves): Gary Cooper, Joan Crawford, Sydney Greenstreet, Danny Kaye, Patricia Neal, Eleanor Parker, Ronald Reagan, Edward G. Robinson, Jane Wyman, and directors David Butler, Michael Curtiz, King Vidor and Raoul Walsh.

1949   TASK FORCE   Warner Brothers

Director: Delmer Daves
Producer: Jerry Wald
Scenarist: Delmer Daves
Photographers: Robert Burks, Wilfrid M. Cline
Editor: Alan Grosland, Jr.
Musical Score: Franz Waxman
Cast: Gary Cooper (Jonathan L. Scott), Jane Wyatt (Mary Morgan), Wayne Morris (McKinney), Walter Brennan (Pete Richard), Julie London (Barbara McKinney), Bruce Bennett (McCluskey), Jack Holt (Reeves), Stanley Ridges (Bentley), John Ridgely (Dixie Rankin), Richard Rober (Jack Southern), Art Baker (Senator Vincent), Moroni Olsen (Ames), Ray Montgomery (Pilot), Harlan Wade (Timmy), James Holden (Tom Cooper), Rory Mallinson (Jerry Morgan), John Gallaudet (Jennings), Warren Douglas (Winston), Charles Waldreon, Jr. (Aide), Robert Rockwell (Lt. Kelley), William Gould (Mr. Secretary), Sally Corner (Mrs. Secretary), Kenneth Tobey (Capt. Williamson), Tetsu Komai (Japanese Representative), Beal Wong (Japanese Naval Attaché), Laura Treadwell (Mrs. Ames), Roscoe J. Behan (Ames' Attaché), Basil Ruysdael (Admiral), Reed Howes (Officer), Edwin Fowler (Commander Price), William Hudson (Lt. Leenhouts), Mary Lawrence (Ruth Rankin), John McGuire (Supply Officer), Charles Sherlock (Capt. Wren), Charles Williams (Luggage Clerk), Brad Evans, Gerard Waller (Midshipmen), Richard A. Paxton (Pilot), Tommy Walker (Lieutenant).

1949   SNOW CARNIVAL   Warner Brothers

Cooper narrated, produced and acted in this sports short.

1950   BRIGHT LEAF   Warner Brothers

Director: Michael Curtiz
Producer: Henry Blanke
Scenarist: Ronald MacDougall
Photographer: Karl Freund
Editor: Owen Marks
Art Director: Stanley Fleisher
Set Decorator: Ben Bone
Musical Score: Victor Young
Second Unit and Montage Director: David Gardner
From the novel by Foster Fitz-Simons
Cast: Gary Cooper (Brant Royle), Lauren Bacall (Sonia Kovac), Patricia Neal (Margaret Jane), Jack Carson (Chris Malley), Donald Crisp

(Major Singleton), Gladys George (Rose), Elizabeth Patterson (Tabitha Jackson), Jeff Corey (John Barton), Taylor Holmes (Lawyer Calhoun), Thurston Hall (Phillips), James Griffith (Ellery), Marietta Canty (Queenie), William Walker (Simon), Charles Meredith (Pendleton), Leslie Kimmel (Hokins), John Pickard (Devers), Elzie Emanuel (Negro Boy), James Adamson, Ira Buck Woods (Negro Peddlers), Paul Newland (Blacksmith), J. Lewis Johnson (Negro Grandpa), Jessie Lee Hunt (Boy), Lyle Latell (Clay), Eddie Parkes (Hotel Clerk), Celia Lovsky (Dressmaker), Selby Bacon (Fauntleroy), Pat Flaherty (Farmer), Peter Kellett, Hubert Kerns (Farmer's Sons), Rene De Voux (Cousin Emily), Eileen Coughlan (Cousin Pearl), Cleo Moore (Cousin Louise), Nita Talbot (Cousin Theodora), Pat Goldin (Cousin Arthur), Chalky Williams (Sheriff), Chick Chandler (Tobacco Auctioneer), Marshall Bradford (Farmer), John Alvin, John Morgan, Benny Long (Poker Players), Ed Peil, Sr. (Conductor), Charles Conrad (Edwards), Sam Flint (Johnson), Boyd Davis (Official), Kermit Whitfield (Detective Curson).

1950   DALLAS   Warner Brothers

Director: Stuart Heisler
Producer: Anthony Veiller
Scenarist: John Twist
Photographer: Ernest Haller
Art Director: Douglas Bacon
Musical Score: Max Steiner
Editor: Clarence Kolster
Second Unit Director: B. Reeves Eason
Cast: Gary Cooper (Blayde ("Reb" Hollister), Ruth Roman (Tonia Robles), Steve Cochran (Brant Marlow), Barbara Payton (Flo), Leif Erickson (Martin Weatherby), Antonio Moreno (Felipe), Jerome Cowan (Matt Coulter), Reed Hadley (Wild Bill Hickok), Gil Donaldson (Luis), Zon Murray (Cullen Marlow), Will Wright (Judge Harper), Monte Blue (The Sheriff), Byron Keith (Jason Trask), Steve Dunhill (Dink), Charles Watts (Bill Walters), Jose Dominguez (Carlos), Gene Evans (Drunk), Jay "Slim" Talbot (Stage Driver), Billie Bird (School Teacher), Frank Kreig (Politician), Tom Fadden (Mountaineer), Hal K. Dawson (Drummer), Buddy Roosevelt (Northerner), Alex Montoya (Vaquero), Dolores Corvall (Mexican Servant), Fred Graham (Lou), Charles Horvath, Winn Wright, Carl Andre (Cowpunchers), Ann Lawrence (Mrs. Walters), O. Z. Whitehead (Settler), Mike Donovan (Citizen), Glenn Thompson (Guard), Frank McCarroll, Larry McGrath, Al Ferguson (Citizens), Dewey Robinson, Roy Bucko, Buddy Shaw, Dave Dunbar, Oscar Williams (Prisoners), Fred Kelsey (Carter), Benny Corbett (Bystander).

1951   YOU'RE IN THE NAVY NOW

Twentieth Century Fox

First released under the title: *U.S.S. Teakettle*

Director: Henry Hathaway
Producer: Fred Kohlmar
Scenarist: Richard Murphy
Photographer: Joe MacDonald
Musical Score: Cyril Mockridge
Art Directors: Lyle Wheeler, J. Russell Spencer
Editor: James B. Clark
From an article in *The New Yorker* by John W. Hazard
Cast: Gary Cooper (Lt. John Harkness), Jane Greer (Ellie), Millard Mitchell (Larrabee), Eddie Albert (Lt. Bill Barron), John McIntyre (Commander Reynolds), Ray Collins (Admiral Tennant), Harry Von Zell (Capt. Eliot), Jack Webb (Ensign Anthony Barbo), Richard Erdman (Ensign Chuck Dorrance), Harvey Lembeck (Norelli), Henry Slate (Ryan—Chief Engineer), Ed Begley (Commander), Fay Roope (Battleship Admiral), Charles Tannen (Houlihan), Charles Buchinski (later Bronson) (Wascylewski), Jack Warden (Morse), Ken Harvey, Lee Marvin, Jerry Hausner, Charles Smith (Crew Members), James Cornell (New Boy—Sailor), Glen Gordon, Laurence Hugo (Shore Patrolmen), Damian O'Flynn (Doctor), Biff McGuire (Sailor Messenger), Norman McKay (Admiral's Aide), John McGuire (Naval Commander), Elsa Peterson (Admiral's Wife), Joel Fluellen (Mess Boy), Herman Canton (Naval Captain), Rory Mallinson (Lieutenant Commander), William Leicester (C.P.O.), Ted Stanhope (Naval Officer).

1951   STARLIFT   Warner Brothers

Director: Roy Del Ruth
Producer: Robert Arthur
Scenarists: John Klorer, Karl Kamb
Photographer: Ted McCord
Art Director: Charles H. Clarke
Editor: William Ziegler
"Look Out, Stranger, I'm a Texas Ranger" by Ruby Ralesin and Phil Harris
From a story by John Klorer
Cast: Doris Day, Gordon MacRae, Virginia Mayo, Gene Nelson, Ruth Roman (Themselves), Janice Rule (Nell Wayne), Dick Wesson (Sgt. Mike Nolan), Ron Hagerthy (Cpl. Rick Williams), Richard Webb (Col. Callan), Hayden Rorke (Chaplain), Howard St. John (Steve Rogers), Ann Doran (Mrs. Callan), Tommy Farrell (Turner), John Maxwell (George Norris), Don Beddoe (Bob Wayne), Mary Adams (Sue Wayne), Bigelowe Sayre (Dr. Williams), Eleanor Audley (Mrs. Williams), Pat

Henry (Theatre Manager), Gordon Polk (Chief Usher), Robert Hammack (Piano Player), Ray Montgomery (Capt. Nelson), Bill Neff (Co-Pilot), Stan Holbrook (Ground Officer), Jill Richards (Flight Nurse), Joe Turkel (Litter Case), Rush Williams (Virginia Boy), Brian McKay (Pete), Jack Larson (Will), Lyle Clark (Nebraska Boy), Dorothy Kennedy, Jean Dean, Dolores Castle (Nurses), William Hunt (Boy with Cane), Elizabeth Flournoy (Army Nurse), Walter Brennan, Jr. (Driver), Robert Karns, John Hedloe (Lieutenants), Steve Gregory (Boy with Camera), Richard Monohan (Morgan), Joe Recht, Herb Latimer (Soldiers in Bed), Dick Ryan (Doctor), Bill Hudson (Crew Chief), Sarah Spencer (Miss Parson's Asst.), James Brown (Non-Com), Ezelle Poule (Waitress).
Guest Stars: James Cagney, Gary Cooper, Virginia Gibson, Phil Harris, Frank Lovejoy, Lucille Norman, Louella Parsons, Randolph Scott, Jane Wyman and Patrice Wymore.

1951   IT'S A BIG COUNTRY   Metro-Goldwyn-Mayer

Directors: Richard Thorpe, John Sturges, Charles Vidor, Don Weis, Clarence Brown, William A. Wellman, Don Hartman.
Producer: Robert Sisk Scenarists: William Ludwig, Helen Deutsch, George Wells, Allen Rivkin, Dorothy Kingsley, Dore Schary, Isobel Lennart
Photographers: John Alton, Ray June, William Mellor, Joseph Ruttenberg
Editors: Ben Lewis, Frederick Y. Smith
Cast: Ethel Barrymore (Mrs. Brian Patrick Riordan), Keefe Brasselle (Sgt. Maxie Klein), Gary Cooper (Texas), Nancy Davis (Miss Coleman), Van Johnson (Adam Burch), Gene Kelly (Icarus Xenophon), Janet Leigh (Rosa Szabo), Marjorie Main (Mrs. Wrenley), Fredric March (Papa Esposito), George Murphy (Mr. Callaghan), William Powell (Professor), S. Z. Sakall (Stefan Szabo), Lewis Stone (Sexton), James Whitmore (Mr. Stacey), Keenan Wynn (Michael Fisher), Leon Ames (Secret Service Man), Angela Clarke (Mama Esposito), Bobby Hyatt (Joseph Esposito), Sharon McManus (Sam Szabo), Elisabeth Risdon (Woman), Bill Baldwin (Austin), Mickey Martin (Copy Boy), William H. Walsh (Official), Ned Glass (Receptionist), Sherry Hall, Fred Santley, Henry Sylvester, Roger Moore, Roger Cole, Harry Stanton (Officials), June Hedin (Kati), Luana Mehlberg (Lenka), Jeralyn Alton (Yolande), Jacqueline Kenley (Margit), Tonly Taylor (Baby Sitter), Benny Burt (Soda Jerk), George Economides (Theodore), Hal Hatfield, George Conrad, Richard Grindle, Anthony Lappas, Tom Nickols, Costas Morfis (Greek Athletes), A. Cameron Grant (Proprieter of Inn), David Alpert (Greek Athlete), Don Fields (George), Jerry Hunter (Frank Grillo), Donald Gordon (Mervin), Lucile Curtis (Miss Bloomburg), Dolly Arriage (Concetta Esposito), Elena Savanarola (Amelia Esposito), Carol Nugent (Girl), George McDonald, Charles Myers,

David Wyatt, Mickey Little (Boys), Tiny Francone (Girl in Classroom), Rhea Mitchell (School Teacher).

1951   DISTANT DRUMS   Warner Brothers

Director: Raoul Walsh
Producer: Milton Sperling
Scenarists: Niven Busch, Martin Rackin
Photographer: Sid Hickox
Art Director: Douglas Bacon
Editor: Folmer Blangsted
Musical Score: Max Steiner
Cast: Gary Cooper (Capt. Quincy Wyatt), Mari Aldon (Judy Beckett), Richard Webb (Lt. Richard Tufts), Ray Teal (Private Mohair), Arthur Hunnicutt (Monk), Robert Barrat (General Zachary Taylor), Clancy Cooper (Sgt. Shane), Larry Carper (Chief Ocala), Dan White (Cpl. Peachtree), Mel Archer (Pvt. Jeremiah Hiff), Angelita McCall (Amelia), Lee Roberts (Pvt. Tibbett), Gregg Barton (Pvt. James Tasher), Sheb Wooley (Pvt. Jessup), Warren MacGregor (Pvt. Sullivan), George Scanlan (Bosun), Carl Harbaugh (M. Duprez), Beverly Brandon (Mme. Duprez), Sidney Capo (Indian Boy).

1952   HIGH NOON   United Artists

Director: Fred Zinnemann
Producer: Stanley Kramer
Scenarist: Carl Foreman
Photography: Floyd Crosby
Art Director: Rudolph Sternad
Musical Score: Dimitri Tiomkin
Editor: Elmo Williams
Song: "Do Not Forsake Me, Oh My Darlin' " by Dimitri Tiomkin and Ned Washington, sung by Tex Ritter
Based on the story "The Tin Star" by John W. Cunningham
Cast: Gary Cooper (Will Kane), Thomas Mitchell (Jonas Henderson), Lloyd Bridges (Harvey Pell), Katy Jurado (Helen Ramirez), Grace Kelly (Amy Kane), Otto Kruger (Percy Mettrick), Lon Chaney (Martin Howe), Henry Morgan (William Fuller), Ian MacDonald (Frank Miller), Eve McVeagh (Mildred Fuller), Harry Shannon (Cooper), Lee Van Cleef (Jack Colby), Robert Wilke (James Pierce), Sheb Wooley (Ben Miller), Tom London (Sam), Ted Stanhope (Station Master), Larry Blake (Gillis), William Phillips (Barber), Jeanne Blackford (Mrs. Henderson), James Millican (Baker), Cliff Clark (Weaver), Ralph Reed (Johnny), William Newell (Drunk), Lucien Prival (Bartender), Guy Brach (Fred), Howland Chamberlin (Hotel Clerk), Morgan Farley (Minister), Virginia Christine (Mrs. Simpson), Virginia Farmer (Mrs.

Fletcher), Jack Elam (Charlie), Paul Dubov (Scott), Harry Harvey (Coy), Tim Graham (Sawyer), Nolan Leary (Lewis), Tom Greenway (Ezra), Dick Elliott (Kibbee), John Doucette (Trumbull).

1952   SPRINGFIELD RIFLE   Warner Brothers

Director: Andre De Toth
Producer: Louis F. Edelman
Scenarists: Charles Marquis Warren, Frank Davis
Photographer: Dewin DuPar
Editor: Robert L. Swanson
Musical Score: Max Steiner
Art Director: John Beckman
From a story by Sloan Nibley
Cast: Gary Cooper (Major Alex Kearney), Phyllis Thaxter (Erin Kearney), David Brian (Austin McCool), Paul Kelly (Lt. Col. Hudson), Philip Carey (Capt. Tennick), Lon Chaney (Elm), James Millican (Matthew Quinn), Martin Milner (Olie Larsen), Guinn "Big Boy" Williams (Sgt. Snow), Jerry O'Sullivan (Lt. Evans), James Brown (Pvt. Ferguson), Jack Woody (Sims), Alan Hale, Jr. (Mizzell), Vince Barnett (Cook), Fess Parker (Jim Randolph), Richard Benjamin (later Lightner) (Lt. Johnson), Ewing Mitchell (Spencer), Poodles Hanneford (Cpl. Hamel), George Ross (Riley), Eric Hoeg (Southerner), Wilton Graff (Col. Sharpe), Ned Young (Sgt. Poole), William Fawcett (Cpl. Ramsey), Richard Hale (General Halleck), Ben Corbett (Sgt. Major), Guy E. Hearne (Calhoun), George Eldredge (Judge Advocate), Rory Mallinson (Barfly), Paula Sowl (Bit Woman), Ric Roman, Jack Mower (Guards), Michael Ragan (later Holly Bane) (Red), Ray Bennett (Commissioner), Michael Chapin (Jamie), Ralph Sanford (Barfly).

1953   RETURN TO PARADISE   United Artists

Director: Mark Robson
Producers: Theron Warth, Robert Wise and Mark Robson
Scenarist: Charles Kaufman
Photographer: Winton Hoch
Musical Score: Dimitri Tiomkin
Editor: Daniel Mandell
Based on the book by James A. Michener
Cast: Gary Cooper (Mr. Morgan), Roberta Haynes (Maeva), Barry Jones (Pastor Corbett), Moira MacDonald (Turia), John Hudson (Harry Faber), Va'a (Rori, age 9), Hans Kruse (Rori, age 21), Mamea Mataumua (Tonga), Herbert Ah Sue (Kura), Henrietta Godinet (Povana), La'ili (Kim Ling), Ezra Williams (Interpreter), George Miedeske (Hawkins), Donals Ashford (Cutler), Terry Dunleavy (Mac),

Howard Poulson (Russ), Malia (Maeva's Aunt), Webb Overlander (Will Talbot), Frances Gow (Mrs. Talbot), Brian McEwen (Hank Elliott), Kathleen Newick (Mrs. Elliott), Kalapu (Tomare).

1953   BLOWING WILD   Warner Brothers

Director: Hugo Fregonese
Producer: Milton Sperling
Scenarist: Philip Yordan
Photographer: Sid Hockox
Art Director: Al Ybarra
Editor: Alan Crosland, Jr.
Set Decorator: William Wallace
Musical Score: Dimitri Tiomkin
Song: "Blowing Wild—The Ballad of Black Gold" by Dimitri Tiomkin and Paul Francis Webster, sung by Frankie Laine
Cast: Gary Cooper (Jeff Dawson), Barbara Stanwyck (Marina Conway), Ruth Roman (Sal), Anthony Quinn (Ward "Paco" Conway), Ward Bond (Dutch), Ian MacDonald (Jackson), Richard Karlan (Henderson), Juan Garcia (El Gavilan).

1954   GARDEN OF EVIL   Twentieth Century Fox

Director: Henry Hathaway
Producer: Charles Brackett
Scenarist: Frank Fenton
Musical Score: Bernard Herrmann
Photographers: Milton Krasner, Jorge Stahl, Jr.
Art Directors: Lyle Wheeler, Edward Fitzgerald
Editor: James B. Clark
Associate Producer: Saul Wurtzel
From a story by Fred Freiberger and William Tunberg
Cast: Gary Cooper (Hooker), Susan Hayward (Leah Fuller), Richard Widmark (Fiske), Hugh Marlowe (John Fuller), Cameron Mitchell (Luke Daly), Rita Moreno (Singer), Victor Manuel Mendoza (Vincente Madariaga), Fernando Wagner (Captain), Arturo Soto Bangel (Priest), Manuel Donde (Waiter), Antonio Bribiesca (Bartender), Salvado Terroba (Victim).

1954   VERA CRUZ   United Artists

Director: Robert Aldrich
Producer: James Hill
Co-Producers: Harold Hecht, Burt Lancaster

Scenarists: Roland Kibbee, James R. Webb
Photographer: Ernest Laszlo
Editor: Alan Crosland, Jr.
Musical Score: Hugo Friedhofer
Orchestrator and Conductor: Raul Lavista
From a story by Borden Chase
Cast: Gary Cooper (Benjamin Trane), Burt Lancaster (Joe Erin), Denise Darcel (Countess Marie Duvarre), Cesar Romero (Marquis de Labordere), Sarita Montiel (Nina), George Macready (Emperor Maximilian), Ernest Borgnine (Donnegan), Henry Brandon (Danette), Charles Buchinski [Charles Bronson] (Pittsburgh), Morris Ankrum (General Aguilar), James McCallion (Little-Bit), Jack Lambert (Charlie), Jack Elam (Tex), James Seay (Abilene), Archie Savage (Ballard), Charles Horvath (Reno), Juan Garcia (Pedro).

1955   THE COURT-MARTIAL OF BILLY MITCHELL
Warner Brothers

Director: Otto Preminger
Producer: Milton Sperling
Scenarists: Milton Sperling, Emmet Lavery
Photographer: Sam Leavitt
Art Director: Malcolm Bert
Editor: Folmar Blangsted
Musical Score: Dimitri Tiomkin
Second Unit Director: Russ Saunders
From an original story by Milton Sperling and Emmet Lavery
Cast: Gary Cooper (Billy Mitchell), Charles Bickford (General Guthrie), Ralph Bellamy (Congressman Reid), Rod Steiger (Allan Guillion), Elizabeth Montgomery (Margaret Lansdowne), Fred Clark (Colonel Moreland), James Daly (Colonel White), Jack Lord (Zach Lansdowne), Peter Graves (Captain Elliott), Herbert Heyes (General John J. Pershing), Darren McGavin (Russ Peters), Robert Simon (Admiral Gage), Charles Dingle (Senator Fullerton), Will Wright (Admiral William S. Sims), Dayton Lummis (General Douglas MacArthur), Ian Wolfe (President Collidge), Griff Barnett (Civilian Steno), Edward Keane, Anthony Hughes, John Maxwell, Ewing Mitchell (Court Judges), Max Wagner (Sergeant Major), Adam Kennedy (Yip Ryan), Steve Holland (Stu Stewart), Manning Ross (Ted Adams), Jack Perrin (Court Reporter), Gregory Walcott (Reporter Millikan), Robert Williams (Reporter Tuttle), Edna Holland (Woman Secretary), William Forrest (Commandant F.S.H.), Frank Wilcox (Officer Tom), Carleton Young (Pershing's Aide), Tom McKee (Capt. Eddie Rickenbacker), Phil Arnold (Fiorello La Guardia), Robert Brubaker (Major Hap Arnold), William Henry, Peter Adams (Officers), Charles Chaplin, Jr., Joel Smith,

Al Page, Jordan Shelley, Fred Perce, William Fox, Lars Hansen, George Mayon, Michael Lally, Cy Malis (Reporters).

1956   FRIENDLY PERSUASION   Allied Artists

Director: William Wyler
Producer: William Wyler
Associate Producer: Robert Wyler
Photographer: Ellsworth Fredricks
Editors: Robert Swink, Edward A. Biery, Robert A. Belcher
Art Director: Edward S. Haworth
Technical Advisor: Jessamyn West
Musical Score: Dimitri Tiomkin
Songs: "Friendly Persuasion (Thee I Love)," "Mocking Bird in a Willow Tree," "Coax Me a Little," "Indiana Holiday," "Marry Me, Marry Me" by Dimitri Tiomkin and Paul Francis Webster. Title song sung by Pat Boone
From *The Friendly Persuasion* by Jessamyn West.
Cast: Gary Cooper (Jess Birdwell), Dorothy McGuire (Eliza Birdwell), Marjorie Main (Widow Hudspeth), Anthony Perkins (Josh Birdwell), Richard Eyer (Little Jess), Phyllis Love (Mattie Birdwell), Robert Middleton (Sam Jordan), Mark Richman (Gard Jordan), Walter Catlett (Professor Quigley), Richard Hale (Elder Purdy), Joel Fluellen (Enoch), Theodore Newton (Army Major), John Smith (Caleb), Mary Carr (Quaker Woman), Edna Skinner, Marjorie Durant, Frances Farwell (Widow Hudspeth's Daughters), Samantha (The Goose), Russell Simpson, Charles Halton, Everett Glass (Elders), Richard Garland (Bushwhacker), James Dobson (Rebel Soldier), John Compton (Rebel Lieutenant), James Seay (Rebel Captain), Diane Jergens (Young Girl —Elizabeth), Ralph Sanford (Businessman), Jean Inness (Mrs. Purdy), Nelson Leigh (Minister), Helen Kleeb (Old Lady), William Schallert (Young Husband), John Craven (Leader), Frank Jenks (Shell Game Man), Frank Hagney (Lemonade Vendor), Jack McClure (Soldier), Charles Courtney (Reb Courier), Tom Irish (Young Rebel), Mary Jackson (Country Woman).

1957   LOVE IN THE AFTERNOON
A Billy Wilder Production
An Allied Artists Pictures Corp. Film

Director and Producer: Billy Wilder
Scenarists: Billy Wilder, I. A. L. Diamond
Photographer: William Mellor
Editor: Leonid Azar
Art Director: Alexandre Trauner

Musical Adaptation: Franz Waxman
Based on the novel *Ariane* by Claude Anet
Cast: Gary Cooper (Frank Flannagan), Audrey Hepburn (Ariane Chavasse), Maurice Chevalier (Claude Chavasse), John McGiver (Monsieur X), Lise Bourdin (Madame X), Bonifas (Commissioner of Police), Audrey Wilder (Brunette), Gyula Kokas, Michel Kokas, George Cocos and Victor Gazzoli—The Four Gypsies (Themselves), Olga Valery (Lady Hotel Guest), Leila Croft, Valerie Croft (Swedish Twins), Charles Bouillard (Valet at the Ritz), Filo (Flannagan's Chauffeur), Andre Priez (First Porter at the Ritz), Gaidon (Second Porter at the Ritz), Gregory Gromoff (Doorman at the Ritz), Janine Dard, Claude Ariel (Existentialists), Francois Moustache (Butcher), Gloria France (Client at Butcher's), Jean Sylvain (Baker), Annie Roudier (First Client at Baker's), Jeanne Charblay (Second Client at Baker's), Odette Charblay (Third Client at Baker's), Gilbert Constant, Monique Saintey (Lovers on Left Bank), Jacques Preboist, Anne Laurent (Lovers Near the Seine), Jacques Ary, Simone Vanlancker (Lovers on Right Bank), Richard Flagy (Husband), Jeanne Papir (Wife), Marcelle Broc, Marcelle Praince (Rich Women), Guy Delorme (Gigolo), Olivia Chevalier, Solon Smith (Little Children in the Gardens), Eve Marley, Jean Rieubon (Tandemists), Christian Lude, Charles Lemontier, Emile Mylos (Generals), Alexander Trauner (Artist), Betty Schneider, Georges Perrault, Vera Boccadoro, Marc Aurian (Couples Under Water Wagon), Bernard Musson (Undertaker), Michele Selignac (Widow).

1958   TEN NORTH FREDERICK   Twentieth Century Fox

Director and Scenarist: Philip Dunne
Producer: Charles Brackett
Photographer: Joe MacDonald
Musical Score: Leigh Harline
Art Directors: Lyle R. Wheeler, Addison Hehr
Editor: David Bretherton
From the novel by John O'Hara
Cast: Gary Cooper (Joe Chapin), Diane Varsi (Ann Chapin), Suzy Parker (Kate Drummond), Geraldine Fitzgerald (Edith Chapin), Tom Tully (Slattery), Ray Stricklyn (Joby), Philip Ober (Lloyd Williams), John Emery (Paul Donaldson), Stuart Whitman (Charley Bongiorno), Linda Watkins (Peg Slattery), Barbara Nichols (Stella), Joe McGuinn (Dr. English), Jess Kirkpatrick (Arthur McHenry), Nolan Leary (Harry Jackson), Beverly Jo Morror (Waitress), Buck Class (Bill), Rachel Stephens (Salesgirl), Bob Adler (Farmer), Ling Foster (Peter), John Harding (Robert Hooker), Dudley Manlove (Ted Wallace), Mack Williams (General Coates), Vernon Rich (Board Chairman), Mary Carroll (Nurse), George Davis (Waiter), Joey Faye (Taxi Driver), Fred

Essler (Hoffman), Irene Seidner (Wife), Melinda Byron (Hope), Sean Meaney (Sax Player), John Indrisano, Michael Pataki, Michael Morelli (Men).

1958   **MAN OF THE WEST**   An Ashton Picture
A Walter M. Mirisch Production
Released Through United Artists

Director: Anthony Mann
Producer: Walter M. Mirisch
Scenarist: Reginald Rose
Photographer: Ernest Haller
Editor: Richard Heermance
Musical Score: Leigh Harline
Art Director: Hillyard Brown
Song: "Man of the West" by Bobby Troup, sung by Julie London
Based on a novel by Will C. Brown
Cast: Gary Cooper (Link Jones), Julie London (Billie Ellis), Lee J. Cobb (Dock Tobin), Arthur O'Connell (Sam Beasley), Jack Lord (Coaley), John Dehner (Claude), Royal Dano (Trout), Robert Wilke (Ponch), Jack Williams (Alcutt), Guy Wilkerson (Conductor), Chuck Roberson (Rifleman), Frank Ferguson (Marshal), Emory Parnell (Gribble), Tina Menard (Mexican Woman), Joe Dominquez (Mexican Man).

1959   **THE HANGING TREE**   A Baroda Production
Released Through Warner Brothers

Director: Delmer Daves
Producers: Martin Jurow, Richard Shepherd
Scenarists: Wendell Mayes, Halsted Welles
Photographer: Ted McCord
Art Director: Daniel B. Cathcart
Editor: Owen Marks
Musical Score: Max Steiner
Song: "The Hanging Tree" by Mack David and Jerry Livingston, sung by Marty Robbins
From the novelette "The Hanging Tree" by Dorothy M. Johnson
Cast: Gary Cooper (Doc Joseph Frail), Maria Schell (Elizabeth Mahler), Karl Malden (Frenchy Plante), Ben Piazza (Rune), George C. Scott (Dr. George Grubb), Karl Swenson (Tom Flaunce), Virginia Gregg (Edna Flaunce), John Dierkes (Society Red), King Donovan (Wonder), Slim Talbot (Stage Driver), Guy Wilkerson (Home Owner), Bud Osborne (Horseman), Annette Claudier (Dance Hall Girl), Clarence Straight (Dealer).

1959   ALIAS JESSE JAMES
A Hope Enterprises Production Released Through
United Artists

Director: Norman McLeod
Producer: Jack Hope
Executive Producer: Bob Hope
Scenarists: William Bowers, Daniel D. Beauchamp
Photographer: Lionel Lindon
Art Directors: Hal Pereira, Roland Anderson
Editors: Marvin Coil and Jack Bachom
"Alias Jesse James Theme" by Marilyn and Joe Hooven (Music) and
Dunham (Lyrics), sung by Guy Mitchell over title credits
Based on a story by Robert St. Aubrey and Bert Lawrence
Cast: Bob Hope (Milford Farnsworth), Rhonda Fleming (The Duchess),
Wendell Corey (Jesse James), Jim Davis (Frank James), Gloria Talbott
(Indian Maiden), Will Wright (Titus Queasley), Mary Young ("Ma"
James), Sid Melton (Fight Fan), George E. Stone (Gibson Girl Fan),
James Burke (Charlie, bartender), Joe Vitale (Sam Hiawatha), Lyle
Latell (Conductor), Harry Tyler (Elmo, Station Master), Mike
Mazurki, Mickey Finn (Toughs), Nestor Paiva (Bixby), Mike Ross
(Killer), Emory Parnell (Sheriff), Stan Jolley (Conductor), Dick Alex-
ander (Jeremiah Cole), Oliver Blake (Undertaker), Jack Lambert
(Snake Brice), Ethan Laidlaw, Glenn Strange (Henchmen), J. Anthony
Hughes (Dirty Dog Saloonkeeper), Bob Gunderson, Fred Kohler, Jr.,
and Iron Eyes Cody.
Guest Stars: Hugh O'Brian (Wyatt Earp), Ward Bond (Major Seth
Adams), James Arness (Matt Dillon), Roy Rogers (Himself), Fess
Parker (Davy Crockett), Gail Davis (Annie Oakley), James Garner
(Bret Maverick), Gene Autry (Himself), Jay Silverheels (Tonto), Bing
Crosby (Himself), Gary Cooper (Himself).

1959   THE WRECK OF THE MARY DEARE
A Blaustein-Baroda Production
A Metro-Goldwyn-Mayer Picture

Director: Michael Anderson
Producer: Julian Blaustein
Scenarist: Eric Ambler
Photographer: Joseph Ruttenberg
Musical Score: George Duning
Art Directors: Hans Peters, Paul Groesse
Based on a novel by Hammond Innes
Cast: Gary Cooper (Gideon Patch), Charlton Heston (John Sands),
Michael Redgrave (Mr. Hyland), Emlyn Williams (Sir Wildred Fal-
cett), Cecil Parker (The Chairman), Alexander Knox (Petrie), Virginia

McKenna (Janet Taggart), Richard Harris (Higgins), Ben Wright (Mike Duncan), Peter Illing (Gunderson), Terence De Marney (Frank), Ashley Cowan (Burrows), Charles Davis (Yules), Alexander Archdale (Lloyd's Counsel), John LeMesurier (M.O.A. Lawyer), Louis Mercier (Comm. de Police), Albert Carrier (Ambulance Attendant), Lilyan Chauvin (Nun), Paul Bryar (Port Official), Lomax Study (Photographer), Jean del Val (Javot), Kalu K. Sonkur (Lascar), Noel Drayton (Bell), Charles Lamb (Court Clerk), John Dearth (Reporter), George Dee (French Captain).

1959   THEY CAME TO CORDURA
A Goetz-Baroda Production
Released by Columbia Pictures

Director: Robert Rossen
Producer: William Goetz
Scenarists: Ivan Moffat, Robert Rossen
Photographer: Burnett Guffey
Editor: William A. Lyon
Musical Score: Elie Siegmeister
Art Director: Cary Odell
Based on the novel by Glendon Swarthout
Cast: Gary Cooper (Major Thomas Thorn), Rita Hayworth (Adelaide Geary), Van Heflin (Sgt. John Chawk), Tab Hunter (Lt. William Fowler), Richard Conte (Cpl. Milo Trubee), Michael Callan (Pvt. Aubrey Hetherington), Dick York (Pvt. Renziehausen), Robert Keith (Col. Rogers), Carlos Romero (Arrsaga), James Bannon (Capt. Raltz), Edward Platt (Col. DeRose), Maurice Jara (Mexican Federale), Sam Buffington (First Correspondent), Arthur Hanson (Second Correspondent).

1961   THE NAKED EDGE
A Pennebaker-Baroda Production
Released Through United Artists

Director: Michael Anderson
Producers: Walter Seltzer, George Glass
Executive Producer: Marlon Brando, Sr.
Scenarist: Joseph Stefano
Photographer: Edwin Hillier
Editor: Gordon Pilkington
Musical Score: William Alwyn
Art Director: Carmen Dillon
Based on the novel *Last Train to Babylon* by Max Ehrlich
Cast: Gary Cooper (George Radcliffe), Deborah Kerr (Martha Radcliffe)

Eric Portman (Jeremy Clay), Diane Cilento (Mrs. Heath), Hermione Gingold (Lilly Harris), Peter Cushing (Mr. Wrack), Michael Wilding (Morris Brooke), Ronald Howard (Mr. Claridge), Ray McAnally (Donald Heath), Sandor Eles (Manfridi), Wilfrid Lawson (Mr. Pom), Helen Cherry (Miss Osborne), Joyce Carey (Victoria Hicks), Diane Clare (Betty), Frederick Leister (Judge), Martin Boddey (Jason Roote), Peter Wayn (Chauffeur).

INDEX